THE

COOKBOOK

MARY FARRELL

GILL & MACMILLAN

Gill & Macmillan Ltd

Hume Avenue

Park West

Dublin 12

with associated companies throughout the world

www.gillmacmillan.ie

© 2006 Mary Farrell

ISBN-13: 978 0 7171 4107 4

ISBN-10: 0 7171 4107 1

Photographs by John Jordan

Index compiled by Cover to Cover

Design by Anú Design, Collierstown, Co. Meath

Typesetting by O'K Graphic Design, Dublin

Printed by GraphyCems Ltd, Spain

Contents

SALADS

SOUPS

FRITTATAS, TARTS AND QUICHES

Acknowledgments

This labour of love is dedicated to my wonderful husband Richard, the calming influence on my life.

There are many people to whom I owe a great debt of gratitude for their help in writing this book. I would be nowhere without my family. My mum and dad have been my inspiration all my life. They have given me a passion for food, a dedication to work and the confidence and self-belief that allows me to fulfil my dreams and ambitions.

A special thanks to my siblings Cathy, Sean, David, Audrey, Alma, Hazel and Carol for their advice and constructive criticism. They all live very different lives and in conversation with them I have learned to adapt to the reality of cooking for different lifestyles.

Children have a beautiful honesty; they won't eat something that is good for them if it doesn't taste good. My nieces and nephews, Peter, Emma, Ciara, David, Grace and Anna, have enlightened me to the taste buds of the younger family members.

I would like to thank the staff (past and present) of Café Fresh, without whom none of this would be possible. My excellent staff have allowed me the free time to write this book, safe in the knowledge that they will ensure the quality of food in Café Fresh is at its highest at all times.

A special thanks to the customers of Café Fresh. Ninety per cent of our clientele are regular, loyal lunchtime grazers. I rely on their feedback and comments for much of how the recipes and menu in Café Fresh develop and we hope to continue to excite and please your taste buds.

Many thanks to my dear friends Thea Gilien, Tina Convey and Declan Long, who have added value to my work with their helpful comments over many glasses of wine!

I am thankful to Gill & Macmillan for taking my work on and publishing my book. A special mention to Michael Gill, Anita Ruane, Emma Farrell, Fergus O'Keeffe and Anú Design. John Jordan deserves special thanks for much patience and long hours of work that have resulted in wonderful photography for this book.

A Brief Background

Café Fresh opened its doors on 9 June 2001. My life's journey has taken many twists and turns before arriving here to welcome patrons through these doors. I worked with my two passions, politics and food, for many years before finally focusing my career in the food business.

My love of food began at a very young age. I'm the oldest of a farming family of eight children where meal time was an extremely important part of the day. My mother worked her kitchen with precision-like effect to produce healthy, fresh, tasty meals every day. Our family garden was the source of the fresh vegetables and fruit. My youngest brother was diagnosed as diabetic at the age of two, so my mother had to cater for a diabetic diet. The family became accustomed to and benefited from a sugar-free diet at a very young age and we learned how to cook dishes, particularly desserts, without sugar. Early on I became familiar with the idea that certain ingredients can be excluded from the diet without sacrificing flavour and quality.

I have developed my skills through my experiences working in different restaurants for over ten years. On leaving school, I spent a brief but unsuccessful period studying computer science. I worked in an office environment for a few years, which proved to be not to my liking. I then embarked on a travelling expedition to find myself! I travelled through France, Germany and Holland, but unlike most people, I travelled through the kitchens of Europe, financing my travel by working in the catering industry. I quickly broadened my knowledge of food, diverse methods of cooking and innovative dishes from the various countries. On returning to Dublin I worked at The Well Fed Café, Crowe Street in Temple Bar for five years while studying history and politics in UCD. After completing an MA in politics, I headed to Australia for a well-earned break. In Australia I was fascinated with the diversity and ingenuity of the 'East meets West' cuisine which has developed as a result of Asian immigration, ideas that are now reflected in the menu at Café Fresh. During this trip I decided that it was time to focus on my career in catering and leave politics for another day.

I am now the proud owner and chef of Café Fresh. In 1999 I set out with the objective of running a vegetarian restaurant which would appeal to carnivores and herbivores alike, providing a high-quality, innovative lunch menu where everyone would find something to eat, regardless of diet restrictions. My menu showcases seasonal and organic ingredients through salads, soups, sandwiches and a plethora of ever-changing selections of hot dishes. The popularity of Café Fresh with a diverse group of new and loyal customers reflects the success of the food. Everything is made from raw ingredients. Café Fresh is a food-focused restaurant; we cater for the public who love to eat good food and don't have to feel guilty about it! They also can feel good about the organic *local* products and purveyors Café Fresh supports.

Café Fresh has been awarded the Bridgestone Food Award for 2003, 2004, 2005 and 2006. Café Fresh also features in *The Dubliner Best Places to Eat Guide 2006* and is a member of the Slow Food movement and the Vegetarian Societies in Ireland and the United Kingdom. Café Fresh features in many guide books for tourists. I run a full catering service, catering for small groups, large parties and people on special diets. Due to demand from my customers, from September to May I run cookery courses for beginner and intermediate level, which are extremely popular. I also give individual private cookery classes to people on special diets. This cookery book is a culmination of the many tried and tested recipes at Café Fresh. I am currently studying nutritional therapy, thus there is a focus on the nutritional content of the recipes in this book.

This book is for friends and family, my customers who have been eating at Café Fresh for years and for those who may be discovering the tastes of the Café Fresh kitchen for the first time in the recipes on these pages.

The Purpose of the Book

I have been asked about a cookery book ever since I opened the doors of Café Fresh in 2001. Last year I decided to dedicate time, thought and care to sharing the wonderful recipes of Café Fresh.

This book is a no-nonsense cookbook for those who are interested in tasty, seasonal food, eating healthily and understanding the benefits of incorporating a meat-free meal in the present health-obsessed climate. This book emphasises the use of natural, seasonal ingredients, easy methods of cooking and the use of the senses to guide you in your cooking experiments. I use my senses of smell, sight, touch, sound and taste as tools to guide me through my cooking process. This begins with the selection of the ingredients, cooking, presentation and final eating of the meal.

The book will give you the means of incorporating more vegetables, pulses, grains and fruit into your diet in an interesting way, as is done on a daily basis at Café Fresh. The recipes demonstrate how you can remove sugars, fat, flours and many other foods from meals without compromising on flavour or nutrition.

In this book, I share my knowledge of food with you. I love food, but I don't want to spend hours in the kitchen. Around the table with family and friends, I want to maintain a healthy diet and I want my food to taste great. Through my cookery courses, I have learned that people are time-poor when it comes to cooking. The concept of the family has become much more fluid in twenty-first-century Ireland. As a result, there is little time in the family home to prepare meals. For the every-day evening meal or lunch, the cook is looking for a recipe that's quick, easy, healthy and that tastes great. The recipes in this book will aid the cook who strives for a healthy lifestyle where good food is a pleasure to eat and quick and easy to create. Time-poor people will find this book invaluable, as all recipes are laid out simply and require the minimum amount of time to prepare and cook. All you need is a basic kitchen and utensils, fresh ingredients and 30–45 minutes to prepare a healthy, tasty meal for everyone.

There is currently huge media and government focus on healthy eating. As our society becomes more affluent, we acquire more health problems that are directly related to our lifestyle choices, such as obesity and diabetes. The media focus on obesity and health urges people to eat more nutritious, low-fat meals. Scientific research constantly reveals links between diet and various illnesses. Reduced meat intake is encouraged to prevent bowel cancers. Research at Yale University in the US has shown the nutritional value of sprouts and sprouted beans, identifying them as the new 'superfood'. We are encouraged to eat more vegetables, fruit and whole foods for optimum health. New trends are emerging in the food industry, where the focus is turning away from fad diets to healthy eating programmes that promote health and wellness. The time is right for this cookbook.

This cookery book reflects the food focus of Café Fresh – the healthy, wholesome recipes which can now be recreated in your own kitchen. It showcases the recipes which have been tried and tested over the past five years. The recipes aren't difficult, but rather the result of combinations that allow the flavours of the ingredients to shine and allow your senses to delight in the food.

A Note on the Five Senses

What I do consider absolutely essential to create tasty dishes is the ability to use your senses to guide you through your kitchen. 'The senses' is a general term for the faculties of perception: taste, smell, touch, sight and sound. Each of these senses play their own individual roles separately and in conjunction with each other when cooking, from the purchase of the ingredients to the preparation, cooking, presentation and eating of the final dish.

Taste: This, of course, is the most obvious sense, as it's with the tongue that we taste the food we've made and decide if it appeals to us or not. When cooking, you should taste the food at different stages to ensure the flavours are developing as they should be. Once you do this regularly, you'll get a feel for the ingredients and learn how to make the dish taste really good.

Hearing: Your sense of hearing is very important in the kitchen. There are many sounds in cooking, such as water boiling or oil sizzling. Once you become aware of the cooking sounds, you'll understand your ingredients and the process of cooking better. When sautéing onions, the oil must be hot enough so that they cook in the oil. You cannot touch the oil, so the best way to test it is to drop a piece of onion into the oil. If it sits in the oil making no sound, it's absorbing the oil and the oil isn't hot enough. If it sizzles, then the oil is just right.

Smell: The smell of food is just as important as the taste. The sense of smell prepares the body for what's about to be eaten. If the smell isn't pleasing, then the food won't be eaten with enthusiasm, if at all. Your sense of smell will tell you when something is burning or if a vegetable has gone rancid and will delight in the aroma of fresh herbs. When cooking, your sense of smell should be on high alert. When sautéing vegetables, a pleasant aroma is given off as they cook. When preparing spices for a curry, your nose will tell you when they're heating up and releasing their flavour, as the smell should be pungent and aromatic.

Touch: Hands are extremely sensitive and sophisticated cooking tools. You can develop this sense of touch by paying attention to how different foods feel at different stages of cooking. Touch can indicate when a cake is baked, if a dough is kneaded enough and whether an avocado is ripe.

Sight: When I think of sight, I immediately think of colour. This is a very important theme in my cooking. When you sit down to eat something, your eyes immediately respond to how the food looks. If the food looks appealing, you'll be looking forward to tasting the dish. Colour plays an important factor in stimulating our senses when we think about food. When choosing vegetables or fruit, your eyes will immediately tell you if it's worth it to check the quality with your sense of touch and smell.

Conversion Charts

Weight

oz	grams
1	25
2	50
3	75
4	110
5	150
6	175
7	200
8	225
9	250
10	275
11	300
12	350
13	365
14	400
15	425
16/1 lb	450

Volume

fl oz	ml
1	25
2	60
3	90
4	120
5	150
6	175
7	200
8	225
9	250
10	275
15	425
20/1 pint	570
1¼ pints	725
1½ pints	850
1¾ pints	1 litre
1 tbsp =	15 ml

Oven Temperatures

	Fahrenheit	Celsius	Gas mark
Very cool	225–250	110–130	¼–½
Cool	275–300	140–150	1–2
Warm	325	160	3
Moderate	350	180	4
Fairly hot	375–400	190–200	5–6
Hot	425	220	7
Very hot	450–475	230–240	8–9

condiments
and buffet
dishes

Introduction

A **condiment** is a savoury, piquant, spicy or salty accompaniment to food, such as a relish, sauce, mixture of spices and so on. The idea of adding a condiment to food is that it will enhance or improve the flavour and add colour to a dish. Many of the condiments that follow serve well as dips for crudités or breads as an aperitif accompaniment for a dinner party.

In Café Fresh we use various condiments as dips, spreads and additions to sauces and dishes. Use them as you feel suits your kitchen.

pesto

A pesto is an uncooked sauce made with fresh basil, garlic, pine nuts, Parmesan and olive oil. The ingredients can either be crushed with a pestle and mortar or finely chopped with a food processor. This classic, fresh-tasting sauce originated in Genoa, Italy, and although used on a variety of dishes, it's a favourite with pasta in Italy. Now there are a myriad of pestos made from various herbs and nuts.

In Café Fresh we don't use Parmesan – we rely on the quality of the herbs, nuts and olive oil to make a wonderful pesto. We use pestos as sandwich spreads, condiments for main dishes, dips or added to soup or other sauces for extra richness and flavour. Pestos are very versatile and very easy to make. What follows is a selection of those we use in Café Fresh. There are endless combinations, and once you're confident, you can experiment yourself.

A pesto can be as smooth, chunky or thick as you like. It will also depend on what you're using it for. I find that if I'm using it for a spread on a sandwich, it needs to be quite thick or else the bread will absorb the olive oil and become soggy. If I'm using it for a salad dressing, it should be more oily so as to mix well with the salad ingredients or pasta.

The quantities here are small, so this quantity can be difficult to work with in a food processor. Personally, I find the hand blender or pestle and mortar is better for smaller quantities.

Pesto is best eaten fresh, but it will keep in the fridge for two to three days, though it will lose some of its colour.

Basil Pesto

serves 4 as an accompaniment to a main dish
ready in 10 minutes

50 g (2 oz) fresh basil
50 g (2 oz) pine nuts, toasted
1 garlic clove
2 tbsp olive oil
sea salt and freshly ground black pepper

Place all ingredients in a food processor and blend until smooth. Alternatively, you can use an electric hand blender or pestle and mortar and grind to a smooth paste. Add more olive oil if you like a thinner pesto.

Vegan. Dairy, gluten, sugar, wheat and yeast free.
Freezing: Can be frozen for up to 1 month but will lose some of its colour.
Cook's Tips: Spend a little extra on good-quality olive oil here – it will pay off in the flavour. This quantity can be difficult to work with in a food processor. Personally, I find the hand blender is better for smaller quantities. To make rocket pesto, simply replace the basil with rocket.
Nutritional Content: Antioxidants, fat, fibre, flavonoids.
Note to the Senses: Basil is unmistakable for its sweet, fragrant smell and this should be reflected in the vibrant colour and pungent taste of the pesto. Pine nuts are a delicate, creamy nut and are the perfect compliment for basil. The secret to good pesto is fresh basil, fresh pine nuts and good-quality olive oil.

Sun-Dried Tomato Pesto

serves 4 as an accompaniment to a main dish
ready in 10 minutes

50 g (2 oz) drained semi-sun-dried tomatoes
50 g (2 oz) cashew nuts
2 garlic cloves
2 tbsp olive oil

Place all ingredients in a food processor and blend to a smooth consistency. Taste and season if required. You can also use an electric hand blender or pestle and mortar.

Vegan. Dairy, gluten, sugar, wheat and yeast free.
Freezing: Can be frozen for up to 1 month but will lose some of its colour.
Cook's Tips: You can use the oil from the semi-sun-dried tomatoes and then use less olive oil. This oil will have lots of flavour from the marinating process. Some would suggest adding a dash of lemon juice to balance the sweetness of the tomatoes – try it and see what you think.
Nutritional Content: Antioxidants, copper, lycopene, magnesium, tryptophan, vitamin C.
Note to the Senses: Sun-dried tomatoes have a wonderful orange-red colour. This pesto is very rich in flavour as the dehydrating process has intensified the flavour of the tomatoes. It has a sweetish taste and the cashew nuts add charac- ter to the pesto. If you're using this as a spread, don't over-blend the cashew nuts so that small pieces are visible and come through in the texture. Making the pesto this way is perfect as an accompaniment to the Middle Eastern Filo Rice Torte (p. 140).

Parsley Pesto

serves 4 as an accompaniment to a main dish
ready in 10 minutes

50 g (2 oz) fresh parsley
50 g (2 oz) walnuts
2 garlic cloves
2 tbsp olive oil

Place all ingredients in a food processor and blend to a smooth consistency. Taste and season if required. You can also use an electric hand blender or pestle and mortar.

Vegan. Dairy, gluten, sugar, wheat and yeast free.
Freezing: Can be frozen for up to 1 month but will lose some of its colour.
Cook's Tips: Flat-leaf parsley gives better flavour.
Nutritional Content: Copper, manganese, omega 3 fatty acids, tryptophan and vitamins A, C and K.
Note to the Senses: Parsley is the world's most popular herb. This is a great winter pesto. If you can get flat-leaf parsley, all the better, but it's not essential. Walnuts give this pesto an earthiness that's ideal for the humble parsley.

tahini dressings

Tahini is a sesame paste. There are two types – hulled (husks removed) and unhulled. The dark tahini is unhulled and has a richer flavour. The hulled is less bitter and lighter in colour. However, it's also less nutritious because a lot of the vitamins and protein are contained in the outer hull. If you find the darker tahini too strong in flavour, you can start with the light first.

The following dressings are good used as a mayonnaise substitute or as a dip for crudités. The dressing quantities below will serve four to six people as a dip or dressing for salad.

Tahini and Apple Dressing

serves 4–6
ready in 10 minutes

3 tbsp tahini
½ small onion, finely chopped
1 tsp concentrated apple juice
sea salt to taste
½ tsp miso
1–2 tbsp water, as necessary

Place all ingredients except water in a blender. Add the water 1 tablespoon at a time until you get a smooth consistency. Use as a salad dressing or as a mayonnaise dressing for sandwiches. Store in an airtight container in the fridge for up to three days.

Vegan. Dairy, gluten, sugar and wheat free.
Freezing: Can be frozen for up to 1 month.
Nutritional Content: Calcium, copper, magnesium, manganese and tryptophan.

Tahini and Lemon Dip/Dressing

serves 4–6
ready in 5 minutes

120 ml (4 fl oz) tahini
1 garlic clove, crushed
55 ml (2 fl oz) water
juice of 1 lemon
1½ tbsp sunflower oil/olive oil
chopped parsley, to garnish
pinch of cayenne pepper, to garnish

Thoroughly blend the tahini, garlic, water, lemon juice and oil. A hand blender or a whisk will work well here. Add more water if the dip is too thick. Season to taste. Serve garnished with parsley and a sprinkle of cayenne.

Vegan. Dairy, gluten, sugar, wheat and yeast free.
Freezing: Can be frozen for up to 1 month.
Nutritional Content: Calcium, copper, magnesium, manganese and tryptophan.
Note to the Senses: Remember, this should have a tangy flavour and feel clean on the palate.

Tofu Dressing/Mayo Substitute

serves 4–6
ready in 2 minutes

200 g (7 oz) firm or silken tofu, drained
1 tbsp chopped chives
1 tbsp olive oil
1 tsp honey
1 tsp lemon juice

Blend all ingredients together in a liquidiser for 1 minute or until smooth. Season to taste.

Vegan. Dairy, gluten, wheat and yeast free.
Freezing: Can be frozen for up to 1 month but is always better made fresh.
Cook's Tips: 1 teaspoon of tahini is good added to this.
Nutritional Content: Calcium, copper, magnesium, manganese and tryptophan.
Note to the Senses: The texture won't be exactly like mayonnaise, but very nearly like it. You can add a little seasoning if you feel it needs it.

Aioli

serves 4 as a condiment
ready in 10 minutes

This is a Provençal garlic paste.

2 garlic cloves, peeled and squashed to purée consistency
pinch of salt
juice of ½ lemon
55 ml (2 fl oz) olive oil

Place the garlic, salt and lemon juice in a pestle and mortar and combine well. Slowly add the olive oil drop by drop, whisking the garlic constantly until a dropping consistency is obtained. It should have the consistency of thin mayonnaise.

Vegan. Dairy, gluten, sugar, wheat and yeast free.
Freezing: Can be frozen for up to 1 month.
Cook's Tips: For a richer mayonnaise like aioli, you can add 2 egg yolks to the garlic and lemon before adding the olive oil very slowly. This is similar to the mayonnaise-making process. When making aioli, the utensils should be at room temperature, as variations in temperatures can cause the aioli to separate. Add some freshly chopped parsley or coriander for an herb aioli.

Nutritional Content: Manganese, monounsaturated fats and vitamins B$_6$, C and E.

Note to the Senses: This condiment is all about the garlic. When you taste this, there should be a good hit of garlic to the taste buds and it should have a creamy consistency.

Salsa Verde

serves 4 as a condiment
ready in 10 minutes

This is basically a green spicy condiment.

2 tsp parsley, chopped
2 tsp basil, chopped
2 tsp celery leaves, chopped
1 tsp mint, chopped
1 tbsp chives, chopped
1 tbsp capers, washed and chopped
1 small green chilli, deseeded and chopped
120 ml (4 fl oz) extra virgin olive oil
1 tbsp balsamic vinegar

Put the herbs, capers and chilli in a bowl and gradually stir in the oil until it's combined. Season with salt and pepper and leave to marinate for at least 30 minutes. Stir in the balsamic vinegar just before serving.

Vegan. Dairy, gluten, sugar, wheat and yeast free.
Freezing: Not suitable for freezing.
Cook's Tips: Do not add salt. The capers will have some residual salt.
Nutritional Content: Calcium, dietary fibre, iron, vitamins A and C.
Note to the Senses: This condiment has such a wonderfully fresh aroma and it will enhance the flavour of a frittata or tart. You can use it as a dip for bread or crudités just as successfully. It simply oozes freshness.

tapenade

Again I turn to France's Provence region for this wonderful thick paste made from capers, ripe olives, olive oil and lemon juice. It's ideal as a condiment, added to pasta salads and as a sandwich spread.

Black Olive Tapenade

serves 4 as a condiment
ready in 10 minutes

250 g (9 oz) black stoned olives
½ tsp capers, rinsed
3 garlic cloves
3–4 tbsp olive oil

Put all ingredients in a food processor or blender and blend to a smooth paste. Refrigerate for up to 2 weeks.

Vegan. Dairy, gluten, sugar, wheat and yeast free.
Freezing: Can be frozen for up to 1 month.
Cook's Tips: You can use green olives if preferred for green olive tapenade. There's no need to add salt here, as the olives and capers are salty enough.
Nutritional Content: Fibre, iron and vitamin E.
Note to the Senses: The taste of the tapenade depends on the olive used. You can have sour or bitter, piquant or sweet. Choose an olive that you like the taste of for a tangy tapenade. It's advisable to use the tapenade sparingly if using as a spread on sandwiches, as the flavour is intense and can overwhelm the rest of the sandwich ingredients.

hummus

This thick Middle Eastern sauce is made from mashed chickpeas seasoned with lemon juice, garlic and olive or sesame oil and tahini. It's usually served as a dip with pieces of pitta bread or as a sauce. In Café Fresh we also use it on sandwiches.

Oil-Free Hummus

serves 4–6 as a condiment
ready in 10 minutes

250 g (9 oz) cooked chickpeas or 400 g (14 oz) can chickpeas, drained
2 garlic cloves
juice of 1 lemon
1 tsp tahini
2 tbsp water

Place all ingredients except water in a blender. Turn on blender and add 1 tbsp water and blend. Add more water slowly until the texture is a thick paste. Taste and season as required. Refrigerate for up to 3 days.

Vegan. Dairy, gluten, sugar, wheat and yeast free.
Freezing: Can be frozen for up to 1 month.
Cook's Tips: A pinch of ground cumin, coriander or chilli powder can be added for a more North African flavour.
Nutritional Content: Copper, dietary fibre, folate, manganese, molybdenum, protein.
Note to the Senses: This is a smooth, creamy paste, which for some reason really appeals to children, probably due to the texture. I suppose it's not dissimilar to puréed baby food, though of course it tastes infinitely better.

Cucumber Raita

serves 4 as a condiment
ready in 10 minutes

Raita is a yoghurt salad condiment common in India. Raita is a combination of thick, whole-milk yoghurt and various chopped vegetables like cucumbers, aubergines, potatoes or spinach, or fruits such as bananas or tomatoes. These salads are variously seasoned with black mustard seeds, garam masala and herbs such as chervil, coriander, cumin, dill, mint, parsley or tarragon. Raitas are designed to be a cooling counterbalance for many spicy Indian dishes. Here I give a simple cucumber raita.

1 cucumber, finely diced
½ onion, peeled and chopped
1 tbsp chopped fresh mint
175 g (6 oz) Greek-style yoghurt
juice of ½ lemon

Place the cucumber, onion and mint leaves into a bowl. Add the Greek-style yoghurt, seasoning to taste and lemon juice and mix together until combined. Spoon into a serving dish and serve at once.

Gluten, sugar, wheat and yeast free.
Freezing: Not suitable for freezing.
Cook's Tips: This raita will become watery if left for any length of time before using. It really has to be eaten as soon as it's made.
Nutritional Content: Calcium, iodine, phosphorous and vitamin B_2 (riboflavin).
Note to the Senses: The word I use to describe this raita is refreshing. Mint is such a fresh and cooling herb and the light green colour emphasises the cooling nature of this raita.

Beetroot Relish

serves 4 as a condiment for burgers
ready in 10 minutes

1½ tsp olive oil
¼ red onion, finely chopped
1½ tsp red wine vinegar
1 tsp maple syrup or concentrated apple juice
2 small cooked beetroot, finely diced

Heat the oil in a pan and add the onion. Sauté until soft. Add the red wine vinegar and maple syrup and sauté for another 3–5 minutes, until reduced by half. Add beetroot and mix well to heat through. Serve with burgers.

Vegan. Dairy, gluten and wheat free.
Freezing: Not suitable for freezing.
Cook's Tips: Vacuum-packed cooked beetroot is ideal for making relish.
Nutritional Content: Fibre, folate, magnesium, manganese, vitamin C.
Note to the Senses: This relish has an earthy flavour, adding a tangy sweetness to your burger. It's equally good added to a mature Cheddar cheese sandwich.

Tomato Relish

serves 4 as a condiment for curry or burgers
ready in 10 minutes

6 large ripe tomatoes, quartered, deseeded and diced
200 g (7 oz) Greek-style yoghurt (optional)
handful of fresh coriander, roughly chopped
1 small red onion, finely chopped
1 spring onion, finely chopped
squeeze of lemon or lime juice

Mix together all the ingredients and season to taste.

Gluten, wheat and yeast free.
Freezing: Not suitable for freezing.
Cook's Tips: This tomato relish is very good without yoghurt. If you don't have coriander, flat-leaf parsley is a good substitute. Deseeding the tomatoes isn't absolutely necessary either, but if you don't, the relish will be less thick. Add a drop of balsamic vinegar for an interesting variation. If you're using this as a condiment or a dip for crisps, nachos and crudités, then I suggest adding a sprinkle of chilli powder or half a finely diced chilli (deseeded for less piquancy).
Nutritional Content: Lycopene, molybdenum, potassium and vitamins A, C and K.
Note to the Senses: This relish should have a vibrant red colour. The tomatoes must be ripe and firm with a good colour. Beef tomatoes work well here, as do vine tomatoes, as they have a great colour. Don't use watery-coloured tomatoes – it's better not to make this at all than use them. In the farmers' markets you can find green tomatoes, which are fantastic as a green tomato relish and it will surprise everyone.

Guacamole

serves 4 as a condiment
ready in 10 minutes

1 avocado, peeled and mashed
1 shallot or small white onion, finely chopped
pinch of cumin seeds, toasted
pinch of chilli flakes or ½ chilli, finely chopped
juice of 1 lime
1 tomato, finely diced
1 tsp olive oil

Mix all the ingredients together. Taste and season as required.

Vegan. Dairy, gluten, sugar, wheat and yeast free.
Freezing: Not suitable for freezing.

Cook's Tips: To help avoid the guacamole blackening, place the stone of the avocado in the centre of the guacamole.

Nutritional Content: Fibre, folate, potassium and vitamin K.

Note to the Senses: The avocado is colloquially known as the alligator pear, reflecting its shape and its leather-like appearance. When purchasing avocados, it's essential that you pick it up, place it in the palm of your hand and squeeze gently. A ripe avocado will appear firm but will yield to gentle pressure. It should be reasonably soft, definitely not hard (some can be rock hard), but not so soft it seems mushy.

buffet dishes

Grilled Aubergine Terrine

serves 4–6
ready overnight

4 large aubergines, cut into 3 mm (⅛ in) slices
6 tbsp olive oil
4 plum tomatoes, cored and cut into 3 mm (⅛ in) slices
135 g (4 ¾ oz) olive tapenade
18–20 large fresh basil leaves

for vinaigrette:
2 tbsp olive oil
1½ tsp cider vinegar
½ tsp Dijon mustard

Arrange the aubergine slices on a baking tray. Brush them with olive oil and season with salt and pepper. Grill under a preheated hot grill for 3–4 minutes. Alternatively, place in a hot oven for approximately 10 minutes, until golden brown. Drain on kitchen paper.

Line a 2-lb terrine/loaf tin with cling film, leaving a good overlap of cling film. Layer the base and sides of the tin with overlapping layers of aubergines.

Arrange a layer of tomato slices over the aubergines, then spread one-third of the tapenade over the tomato. Scatter over one-third of the basil.

Cover with a layer of aubergines. Repeat the layering twice more, finishing with a layer of aubergines.

Cover with the cling film that overlaps the tin. Place a weight such as a litre of milk over the dish and refrigerate for at least 4 hours, or ideally, overnight.

Remove from fridge, loosen the cling film from around the top and turn out onto a board, carefully removing the cling film.

Mix the dressing ingredients together in a bowl and whisk to combine. Season to taste.

To serve, unmould the terrine onto a board or plate and cut into thick slices. Serve drizzled with the dressing.

Vegan. Dairy, gluten, sugar, wheat and yeast free.
Freezing: Not suitable for freezing.
Cook's Tips: Add a layer of mozzarella cheese or smoked tofu in the centre for an alternative. When you remove the terrine from the tin, there will probably be some liquid in the base of the terrine. This is normal, as the juices form the vegetables sink to the bottom from the pressure of the weight. You can add this juice to the vinaigrette for more flavour. This terrine will keep in the fridge for up to 3 days. It's good as a summer lunch with some salad and cheese.
Nutritional Content: Iron, lycopene, molybdenum, potassium and vitamins A, C and K.
Note to the Senses: Terrines are very visual. When you cut a slice, you can see the various layers and it's very attractive to the eye. This terrine combines well as a summer buffet dish and looks good beside a bowl of green leaves.

Grilled Vegetable Terrine with Ricotta

serves 4–6
ready overnight

2 large red peppers, quartered, cored and seeded

2 large yellow peppers, quartered, cored and seeded

1 large aubergine, sliced lengthways

2 large courgettes, sliced lengthways

6 tbsp olive oil

1 large red onion, thinly sliced

1 tbsp tomato purée

1 tbsp red wine vinegar

150 g (5 oz) ricotta cheese

2 tbsp freshly chopped basil

fresh basil leaves, to garnish

for dressing:

6 tbsp olive oil

2 tbsp red wine vinegar

Place the peppers skin side up on a baking tray and place under a hot grill and cook until blackened. Put in a bowl and cover or a sealed plastic bag and leave to cool. Peel the peppers when they are cooled.

Arrange the aubergine and courgette slices on separate baking trays. Brush them with olive oil and cook under the grill.

Heat the remaining olive oil in a frying pan. Add the onion, tomato purée and red wine vinegar. Cook until onions are soft.

Mix the ricotta and 2 tablespoons chopped basil together.

Line a 2-lb terrine/loaf tin with cling film, leaving a good overlap of cling film. Place a layer of red peppers on the bottom, then yellow peppers, then a layer of aubergines and then courgettes. Spread the ricotta cheese over the vegetables. Now add a layer of the onion mixture. Finally, finish with a layer of peppers. Press the vegetables down well.

Cover the vegetables with the overlap of cling film. Place a weight such as a litre of milk on top and refrigerate to chill for a minimum of 4 hours, or ideally, overnight.

Remove from fridge, loosen the cling film from around the top and turn out onto a board, removing the cling film.

Mix the dressing ingredients together, whisking with a fork to combine. Season to taste. Drizzle over each slice of terrine as you serve it. Garnish with the fresh basil leaves.

Gluten, sugar, wheat and yeast free.

Freezing: Not suitable for freezing.

Cook's Tips: Replace the ricotta with silken tofu for a vegan option. When you remove the terrine from the tin, there will probably be some liquid in the base of the terrine. This is normal, as the juices form the vegetables sink to the bottom from the pressure of the weight. You can add this juice to the vinaigrette for more flavour.

Nutritional Content: Dietary fibre, lycopene, manganese, potassium, protein and vitamins A, B_6, C and K.

Note to the Senses: This is the quintessential summer buffet dish. Everyone will be automatically drawn to the colourful layers in each slice. It looks and tastes like summer. It's a real winner.

Provençal Stuffed Autumn Vegetables with Tomato and Coriander Salsa

serves 6
ready in 50 minutes

2 aubergines, halved, pulp scraped out and retained
2 courgettes, halved, pulp scraped out and retained
2 peppers, halved and deseeded
1½ tsp olive oil
1 red onion, finely chopped
2 garlic cloves, finely chopped
1 tsp herbs de Provence
2 sticks of celery, finely chopped
1 carrot, peeled and finely chopped
handful of chopped olives

handful of capers, rinsed

25 g (1 oz) sun-dried tomatoes, chopped

lots of chopped fresh basil

100 g (4 oz) cooked rice (brown or basmati) or cooked quinoa

for salsa:

6 tomatoes

1 green pepper, finely chopped

1 small red onion, finely chopped

handful chopped coriander

½ chilli, finely chopped

1 tbsp lemon/lime juice

Preheat the oven to 180°C/350°F/gas 4.

Finely chop the pulp of the aubergines and courgettes and set aside with the peppers.

Heat the oil in a pan and sauté the onion, garlic and herbs de Provence until cooked. Add the celery and carrot and sauté for 7 more minutes, or until vegetables are cooked. Add the pulp of the aubergines and courgettes, olives, capers and sun-dried tomatoes. Mix well and cook for a further 5 minutes, until the pulp has cooked down. Add the chopped basil and combine the vegetable mix with the rice.

Lay the empty aubergines, courgettes and peppers on a greased baking tray. Spoon the rice filling into the vegetables. Cover with tin foil and bake for 25–30 minutes, until the vegetables are cooked.

Meanwhile, to make the salsa, slice the tomatoes in half, scoop out the insides and discard, or use for the vegetable rice filling. Finely chop the tomatoes and place in a bowl. Add the finely chopped pepper, red onion, fresh coriander and chilli. Season and drizzle over with lemon/lime juice. Leave to stand for 30 minutes so all the flavours develop.

Optional – once removed, add a slice of feta/brie to the top of the rice filling and allow it to melt a little. Drizzle over with a little basil pesto if available and serve with salsa on the side.

Vegan. Dairy, gluten, sugar, wheat and yeast free.

Freezing: Filling is suitable for freezing for up to 1 month.

Cook's Tips: This is a good recipe for using up leftover rice. Basmati rice is a better choice than brown if you're having guests. Quinoa also works very well here and has an interesting texture.

Nutritional Content: Fibre, lycopene, manganese, selenium, tryptophan and vitamins A, K and B_6.

Note to the Senses: Aubergine, peppers and courgettes herald the onset of summer months, remind us of Mediterranean flavours and combine well together to make a visually delightful dish.

Vegetable and Bean Burger

makes 6 burgers
ready in 20 minutes

1 tbsp sunflower oil

1 onion, finely diced

2 garlic cloves, finely diced

1 tsp ground coriander

1 tsp ground cumin

1 tsp ground curry powder

1 tsp ground chilli powder

1 carrot, peeled and diced

1 stick of celery, diced

1 parsnip, diced

½ small turnip, diced

450 g (16 oz) cooked pinto or kidney beans or 2 x 400 g (14 oz) can beans, drained

Preheat the oven to 180°C/350°F/gas 4.

Heat the oil in a pan and sauté the onion and garlic together. Add the spices, mix well and sauté for 1 minute. Add the vegetables, season lightly, cover and cook until soft. Add 1 tablespoon of water to avoid burning.

Combine the beans and cooked vegetables together in a food processor and pulse to a rough mash texture. Alternatively, you can use a potato masher or hand blender. Don't over-blend – you want to see the bean texture through the mixture.

Taste and season – you'll need to add a good bit of salt as the beans will absorb a lot. The consistency shouldn't be too wet.

Make 6 burger patties, shaping them in the palms of your hands. Leave the burgers to rest for 30 minutes in the fridge. Bake for 35 minutes, until heated through and brown.

For a summer buffet, serve with Garlic Mayonnaise (see p. 59) or Tofu Mayonnaise (see p. 29), Beetroot Relish (see p. 13), sautéed red onions and oven-roasted cherry tomatoes.

Vegan. Dairy, gluten, sugar, wheat and yeast free.
Freezing: Freezes very well for up to 2 months.
Cook's Tips: If you think the mixture appears too wet, add some breadcrumbs or maize flour. This mixture benefits from resting overnight in the fridge if you can wait that long.
Nutritional Content: Antioxidants, dietary fibre, folate, manganese, molybdenum, protein and tryptophan.
Note to the Senses: The presentation is very important here. The flavours of the spices come through in the burger and once combined with the flavours of the Beetroot Relish and Tofu Mayonnaise it becomes a very special burger. If you have time, oven-roasted cherry tomatoes and sautéed red onions are a perfect accompaniment to this burger for a buffet.

Nut, Vegetable and Feta Loaf

serves 6
ready in 50 minutes

A nut loaf in a vegetarian cookbook is almost clichéd at this stage. However, it's still popular and the recipe below gives a few alternatives to make it more interesting. It's also less heavy on the nuts and therefore a better balance in flavours.

200 g (7 oz) maize flour

1 tsp baking powder

1 courgette, grated

1 carrot, peeled and grated

½ red onion, finely chopped

2 garlic cloves, finely chopped

2 medium chillies, finely chopped

250 g (9 oz) toasted mixed nuts and seeds (sunflower seeds, pine nuts, hazelnuts, cashew nuts, sesame seeds)

1½ tsp herbs de Provence

handful of fresh basil

sea salt and pepper, to taste

2 eggs, lightly beaten

100 ml (3½ fl oz) milk/soy milk

175 g (6 oz) feta cheese

Preheat the oven to 180°C/350°F/gas 4. Line a 2-lb terrine/loaf tin with grease-proof paper.

Mix the flour, baking powder, grated vegetables, onion, garlic and chillies together. Add the nuts and seeds, herbs, sea salt and pepper. Add the beaten eggs and enough milk to bind.

Place half the mix in the lined loaf tin and press down. Slice the feta and lay it over the mix. Place the remaining nut mix over the feta and press down.

Bake for 35–40 minutes, until the loaf has risen slightly and is golden. Remove from the oven and allow to cool for 10 minutes, then turn out of the tin.

Each slice should have a layer of feta cheese in the centre. Serve with Sun-Dried Tomato Pesto (see p. 4) or Basil Pesto (see p. 3).

Sugar and wheat free.

Freezing: Freezes well for up to 2 months.

Cook's Tips: For a vegan alternative, replace the feta with smoked tofu or a layer of roasted, peeled peppers and use soy milk and egg replacer to bind. This is a good Christmas solution for a stressed mum catering for a vegetarian. You can make it more seasonal by adding a layer of feta and a layer of parsley pesto over this and some dried cranberries through the centre for an interesting and beautiful slice of loaf.

Nutritional Content: Copper, flavonoids, magnesium, manganese, tryptophan and vitamins B_1 and E.

Note to the Senses: Like terrines and layers, this loaf is visually appealing as the slice is broken in the centre by a layer of feta cheese. You can use alternatives as suggested above. While there's a nutty flavour, it's not overpowering, as there's a good selection of vegetables. This means that it won't feel too heavy when eaten. Don't forget some pesto for extra moisture and flavour.

salads

Introduction

Salads are a fundamental part of our menu at Café Fresh. For me, the words 'salad' and 'fresh' are synonymous. For a good salad you need the freshest seasonal ingredients, fresh herbs and a good salad dressing, where necessary. Salads can be a light accompaniment to a main dish, a substantial lunch or a quick snack.

Salads aren't just confined to the summer months. Of course there is much more choice in the summer, when wonderful fresh fruit and vegetables and salad leaves are available. However, there are plenty of options for the rest of the year. Using seasonal vegetables may seem a little restrictive for salads, but with a bit more creativity you can produce wonderful salads all year round. Winter salads may need a bit more time and imagination, but the final product will be worth it. Salads should never be doused in heavy vinaigrettes. The ideal dressing should be light, with balanced flavours and correct proportions.

Salads are greatly enhanced by the use of fresh herbs. Dried herbs are a very poor substitute for the real thing. Dried herbs have their place in the kitchen, but they shouldn't be used in salads unless they're being cooked. You'll see this in the winter salads. The more exotic flavours can be added once you've mastered the basics of salads – fresh seasonal ingredients, herbs and dressings.

Salads are very visual, so it's important that the combinations of your chosen vegetables and fruit work well together to tickle the senses and make them really appetising. Remember that the recipes can be altered to suit your palate; nothing is written in stone.

This chapter is divided by the main ingredient in the salad. There's a brief description of the vegetable or pulses, together with the nutritional information. There are lots of tips, so take the time to read the details and you'll have great salads.

vinaigrettes and salad dressings

Salad dressings: There are a plethora of salad dressing recipes available, from the classic vinaigrette (see p. 26) to a drizzle of good-quality extra virgin oil, to a mayonnaise or a complex herb tofu dressing. The important thing to remember is that there are many ways to dress a salad. Regardless of your dietary needs, there are many options, and once you marry the right dressing with the right salad, you can be sure to have a salad to tickle any taste buds.

Vinaigrette: As with a lot of Western cuisine, I look to France for the basic recipe for vinaigrette. There are many recipes and variations on the classic French vinaigrette. However, there are a few basic rules that must be adhered to at the outset to make good vinaigrette.

It's difficult when you're first making a vinaigrette to get the quantities right. It can be too sharp or too oily and have no 'edge' it. The general problem is the proportions of oil to acid, i.e. vinegar/lemon juice/lime juice, etc. My basic rule is three parts oil to one part vinegar. Once I start with this rule, I can then be sure I'm on the way to a good, balanced vinaigrette. Don't worry about the types of vinegar or oil at the moment. Getting the quantities right is all important.

Vinegars come in many shades and varieties. I use different types for different salads. However, vinegar isn't suitable for everyone. A person who is yeast sensitive should replace vinegars with lemon or lime juice. In fact, some salads marry much better with lemon or lime juice, as you'll see throughout this chapter.

Oils, like vinegars, come in an abundance of varieties. I use sunflower oil for certain salads, very good-quality extra virgin olive oil for others and sesame oil for the more Asian flavours. For salads it's worthwhile spending a bit more on good-quality oil. The better quality will make all the difference to the flavour. Never buy blended oils; they're a waste of money. Buy the best oils you can afford for your salad dressings.

Mustard is another ingredient in vinaigrette. The basic mustard I use for general vinaigrette is Dijon mustard. English mustard is too sharp and is far too overbearing for salad dressings. Wholegrain mustard adds depth and texture to vinaigrette and suits some salads extremely well.

Basic Vinaigrette

makes 150 ml (5 fl oz)

2 tbsp white wine vinegar or juice of 1 lemon
¼ tsp Dijon mustard
pinch sea salt and pepper
6 tbsp sunflower oil

Place all the ingredients in a bowl except the oil. Combine well. Add the oil and whisk with a fork until evenly blended.

Alternatively, you can place all the ingredients in a blender and blend for a few seconds. You'll get a thicker consistency. Or you can shake all the ingredients together in a screw-top jar.

Store in the fridge for no more than 2 days, as the taste will diminish after this. It's best to make vinaigrette the day you need it.

If you're making the dressing for just one person, a good rule to remember is that the quantity of oil to vinegar is about 1 part vinegar to 3 parts oil. You can adjust this slightly depending on how sharp you need it. It just takes a little practice to get it right and then you can make your own vinaigrette whenever you need it.

Balsamic Vinaigrette

makes approx. 150 ml (5 fl oz)

2 tbsp balsamic vinegar
1½ tsp Dijon mustard
6 tbsp olive oil

Place the vinegar and mustard in a bowl. Combine well. Add the oil and whisk with a fork until evenly blended. Season to taste.

Alternatively, you can place all the ingredients in a blender and blend for a few seconds. You'll get a thicker consistency. Or you can shake all the ingredients together in a screw-top jar.

Store in the fridge for no more than 2 days, as the taste will diminish after this. It's best to make vinaigrette the day you need it.

mayonnaise

Mayonnaise dressings have got a lot of bad press in recent years. This is mainly down to the fact that they're used too liberally, with salads practically swimming in industrial-style mayonnaise. This, together with the fact that it's a creamy dressing, makes us think it must be bad for us – all those eggs, all that cholesterol!

In Café Fresh we make our own mayonnaise. To make it lighter we add in the whites of the eggs, which gives it a better consistency for using on salads. We only use it on our coleslaw salad and intermittently throughout the year for very specific salads. We also make a Tofu Mayonnaise (see p. 29) which has a lovely creamy texture without the worry of the cholesterol and is completely vegan. Like all of the good things in life, it's a matter of balance. Mayonnaise has its place in the kitchen, but should be used sparingly and enjoyed for its creamy, naughty flavour.

Mayonnaise can seem like a bit of hard work if you're only making a little amount. There's good-quality organic mayonnaise available now, so you don't have to feel too guilty not making your own, although there's no comparison with the real thing!

Egg-Based Mayonnaise

makes 450 ml (16 fl oz)

2 free-range eggs (organic if possible), separated
1 garlic clove, finely chopped (optional)
1 tsp Dijon mustard
juice of 1 lemon
300 ml (10 fl oz) sunflower or olive oil

In a bowl, combine the egg yolk, garlic (if using), mustard and lemon juice. Whisk together until all are well combined.

While still whisking, very slowly add the oil in a thin stream. Continue whisking until all the oil has been added. Once half has been added, you can add the oil a little faster. As you add the oil, the egg mix will begin to thicken. Take care, though – if you add the oil too fast, the mayonnaise will curdle and you'll have to start again.

Add in the egg whites and whisk rigorously until fully combined. Taste and season as required. Store in a sealed container in the fridge for up to 3 days.

Cook's Tips: Making mayonnaise can seem like a daunting task at first. The best advice is to just take your time. If the mayonnaise starts to curdle, don't panic, all is not lost. You'll need to start again. Start with step 1, then very slowly add in approximately 50 ml (2 fl oz) of oil. If all is going well, then you can add the curdled mayonnaise in a very slow stream until fully combined. You will then have a thick mayonnaise. Add the whites of the eggs, one by one, until fully combined. Once you have mastered this basic recipe, you can experiment by adding in some herbs, a chilli or even some pesto.

Tofu Mayonnaise

makes 450 ml (16 fl oz)

110 g (4 oz) tofu (silken is best)
1 garlic clove, finely chopped
1 tsp Dijon mustard
1 tbsp lemon juice
1 tbsp water
300 ml (10 fl oz) sunflower or olive oil

In a bowl, combine the tofu, garlic, mustard, lemon juice and water. Whisk together until all are well combined. Alternatively, place in a food processor or blender.

While still whisking, very slowly add the oil in a thin stream. Continue whisking until all the oil has been added. Once half has been added, you can add the oil a little faster. You should have a mayonnaise-like consistency.

Taste and season as required. Store in a sealed container in the fridge for up to 5 days.

Cook's Tips: Using silken tofu will make it easier to blend. If the consistency is too thick, add a little more water and whisk. Once you've mastered the knack of making mayonnaise, you can then experiment by adding some chopped fresh herbs.

red cabbage salads

Red cabbage has a wonderful purple colour. It gets its colour from a pigment called anthocyanin, as do all red, blue and purple plants. Red cabbage was even grown in the Middle Ages when botanists learned to encourage its special colour feature. Red cabbage reminds me of Christmas, when it's braised in red wine and sweetened. I love to use it in salads for its wonderful colour, flavour and nutritional value.

The colour of this cabbage is uplifting in a winter salad. Red cabbage is available all year round but is best in the winter and early spring months. Red cabbage, a member of the large family of cruciferous vegetables, is rich in nutrients. Along with significant amounts of nitrogen compounds known as indoles and dietary fibre, red cabbage is a rich source of vitamin C (supplying almost twice as much vitamin C as green cabbage). It is also higher in calcium, iron and potassium than its green cousin. By eating it in its raw state, you keep all the nutrients. It's very economical and a great way of getting good nutrients into the diet during the winter.

When purchasing red or white cabbage, note that there are quarter pieces of cabbages available in the supermarkets. If you feel a full cabbage won't be used within a week, then choose the smaller pieces.

Red cabbage has a mildly sweet flavour and so combines very well with other sweet flavours, particularly fruit. Depending on the salad, I add fresh fruit, dried fruit, fruit juice or a little sweetener.

Below are three recipes that will definitely satisfy.

Red Cabbage and Spinach Salad

serves 6
ready in 15–20 minutes

Baby spinach is best for this salad, but if you're using the more mature leaves, remove any tough stems, wash well and leave to dry.

50 g (2 oz) pine nuts
1 red cabbage, halved, quartered and sliced very thinly
1 medium red onion, sliced thinly
110 g (4 oz) baby spinach
50 g (2 oz) smoked tofu or blue cheese

for balsamic vinaigrette:

1 garlic clove, minced

⅛ tsp sea salt

½ tsp Dijon mustard

½ tsp honey or organic maple syrup

1 tbsp balsamic vinegar

3 tbsp extra virgin olive oil

Toast the pine nuts in a dry pan over moderate heat, stirring frequently until golden, about 2 minutes.

Prepare the cabbage. Cut in half lengthwise and then cut in half again. Remove the core at the end of each quarter. Slice the red cabbage thinly. Alternatively, you can use a food processor with a thin slicing blade.

In a large bowl, combine the cabbage, sliced red onion and baby spinach together. If using tofu, cut into small bite-sized cubes and mix into the cabbage. Once the pine nuts have cooled, toss into the salad. If using blue cheese instead of tofu, crumble it over the leaves.

Make the vinaigrette by whisking together the garlic, salt, mustard, honey or maple syrup and vinegar, then add the oil in a stream, whisking until thickened slightly. If using a food processor or hand blender, simply blend all the ingredients together.

Drizzle the dressing over the salad and gently toss. Serve immediately.

Gluten, sugar and wheat free. If you replace the vinegar with lemon juice, then the dish is yeast free. Vegan and dairy free if using tofu.

Cook's Tips: When Swiss chard (that lovely green leaf with a purple vein going through) is available, I would advise using it as an alternative to spinach. Rocket is also very good with this salad.

Nutritional Content: High vitamin and mineral content, as outlined in the introduction on p. 30, as well as low in calories.

Note to the Senses: This salad should be very crunchy. The dressing is sweet and should compliment the cabbage well.

Red Cabbage, Apple and Pear Salad

serves 6

ready in 15–20 minutes

1 red cabbage

½ head cos lettuce or 1 baby cos lettuce, washed

2 red apples, cored and diced into small cubes

1 pear, cored and diced into small cubes

25 g (1 oz) raisins

25 g (1 oz) toasted pumpkin seeds

25 ml (1 fl oz) concentrated apple juice

75 ml (3 fl oz) orange juice

Prepare the cabbage. Cut in half lengthwise and then cut in half again. Remove the core at the end of each quarter. Slice the red cabbage thinly. Alternatively, you can use a food processor with a thin slicing blade.

Thinly slice the washed cos lettuce and pat dry. Combine the red cabbage, Cos lettuce, cubed apples and pear, raisins and seeds together.

Combine the concentrated apple juice and orange juice together, mixing well. Pour over the cabbage salad and toss. Decorate with some toasted pumpkin seeds and serve immediately.

Vegan. Dairy, gluten, sugar, wheat and yeast free.

Cook's Tips: I've used raisins here, but you can substitute chopped dried dates or figs if you prefer.

Nutritional Content: High vitamin and mineral content, as outlined in the introduction on p. 30, as well as low in calories.

Note to the Senses: This salad has a wonderful fruit flavour, and a good combination of colours makes it very pleasing on the eyes.

Red Cabbage Coleslaw

serves 4–6
ready in 20 minutes

½ section white cabbage
¼ section red cabbage, core removed
1 carrot, peeled and grated
½ shallot, thinly sliced (optional)

for mayonnaise:
1 egg, separated
juice of ½ lemon
½ tsp Dijon mustard
200 ml (7 fl oz) sunflower oil
sea salt

First prepare the salad. Cut the white cabbage in half lengthwise and then cut in half again. Remove the core at the end of each quarter. Slice the cabbage thinly. Alternatively, you can use a food processor with a thin slicing blade. To grate the carrot, you can also use the grating blade of the food processor or use the roughest edge of a hand grater.

Place the cabbage, carrot and shallot in a bowl and combine well.

Make the mayonnaise as instructed on p. 28. Alternatively, you can use the Tofu Mayonnaise on p. 29.

Add half the mayonnaise to the cabbage mix. Mix well (I find that a fork or your hand works well here). You don't want the mayonnaise to remain in clumps in the salad. Add more mayonnaise if the salad is still too dry. You may use all the mayonnaise, but it's best to go slowly to make sure you don't end up with cabbage swimming in mayonnaise. Any leftover mayonnaise will keep in the fridge for up to 3 days in a sealed container.

Cook's Tips: Some people love onion in coleslaw and others think there's no place for it here. It's up to you – simply add in or leave out. My mother makes the most wonderful coleslaw, chopped by hand, and always includes some onion. I love it, and if I'm making it at home I always add some onion to the cabbage before dressing. In the restaurant we leave it out so that anyone sensitive to onions can have the yummy coleslaw.

Nutritional Content: High vitamin and mineral content, but more fat if using mayonnaise. The eggs or tofu add a little protein to the dish.

Note to the Senses: Colourful, creamy and crunchy.

beetroot salads

Beetroot is a wonderful root vegetable. It has a deep burgundy colour and intense, earthy flavour. It's highly nutritious and a wonderful detoxing vegetable. It's now being hailed as a 'superfood'. Beetroot contains folate, manganese and potassium. Experts believe its deep burgundy colour contains certain cancer-fighting agents and beetroot has been used in the treatment of cancer for some years. Beetroot is also low in calories (100 g/4 oz = 36 calories). There are lots of good reasons to include it in your diet. The tastiest way of doing this is to use it in salads. In Café Fresh during the autumn and winter months, a pot of beetroot is boiled each afternoon, peeled and sliced for one of the next day's salads.

Raw beetroot is readily available at the food markets and some supermarkets. There are a few important considerations when using beetroot. Beetroot takes a long time to cook – over 1 hour in general, depending on the size. It also tends to have a strong smell when boiling, which people also find off-putting. I have some solutions to these problems.

Cook's Tips: For the domestic kitchen, a little tip to speed up the cooking time is to top and tail each beetroot before boiling. All you need to do is cover with cold water, bring to the boil and simmer for 30–40 minutes. **Be careful** that the water doesn't boil over onto the cooker, as you will have purple juice everywhere! The boiling time will depend on the size of the beets. Test one and see if it slices very easily – if it does, they're cooked. Once cooked, drain off and leave to cool. The skins will be nice and loose and easy to remove. Remember, beetroot stains very badly. I suggest wearing rubber gloves or some other hand protection to avoid staining. When peeling, simply roll the beets between the palms of your hands and the skin will peel off easily. There's no need to peel with a knife.

If this sounds like too much of a chore for you and you just cannot bear the smell of boiling beetroot, there's an alternative. In supermarkets, you'll find vacuum-packed cooked beetroot. The packs usually contain 4–5 cooked beets and have no additives. You can even get organic vacuum packs in some of the better super-markets. If you're using this for salad, use 1 pack for 2 people. Once opened, it will keep in the fridge for about four days.

When you try these salads, you'll never return to the pickled and sugary vari-ety found in jars in supermarkets. There are much better and infinitely tastier ways to eat beetroot, and of course it can be eaten raw or cooked, as shown below.

Roast Beetroot, Shallot and Mushroom Salad

serves 4
ready in 20 minutes

This is an ideal winter salad. The beets aren't roasted from scratch, as this takes a long time. Young beetroot are delicious if baked in the oven for a time to retain their earthy flavour. Combined with shallots, balsamic vinegar and walnuts (option-al), this make a hearty, warm winter salad.

3 shallots
50 g (2 oz) field/chestnut/Portobello mushrooms
1 tbsp balsamic vinegar
2 tbsp olive oil
sea salt and pepper
6 sprigs fresh marjoram
8 baby beetroot or 4 regular beetroot, cooked, or 2 vacuum packs of beetroot
1 tbsp roughly chopped walnuts (optional)

Preheat the oven to 180°C/350°F/gas 5.

Peel the shallots and cut in half. If they're particularly big, cut them in quarters. Wash the mushrooms and cut in half. Place the shallots and mushrooms on a baking tray and drizzle over with half the balsamic vinegar and olive oil. Season lightly and place 4 marjoram sprigs onto the baking tray and toss well. Cover with foil and bake for 15 minutes, or until tender.

Meanwhile, cut the cooked beets into 5 cm (2 in) cubes.

Once the shallots and mushrooms are cooked, remove from the oven. There should be some nice juices in the tray. Add in the chopped beets and drizzle over with the remaining oil and balsamic vinegar.

Return to the oven without covering for 7–10 minutes, until the beetroot is heated through and they have a nice shine.

Once removed, taste and season if desired. If you think the dish looks a bit too dry, just drizzle a little olive oil over the vegetables and combine well. Add in the chopped walnuts. Roughly chop the remaining marjoram and sprinkle over the beets. Serve immediately.

Vegan. Dairy, gluten, sugar and wheat free.
Cook's Tips: This salad is also very good cold, so if there are any leftovers, refrigerate and use the next day. Remember to remove from the fridge 20–30 minutes before eating so that it's not too cold and the flavours come through.
Nutritional Content: The dish is high in chromium, copper, flavonoids, folate, manganese, selenium and vitamins A and C, as well as all the goodness of beetroot.
Note to the Senses: The marjoram really makes this salad. It's a sweet-smelling herb and works wonderfully with the beetroot. The aroma of the balsamic vinegar and the marjoram roasting together wafts through the kitchen, sending signals to your brain that something wonderful is on the way.

Beetroot and Orange Salad

serves 4
ready in 10 minutes

This is an ideal summer salad.

8 baby or 4 regular cooked beetroot, or 2 vacuum packs of beetroot

2 oranges, peeled, white rind removed and cut into small segments

1 tbsp walnuts, roughly chopped

1½ tsp toasted pumpkin seeds

1½ tsp olive oil (optional)

Cut the beetroot into chunks, then simply combine all the ingredients together in a bowl and coat with olive oil. Season to taste.

Cook's Tips: Add 1 tbsp of Greek-style natural yoghurt to the ingredients and combine well as an alternative. Add some freshly chopped mint for a refreshing finish.

Beetroot, Apple and Carrot Salad

serves 4

ready in 20 minutes

This makes a wonderfully light salad. You can drizzle a little olive oil over this if you like, but it really isn't necessary as the juices from the vegetables and lemon juice combined are wonderful here. This salad won't keep, so eat it all in one sitting. It's very light, low in calories and full of goodness, so there should be no reason to leave any behind.

8 baby or 4 regular raw beetroot

2 carrots, peeled

3 red Cox pippins apples, washed

50 g (2 oz) rocket or baby spinach

sea salt and pepper

juice of ½ lemon

1½ tsp extra virgin olive oil (optional)

Grate the beetroot, carrot and apple on the roughest side of the hand grater. Alternatively, you can use the food processor, but be careful that the apple does not turn into mush.

Roughly chop the rocket or spinach. If you can get wild rocket, then so much the better for flavour. Combine with the other grated vegetables. Season with a little sea salt and pepper and drizzle over with lemon juice and olive oil (optional).

Cook's Tips: If you want a slightly creamy dressing for this salad, you can add a tablespoon of mayonnaise (tofu or egg) to the olive oil and whisk.

chicory salads

Chicory, or French endive, is a member of the lettuce family and is available in red and white varieties. It's only in season for a short time during the year. It's available during the winter months, but generally February is the month to get it at its best. You will find it in the farmers' markets. It's an important salad vegetable in Europe in general, but it doesn't get much space on the Irish table. When purchasing, ensure you pick a tight bulb which only has a few loose leaves. I use chicory in salads when in season, February to March, for its wonderfully crunchy texture and slightly bitter leaves.

Chicory, Beetroot and Fennel Salad

serves 4
ready in 20 minutes

4 heads chicory
1 head baby cos lettuce
2 raw beetroot, peeled
½ fennel bulb
2 shallots, peeled
25 g (1 oz) field mushrooms, washed
handful rocket
handful watercress, if available

for the dressing:
½ tsp Dijon mustard
1 tsp concentrated apple juice
50 ml (2 fl oz) raspberry vinegar
150 ml (5 fl oz) sunflower oil

Slice the chicory and baby cos lengthwise and chop thinly into half-moon shapes, then wash and leave to dry.

Grate the beetroot into a large bowl. Remove the core at the bottom of the fennel bulb, then slice thinly into half-moons and add to the beetroot. Thinly slice the shallots and mushrooms and add to the beetroot.

Add the rocket and watercress (if available) to the bowl and add the dry chicory and cos lettuce.

Make the dressing by combining all the ingredients in a bowl and whisking. Drizzle over the salad and serve immediately.

Vegan. Dairy, gluten, sugar and wheat free.
Cook's Tips: Chop some flat-leaf parsley and add to the salad for extra fresh flavour.
Note to the Senses: The raspberry vinegar adds depth to this salad. It helps to balance the strong aniseed flavour of the fennel and the bitter flavour of the chicory. You need to check out a very good delicatessen or grocery store to get it, but it will be worth it. The beetroot adds colour.

celery salads

Celery is a common vegetable and is available all year round. The green or yellow varieties of celery are available all year and are plentiful in summer, but it's the frost-hardy white celery that's available only in winter.

Celery's nutritional benefits derive from its vitamin C content and other active compounds that promote health, including phalides, which may help lower cholesterol, and coumarins, which may be useful in cancer prevention. Phalides relax the muscles of the arteries that regulate blood pressure, allowing these vessels to dilate. Phalides also reduce stress hormones, one of whose effects is to cause blood vessels to constrict. Courmarins help prevent free radicals from damaging cells, thus decreasing the mutations that increase the potential for cells to become cancerous.

Celery is also very low in calories, so you can eat lots of it. Celery is rich in both potassium and sodium, the minerals most important for regulating fluid balance, and stimulates urine production, thus helping to rid the body of excess fluid.

When buying celery, ensure it has crisp, long stems attached to a sound base and that the leaves are vibrant and green. When using, cut the stalks away from the stem and wash thoroughly, as dirt can get lodged between the stalks. When I'm using celery, I generally like to chop and then wash it to make sure it's thoroughly cleaned. Celery is a great winter vegetable and makes a refreshing salad, emphasising its crispness.

Celery, Apple and Walnut Salad

serves 4–6
ready in 20 minutes

4 sticks of celery
1 baby cos or butterhead lettuce
1 bag rocket salad leaves
3 russet apples, cored
squeeze of lemon juice
1 ripe avocado
handful chopped, toasted walnuts
handful raisins

for the dressing:
1 tsp wholegrain mustard
50 ml (2 fl oz) raspberry vinegar
150 ml (5 fl oz) sunflower oil

Chop the celery into bite-sized pieces and wash thoroughly. Leave to drain. Chop cos or butterhead and rocket and wash thoroughly. Leave to drain. Chop apples into bite-sized pieces and drizzle a little lemon juice over them to prevent them from browning. Peel and chop the avocado and add to the chopped apples. Combine well.

In a bowl, mix all the salad ingredients together, including the walnuts and raisins, keeping a little rocket aside for the dressing.

To make the dressing, in a bowl or blender, combine all the dressing ingredients together, including the remaining rocket. If using a blender, just add the rocket to all the other ingredients. If using a hand whisk, finely chop the rocket and combine with the other ingredients. (The blender works better for this.) Season to taste.

Finally, pour the dressing over the salad ingredients and toss well. Serve with some finely chopped walnuts on top.

Vegan. Dairy, gluten, sugar and wheat free.
Cook's Tips: Replace the raspberry vinegar with lemon and lime juice for a yeast-free salad.
Nutritional Content: Copper, dietary fibre, folate, manganese, omega 3 fatty acids, potassium, and vitamins B_6, C and K.
Note to the Senses: A crunchy, healthy, refreshing salad that cleanses the body, this has been around in various guises for many decades. This salad makes you feel good as you eat it.

Celery, Chicory, Cucumber and Mint Salad

serves 4
ready in 10 minutes

4 medium sticks of celery, washed
1 cucumber, washed
1 head chicory
50 ml (2 fl oz) Greek-style yoghurt
2 tbsp chopped fresh mint (or parsley)
juice of 1 lemon

Slice the celery and cucumber into thin slices. Slice the chicory lengthwise, finely chop and wash thoroughly. Pat dry.

In a bowl, toss the celery, cucumber, chicory, yoghurt, mint, lemon juice and salt and pepper to taste. Garnish with fresh mint leaves.

Gluten, sugar, wheat and yeast free.

Cook's Tips: Chicory adds a bitterness to this salad, which I love. You can omit the chicory if you don't like the flavour.

Nutritional Content: Calcium, dietary fibre, folate, phosphorus, potassium, protein, vitamins B_5, B_{12} and C and zinc.

Note to the Senses: A cooling, refreshing salad, ideal for summer months. Fresh mint combined with Greek yoghurt has a tongue-tingling freshness.

super easy and nutritious salads

Broccoli and Cauliflower Salad with Tahini Dressing

serves 4–6
ready in 20 minutes

1 large head broccoli
1 small head cauliflower
handful of green beans (optional)
50 g (2 oz) flaked almonds
1 punnet cherry tomatoes, halved
1 red pepper, thinly sliced

for the dressing:
2 tbsp tahini
1 garlic clove, crushed
juice of ½ lemon
1½ tsp olive oil
1 tbsp water

Break off the broccoli and cauliflower florets into small bite-sized pieces. Keep the stalks for making soups or vegetable stock.

Place the green beans, broccoli and cauliflower into a bowl and cover with boiling water. Leave to stand for 7 minutes, strain and run under the cold tap until all the vegetables are cold. Leave aside to drain.

Toast the almonds in a dry pan over a low heat. Toss regularly until brown, about 2 minutes. Leave aside to cool.

Make the dressing by combining all the dressing ingredients together except the oil. Whisk in the oil slowly, as for mayonnaise (see p. 28). Season to taste. Add a little cold water if the dressing seems too thick.

In a bowl, combine the drained vegetables with the cherry tomatoes, pepper and three-quarters of the almonds. Pour the dressing over the vegetables and toss. Sprinkle with the remaining toasted almonds and a little chopped fresh coriander. Serve immediately.

Vegan. Dairy, gluten, sugar, wheat and yeast free.
Cook's Tips: You must use really good-quality broccoli and cauliflower for this salad; fresh and crisp for best results.
Nutritional Content: Dietary fibre, folate, manganese, molybdenum, potassium, trypophan and vitamins A, B_2, C, E and K.
Note to the Senses: A healthy-looking salad, crunchy and creamy without all the calories. The blanched green vegetables and cherry tomatoes complement each other perfectly and appeal immediately.

Tomato, Red Onion and Basil Salad

serves 4
ready in 10 minutes

8 tomatoes (2 per person)
1 small red onion
handful fresh basil
sea salt
1½ tsp olive oil (optional)

Slice the tomatoes in half lengthwise and cut away the core at the end. Slice each half into half again. If the tomatoes are large, then cut the tomatoes into 8 pieces.

Slice the onion thinly into half-moons. Gently tear the fresh basil into smaller pieces. Place all the ingredients into a bowl and combine.

Sprinkle a pinch of sea salt over the salad and drizzle over with olive oil. Toss and serve.

Vegan. Dairy, gluten, sugar, wheat and yeast free.
Cook's Tips: If making this salad for guests, it's a good idea to prepare it in advance and leave it to stand for 15–20 minutes before serving. This allows the flavours of the tomatoes to develop. To vary the salad slightly, substitute half the quantity of tomatoes with a punnet of cherry tomatoes (there's no need to cut the cherry tomatoes).
Nutritional Value: Tomatoes are full of vitamins A and C and smaller amounts of chromium, fibre, manganese and potassium.
Note to the Senses: The quality of the tomatoes is all important here. Tomatoes are at their best from July to September. Choose plump, deep-red, sweet-smelling tomatoes. In summer there are lots of varieties available, such as the wonderfully flavoured vine tomatoes and smaller cherry tomatoes. If buying from the farmers' markets, there is a fantastic selection of oddly coloured and shaped tomatoes in summer. These are the best tomatoes to use, both from a taste and visual point of view. Of course, tomatoes are available all year round now, though always choose the best you can find.

Tomato and Cucumber Salad

serves 4
ready in 10 minutes

4 tomatoes
1 cucumber
1 red onion
handful fresh mint
olive oil and sea salt, to taste

Slice the tomatoes in half lengthwise and cut away the core at the end. Slice each half into half again. If the tomatoes are large, then cut the tomatoes into 8 pieces.

Slice the cucumber lengthwise, then finely slice each length into half-moons. Thinly slice the onion into half-moons. Combine all the vegetables in a bowl. Roughly chop the mint and add to the vegetables. Drizzle over with a little olive oil and a sprinkle of sea salt.

Vegan. Dairy, gluten, sugar, wheat and yeast free.
Cook's Tips: This salad also works well with fresh basil.
Nutritional Content: Tomatoes are full of vitamins A and C and smaller amounts of chromium, fibre, manganese and potassium.
Note to the Senses: Cucumber is a cooling, refreshing vegetable. It is excellent in the summer months from May to July but is available all year round. When purchasing, choose a firm, vivid-coloured cucumber.

Cucumber Salad with Yoghurt and Mint

serves 4
ready in 10–15 minutes

2 cucumbers
2 garlic cloves, finely chopped or crushed
handful fresh mint, chopped
1 tbsp Greek-style yoghurt

Slice the cucumber lengthwise, then finely slice each length into half-moons. In a bowl, combine the sliced cucumber and crushed garlic.

Add the chopped mint to the yoghurt. Add the yoghurt to the cucumber, coating well. Season lightly and serve immediately.

Gluten, sugar, wheat and yeast free.
Cook's Tips: This salad is very refreshing in summer. I have adapted this from the traditional tzatziki recipe. It's much quicker and there is no loss of nutrients, as in the traditional recipe.
Nutritional Content: Fibre and vitamin C, as well as smaller amounts of magnesium, potassium and silica. The yoghurt is a good source of B vitamins, calcium and protein and is much more digestible than fresh milk. Yoghurt contains good bacteria which are reputed to keep the intestinal system in healthy condition.
Note to the Senses: This is a very refreshing salad and works well as a side dish to Indian curries.

Carrot, Almond and Parsley Salad

serves 4
ready in 15 minutes

6 medium carrots, peeled and grated
1 tbsp flaked almonds, toasted
bunch of finely chopped parsley (curly or flat-leaf)

for the dressing:
juice of ½ lemon
1 tbsp sunflower oil

Combine the carrots, almonds and parsley. Mix the lemon juice and sunflower oil together, then drizzle over the carrot mixture and mix well. Serve immediately.

Vegan. Dairy, gluten, sugar, wheat and yeast free.

Cook's Tips: Parsley is a wonderful all-year herb. If you can get flat-leaf parsley, it has a more intense flavour. Almonds can be replaced by a tablespoon of toasted sunflower seeds if you like.

Nutritional Content: This is a wonderfully nutritious salad. The combination of carrot and parsley is packed with beta carotene (the precursor to vitamin A), folate and vitamin C. This, together with the reputed healing qualities of their antioxidants and flavonoids, makes this a salad to be eaten daily.

Note to the Senses: The deeper the colour orange of a carrot, the higher the content of beta carotene. When choosing carrots, leave the pale, limp carrots behind.

Green Leaf and Seed Salad

serves 4
ready in 15 minutes

1 head butterhead lettuce
1 head romaine lettuce
1 radicchio
2 tsp toasted pumpkin seeds
2 tsp toasted sesame seeds
1 tsp toasted sunflower seeds
½ cup vinaigrette (see p. 26)

Chop and wash the salad leaves thoroughly. Drain and pat dry with a clean tea towel or use a lettuce spinner. Place all the lettuce in a salad bowl and combine well. Toss the toasted seeds with the salad leaves. Before serving, drizzle over with dressing and gently toss.

Vegan. Dairy, gluten, sugar, wheat and yeast free.

Cook's Tips: You can use any combination of lettuces available. In the summer, there's a greater variety.

Nutritional Content: Romaine lettuce is highly nutritious, containing chromium, folate, manganese and vitamins A (in the form of beta carotene) and C. The seeds add calcium, copper, iron, magnesium, manganese, phosphorous, vitamins B_1 and E and smaller amounts of other minerals.

Note to the Senses: Lettuce is synonymous with salads. A good green leaf salad should be visually appetising with a combination of leaves, should have a light coating of dressing and taste crisp and fresh. Toasted seeds add crunch to the salad.

Spinach, Pine Nut and Organic Feta Cheese Salad

serves 4
ready in 15 minutes

175 g (6 oz) baby spinach, washed
1 red onion, thinly sliced
50 g (2 oz) pine nuts, toasted
a few basil leaves
110 g (4 oz) organic feta cheese

for the dressing:
3 tbsp raspberry vinegar
5 tbsp olive oil

Place the spinach, red onion, pine nuts and basil in a salad bowl. Crumble the feta over the salad.

Make the dressing by combining the raspberry vinegar and olive oil. Whisk together using a fork. Season. Drizzle over salad and serve immediately.

Vegan. Gluten, sugar and wheat free.

Cook's Tips: This is a simple salad which has lots of variations. You can use blue cheese instead of feta cheese. Rocket leaves are also a piquant addition to this salad.

Nutritional Content: Folate, iron, magnesium, manganese, protein and vitamins A and K.

Note to the Senses: This is a very clean-tasting, crisp salad and should be made with only the freshest ingredients.

legumes and pulses

Legumes are defined as plant species that have seed pods that split along both sides when ripe. Some of the more common legumes used for human consumption are beans, lentils, peas and soy beans. When the seeds of a legume are dried, they're referred to as pulses. High-protein legumes are a staple throughout the world.

All pulses except soy beans are very similar in nutritional content. They are high in protein, contain vitamin B, carbohydrates, minerals and are a very good source of cholesterol-lowering fibre. The high fibre content prevents blood sugar levels from rising rapidly after a meal, enabling those with blood sugar problems to manage them effectively. Pulses contain saponins, which are thought to be useful in managing cholesterol. In addition, saponins are now being investigated for their anti-cancer properties, in particular against breast and prostate cancer. The isoflavines in pulses are a weak form of oestrogen and are now thought to compete with the body's own oestrogen at oestrogen receptors sites, in effect blocking the body's stronger version and its potential downside, i.e. tumour growth.

Pulses come in dried, canned or frozen states. There are many advantages in canned pulses. Canning doesn't affect the protein content, eliminates the need for soaking and considerably reduces the cooking time of a dish when compared with dried pulses.

In Café Fresh we soak large pots of beans each night and boil them the following morning. The cooking time ranges from 1–1½ hours, depending on the bean. For the domestic kitchen this can seem like a lot of work, particularly when everyone is working. It requires a good bit of organisation and time. If it's too much like hard work, then you won't do it. We're all constrained by our busy schedules now, so I have allowed for this in the recipes, substituting dried pulses for canned pulses to avoid this. I do suggest that you buy organic versions of the canned pulses wherever possible. They aren't that much more expensive, they have no added sugar or additives and are of excellent quality. Pulses are cheap anyway, so spending a little bit extra for a much more superior product isn't going to break the bank.

Warm Winter Salad of Rosemary Roast Root Vegetable and Puy Lentils

serves 4
ready in 50 minutes

1 carrot
1 parsnip
¼ turnip
1 sweet potato
1 Spanish onion, roughly chopped
3 garlic cloves, finely chopped
1½ tsp sunflower oil
4 sprigs fresh rosemary
175 g (6 oz) Puy lentils, uncooked and washed
handful of parsley
sea salt and freshly ground black pepper

for the dressing:
juice of 1 lemon
1 tsp Dijon mustard
5 cm (2 in) length of ginger, peeled and finely chopped or grated
1 tbsp sunflower oil
handful fresh parsley, finely chopped

Preheat the oven to 180°C/350°F/gas 4.

Prepare the vegetables for roasting. Peel the carrot, parsnip, turnip and sweet potato and cut into large bite-sized pieces. Place all the vegetables in an oven-proof dish, then add the onion and garlic. Combine well and season lightly. Drizzle over with sunflower oil and mix well together. Place the rosemary sprigs throughout the vegetables. Roast for 20 minutes, until vegetables are cooked. Allow to cool slightly.

Bring a pan of water to the boil and add the lentils. Boil for 20–25 minutes or until tender and strain. Rinse well with cold water. This removes any residue. Allow to drain.

Meanwhile, make the dressing by combining the lemon juice, mustard, ginger and sunflower oil together, then add the parsley. Season with sea salt and freshly ground black pepper to taste. Alternatively, you can blend all the ingredients together in a food processor or with a hand blender. You will have a thicker consistency.

Place the cooked lentils in a bowl. Add the warm roast vegetables and combine well. The warmth from the vegetables will heat the lentils. Remove any rosemary sprigs. You'll notice that a lot of the rosemary has fallen off the stalks – leave it in the salad. Combine well together. Add the fresh parsley to the salad and season to taste.

Drizzle the dressing over the salad and combine well. Serve immediately.

Vegan. Dairy, gluten, sugar, wheat and yeast free.
Cook's Tips: I choose Puy lentils as they keep their shape and look very attractive. This salad is just as good eaten cold. It will keep in the fridge for up to 3 days.
Nutritional Content: As for all pulses; see beginning of this section (p. 49).
Note to the Senses: This is a winter salad. The lentils are quite dark, so it's important to ensure the vegetables are visible throughout and that there are lots of herbs to make the salad more appetising. The hint of ginger will give this salad a lovely warming effect on the body.

Butterbean, Green Bean and Basil Pesto Salad

serves 4
ready in 20 minutes

400 g (14 oz) tin organic butter beans, drained and rinsed
100 g (3 ½ oz) green beans
1 punnet cherry tomatoes
1 red pepper

for pesto:
handful basil leaves
2–3 tbsp olive oil
1 garlic clove, finely chopped
25 g (1 oz) pine nuts

Place the drained and rinsed butterbeans in a bowl.

Top and tail the green beans and blanch by placing them in a pot of boiling water for 7 minutes. Drain and pour cold water over them until they're completely cold.

Cut the cherry tomatoes in half and add to the butterbeans.

Slice the pepper in half and then cut into thin strips, then add to the butterbeans. Add the green beans to the other vegetables and combine well.

To make the pesto, place all the ingredients in a blender and blend until smooth. You can also use a pestle and mortar or a hand blender. The consistency shouldn't be too thick, as the pesto has to coat the salad. If it seems too thick, add a little more olive oil. Season to taste.

Pour half the pesto over the salad and combine well. Add some more pesto if the salad is too dry. You may not need to use all the pesto. Serve.

Vegan. Dairy, gluten, sugar, wheat and yeast free.
Cook's Tips: Try a variation on this salad: crumble a little feta cheese on top of the salad and drizzle a little more pesto over the feta. If you're using dried butterbeans, take care when cooking. Soak overnight, rinse and then boil for approximately 1 hour, until cooked but still holding their shape. If you overcook them, they'll turn to mush and can't be used for salad. It's a good idea to stir them frequently while cooking so that they cook evenly. Otherwise the beans on the bottom will overcook, fall apart and release a lot of starch into the liquid and everything will turn to mush.
Nutritional Content: As for all pulses, as outlined at the beginning of this section (see p. 49). Butterbeans are also known as lima beans and are quite a starchy

bean. Interestingly, they are also an excellent source of the trace mineral molybdenum, an integral component of the enzyme sulfite oxidase, which is responsible for detoxifying sulfites. Sulfites are a type of preservative commonly added to prepared foods, dried fruit and some alcohol, especially wine. People who are sensitive to sulfites in these foods may experience sneezing, rapid heartbeat, headache or disorientation when sulfites are consumed. If you have ever reacted to sulfites, it may be because your molybdenum stores are insufficient to detoxify them. Eat your butterbeans and this will help to build up this helpful trace mineral.

Note to the Senses: Butterbeans are a starchy bean with a rich, creamy texture. Generally people that avoid all pulses will succumb to the tasty butterbean. It has a good texture and the colour combinations make this salad very attractive.

Chickpea, Roast Butternut, Spinach and Pine Nut Salad

serves 4
ready in 50 minutes

½ **butternut squash**
4 **sprigs fresh thyme or** ½ **tsp dried thyme**
1 **tbsp olive oil**
1 **red pepper**
50 **g (2 oz) pine nuts**
2 × 400 **g (14 oz) tins organic chickpeas**
large handful of spinach, washed

Preheat the oven to 180°C/350°F/gas 4.

To roast the butternut, peel and cut into 5 cm (2 in) chunks. Put on a baking tray, add the dried or fresh thyme and sprinkle with a little sea salt. Drizzle over with one-third to half of the olive oil. Roast for 15–20 minutes, until the butternut is cooked but still has a bite in it. This will depend on how big you cut the chunks, so after 10 minutes, I would advise testing a piece to see how it's doing.

Cut the red pepper in half, then thinly slice. Toast the pine nuts on a dry pan over a gentle heat for 2–3 minutes, until evenly toasted. In a bowl, combine the peppers, pine nuts and chickpeas.

Remove the sprigs of thyme from the butternut and add the warm roast butternut to the rest of the vegetable mix. A little of the butternut will have broken down – don't worry about this, it will coat the vegetables very nicely.

Roughly chop the spinach and add it to the salad. The spinach will wilt from the heat of the butternut. Taste and season as required. If you think the salad is a bit dry, add the remainder of the olive oil.

Turn the salad into a salad bowl, decorate with a few toasted pine nuts and serve.

Vegan. Dairy, gluten, sugar, wheat and yeast free.

Cook's Tips: This salad is enhanced by adding a little basil or parsley pesto to it if you have some in the fridge. You can replace the butternut with sweet potato if you like.

Nutritional Content: As for all pulses; see beginning of this section (p. 49).

Note to the Senses: Chickpeas, also known as garbanzo beans, have a delicious nutty flavour. The softness of the butternut compliments this wonderfully. The salad should be moist from the butternut, olive oil and wilted spinach.

Mixed Bean Salad

serves 4
ready in 15 minutes

½ **head of broccoli**
1 **carrot**
1 **courgette**
½ **red pepper (optional)**
400 g (14 oz) tin organic cooked chickpeas, drained
400 g (14 oz) tin organic cooked kidney or pinto beans, drained
1 small bag bean sprouts, rinsed
handful finely chopped spinach
1½ tsp toasted sesame seeds
handful fresh coriander

for the dressing:
50 ml (2 fl oz) soy sauce or tamari
150 ml (5 fl oz) sunflower oil
1 tsp Dijon mustard

Remove florets from broccoli and break into small bite-sized pieces. Keep the stalks for making soups or vegetable stock.

Place the broccoli florets in a bowl and cover with boiling water. Leave to stand for 7 minutes, strain and run under the cold tap until all the florets are cold. Leave aside to drain.

Peel the carrot and finely dice into small pieces. Finely dice the courgette and pepper (if using) into small pieces.

Place the prepared broccoli, carrot, courgette and pepper (if using) in a bowl. Add the chickpeas, beans, bean sprouts, spinach and toasted sesame seeds and combine well.

To make the dressing, combine all the dressing ingredients together and mix well with a fork.

Drizzle the dressing over the salad and mix well. Garnish with freshly chopped coriander.

Vegan. Dairy, gluten, sugar and wheat free. Replace soy sauce with tamari for a yeast-free salad.

Cook's Tips: If you have pieces of red or yellow pepper in the fridge, they can be used here. They add a very good colour to this salad when finely diced. The beans soak up this dressing very well, which is why there may appear to be a lot of soy sauce used. You will need this amount for flavour. No salt is added to this salad, as the soy sauce contains salt.

Nutritional Content: As outlined at the beginning of this section (see p. 49). The bean sprouts add more protein as well as vitamins A, the vitamin B complex, C and E, as well as various minerals and enzymes.

Note to the Senses: This salad is quite colourful and is a very popular salad in Café Fresh. The kidney beans and chickpeas marry well together because of their contrasting colours. Adding the various coloured vegetables makes it attractive and appetising. This salad is a very easy way to get beans into your diet.

sprouted beans

Sprouted beans are being hailed as one of the 'superfoods'. Their nutritional value was discovered by the Chinese thousands of years ago. More recently, scientific studies in the US are now highlighting the nutritional importance of this humble food. A Yale University comparative study examined sprouts as compared with seeds or adult vegetables. It found that vitamins B_2 and B_{12} increased by more than 2,000 per cent, folic acid by 600 per cent, vitamin B_6 by 500 per cent and inositol by 100 per cent.

Sprouts are an all-year-round food, so they're a constant source of vitamin C, beta carotene and many B vitamins. Sprouts are a living food, which also helps strengthen the immune system.

You can sprout various seeds and beans yourself. You can purchase sprouting kits in health food stores, which is very economical. Packets of mixed sprouts are also available to buy.

Leslie and Susannah Kenton state in *Raw Energy Recipes* that sprouts are 'a vegetable which will grow in any climate, will rival any meat in nutritive value, will mature in three to five days, may be planted any day, will require neither soil nor sunshine, will rival tomatoes in Vit C, will be free of waste in preparation and can be cooked with little fuel. Sprouts have many times the nutritional efficiency of the seeds from which they grow'.

Sprouted Bean Salad

serves 4–6
ready in 15 minutes

120 g (4 oz) mixed sprouted beans
25 g (1 oz) toasted peanuts
1 bag Chinese bean sprouts
handful freshly chopped coriander

for the dressing:
1 tbsp sesame oil
50 ml (2 fl oz) soy tamari
150 ml (5 fl oz) sunflower oil
2 cm (3/4 in) piece of ginger, peeled and finely grated or juiced
handful fresh coriander

Place all the salad ingredients in a bowl together and combine well.

To make the dressing, place all the ingredients in a small bowl or jug and blend or whisk. Drizzle over the salad dressing, combine well and serve immediately.

Vegan. Dairy, gluten, sugar, wheat and yeast free.
Cook's Tips: The peanuts have a habit of falling to the bottom of the bowl, so when serving, remember to mix well. If you're allergic to peanuts or simply don't like them, you can replace them with roughly chopped toasted cashew nuts or simply leave nuts out altogether. This dressing improves in flavour if it's made a little in advance. It will keep in the fridge for 3 days.
Nutritional Content: As outlined on p. 56.
Note to the Senses: This salad has a wonderful crunchiness and is also light on the digestive system.

potatoes in salads

Potatoes have been an Irish staple for hundreds of years. We Irish love our potatoes – it's our comfort food and I'm a big fan myself. There's one sure thing – in Café Fresh, potato salad will always be a favourite. We don't have it on the menu every day or even every month, but when it's on, it's a winner.

Potatoes are nutritionally very good, despite some who would like us to believe otherwise. Of course, they're a carbohydrate-based food. They also contain copper, manganese, potassium, vitamins B_6 and C and dietary fibre if the skins are eaten.

Potato Salad

serves 4
ready in 25 minutes

600 g (1 lb 5 oz) new baby potatoes, washed
50 g (2 oz) green beans
1 radicchio
1 bunch spring onions
handful fresh parsley, chopped

for the dressing:
handful fresh tarragon
1 garlic clove, finely chopped or grated
1 tsp wholegrain mustard
50 ml (2 fl oz) white wine vinegar or juice of 1 lemon
150 ml (5 fl oz) sunflower oil

Place the unpeeled new baby potatoes in boiling water and boil for 15–20 minutes or until cooked. Don't overcook or they'll be soggy and watery. Once cooked, drain and leave to cool.

Meanwhile, top and tail the green beans and blanch by putting the beans in a bowl of boiling water and allowing to stand for 5 minutes. Drain and pour over with cold water until completely cold. Leave to drain.

Finely chop the radicchio, wash and leave to drain. Thinly slice the spring onions.

Cut the cooled new potatoes into halves or bite-sized pieces and place in a medium-sized bowl. Add the green beans, spring onions, radicchio and freshly chopped parsley to the potatoes. Season lightly.

To make the dressing, finely chop the tarragon. Combine all the dressing ingredients and blend or whisk. Season lightly. Pour over the potato salad and combine well. Taste and season as required. Serve with a little freshly chopped parsley on top.

Vegan. Dairy, gluten, sugar and wheat free. Yeast free if using lemon juice instead of vinegar.

Cook's Tips: If using a blender for the dressing, you'll have a green-coloured dressing that's very attractive on the salad.

Nutritional Content: A complex carbohydrate-based salad, including copper, dietary fibre, manganese, potassium and vitamins B_6 and C.

Note to the Senses: When the new season potatoes are in season, this is a real moreish salad. Tarragon has a good aniseed flavour and is a nice surprise when indulging in this yummy potato salad.

Creamy Garlic Potato Salad

serves 4
ready in 30 minutes

600 g (1 lb 5 oz) rooster potatoes, peeled, washed and cooked
1 bunch spring onions
1 shallot
handful fresh parsley, finely chopped

for the garlic mayonnaise:
2 eggs, separated
2 garlic cloves, finely chopped or grated
1 tsp Dijon mustard
juice of ½ lemon
300 ml (10 fl oz) olive oil

Peel the cooked potatoes and cut into bite-sized pieces. Slice the spring onions and shallots thinly. Combine the potatoes, spring onions, shallots and finely chopped parsley in a bowl.

Make the garlic mayonnaise as outlined on p. 28.

Add the mayonnaise to the salad. This is best done in two stages. Add half the mayonnaise first, combine well and add some more as needed. Garnish with freshly chopped parsley.

Gluten, sugar and wheat free. Yeast free if using lemon juice instead of vinegar.

Cook's Tips: This is a good way of using up leftover potatoes, which work better with mayonnaise. Actually, a good tip is to heat the leftover potatoes in the oven for 10 minutes and then add the vegetables and mayonnaise.

Nutritional Value: A complex carbohydrate-based salad, including copper, dietary fibre, manganese, potassium and vitamins B_6 and C, with added protein from the eggs.

Note to the Senses: This should be a very simple, creamy potato salad. This means that the potatoes aren't swimming in the dressing – this salad should be moist to the taste, but not wet.

Warm Potato Salad with Mint and Peas

serves 4–6
ready in 40 minutes

600 g (1 lb 5 oz) new baby potatoes, washed
1½ tsp white wine vinegar or lemon juice
1 shallot, finely chopped
150 g (5 oz) cooked baby peas, either frozen or fresh
⅓ cup chopped or torn fresh mint
2 tbsp extra virgin olive oil
1 tsp salt
½ tsp black pepper

Place the unpeeled new baby potatoes in boiling water and boil for 15–20 minutes or until cooked. Don't overcook or they'll be soggy and watery. Once cooked, leave to cool slightly.

While the potatoes are still warm, add the vinegar or lemon juice. Add the shallot, cooked baby peas and mint. Add half the olive oil and mix well. Taste and season. Add the rest of the olive oil and mix again. Garnish with a few mint leaves and serve warm.

Vegan. Dairy, gluten, sugar and wheat free. Yeast free if using lemon juice instead of white wine vinegar.

Cook's Tips: The vinegar/lemon juice is added while the potatoes are warm so it's quickly absorbed and the flavour is intensified.

Nutritional Content: A complex carbohydrate-based salad, including copper, dietary fibre, manganese, potassium and vitamins B_6 and C.

Note to the Senses: A warm potato salad with the fresh aroma of mint – need I say more?

grains in salads

Rice Salad

We use only organic brown rice in our salads in Café Fresh. They are highly nutritious salads and are a wonderful all-year-round staple, particularly in winter.

Brown rice is simply the whole grain of rice with only the outermost layer, the hull, of the rice kernel removed. This process is the least damaging to its nutritional value. Rice is a carbohydrate and is an excellent source of fibre. It's also an excellent source of manganese, and a good source of the minerals magnesium and selenium. Brown basmati rice has a very low glyceamic load and is therefore good for controlling blood sugar levels.

Wild rice isn't a rice at all – in actual fact it's a grass seed. Compared to rice, it's richer in protein and other nutrients and has a more distinctive, smoky, nutty flavour. The down side is that it's more expensive, so we use it together with organic brown rice. It's wonderful added to salads.

Organic Brown Rice Salad

serves 4–6
ready in 1 hour (if cooking rice)

75 g (3 oz) organic short grain or basmati brown rice, washed
25 g (1 oz) organic wild rice, washed
3 tbsp arame seaweed
2 carrots, peeled and diced finely
3 sticks of celery, diced finely

for the dressing:
juice of 1 lemon
½ tsp Dijon mustard
175 ml (6 fl oz) sunflower oil
1 tbsp fresh tarragon, finely chopped

First cook the rice. Place the brown rice in a pot of boiling water and boil for 30 minutes. Wild rice takes less time to cook, so add it to the brown rice at this stage and continue cooking for a further 15 minutes. Drain, rinse under a cold tap until completely cold and leave to drain fully.

Meanwhile, place the arame seaweed in a bowl of boiling water and leave to stand for 7 minutes. Drain fully.

Place the diced carrots and celery in boiling water for 5 minutes. Drain and run cold water over the vegetables until completely cold.

Combine the rice, vegetables and seaweed. Finely chop half the fresh tarragon, add to the rice and vegetables and mix well.

To make the dressing, combine the lemon juice, mustard, sunflower oil and remainder of the chopped tarragon together and mix well. Season as required. Pour half the dressing over salad and combine well. Taste again and season with sea salt and freshly ground black pepper if required. Add more dressing to suit your taste.

Vegan. Dairy, gluten, sugar, wheat and yeast free.

Cook's Tips: This is a very versatile salad. Remember, this is just a basic recipe. You can add more vegetables, such as diced peppers, spring onions or even blanched broccoli florets. Toasted sesame seeds are also good. If using brown basmati rice, it takes 10 minutes less cooking time. Add the wild rice to the basmati rice after 20 minutes and continue boiling for a further 15 minutes.

Nutritional Content: As outlined at the beginning of the section (see p. 61). Adding arame seaweed or another sea vegetable of your choice is always good. Sea vegetables are an excellent source of iodine and the B vitamin folate, magnesium and a good source of iron, calcium and the B vitamins riboflavin (B_2) and pantothenic acid (B_5). Seaweeds also contain good amounts of lignans, plant compounds with cancer-fighting properties.

Note to the Senses: This salad looks very wholesome and so particularly appeals in the winter months.

pasta salads

Pasta, like potatoes, is a highly popular salad in Café Fresh. They are quick, easy and very satisfying. There are many brands on the market. I find the Italian brands to be the best quality.

Pasta is a wheat-based carbohydrate. Wholewheat pasta has a higher dietary fibre content than white. There are also more and more wheat-free pasta alternatives available. In the recipes below you can substitute the pasta type that best suits you.

When cooking pasta, there are a few important rules. Always add the pasta to boiling water. On the packet the cooking instructions recommend you cook the pasta until it's 'al dente'. What exactly does this mean? This Italian phrase means 'to the tooth'. Pasta should be cooked only until there is a slight resistance when bitten into, but which isn't soft or overdone. Always try a piece of pasta after 10 minutes. You many need to cook the pasta a little longer for children. For pasta salad it's important to drain the pasta once cooked and run the cold tap over the pasta until completely cold, then leave to drain. If you don't do this the pasta will continue cooking in its own heat and will be overdone. You can drizzle a little olive oil over cold pasta to prevent it from sticking.

Pasta Salad with Sun-Dried Tomatoes and Olives

serves 4
ready in 20 minutes

100 g (4 oz) penne pasta
50 g (2 oz) black olives
75 g (3 oz) semi-sun-dried tomatoes
large handful chopped basil
1 tbsp extra virgin olive oil

Cook the pasta as per packet instructions. Drain the pasta once cooked and run the cold tap over the pasta until completely cold, then leave to drain. You can drizzle a little olive oil over cold pasta to prevent it from sticking.

Cut the olives in halves and finely chop the semi-sun-dried tomatoes, then add to the pasta. Roughly tear the basil leaves and add to the salad. Drizzle over with extra virgin olive oil. Season, toss well and serve.

Vegan. Dairy and sugar free. You can choose wheat- and gluten-free pasta if your diet requires.
Cook's Tips: It's really worth using a very good-quality olive oil here. This is the dressing, so we want a good flavour. Semi-sun-dried tomatoes are widely available now. The best quality are found in good delicatessens. This recipe can also be used as a main dish. Replace 100 g (4 oz) penne with 250 g (9 oz) tagliatelle pasta. Cook as per packet instructions. Do not cool, simply add ingredients to the cooked pasta for a simple main meal.
Nutritional Content: Carbohydrate-based dish with a carotenoid from the tomatoes, lycopene, monounsaturated fat and vitamin C, and vitamin E from the olives and extra virgin olive oil.
Note to the Senses: This is a simple salad. The pungent aroma of the basil and sweetness of the tomatoes are tempered by the slight bitterness of the olives.

Warm Roast Vegetable Pasta Salad

serves 4
ready in 40 minutes

100 g (4 oz) penne pasta or farfalle
1 courgette
½ butternut squash or 1 sweet potato
1 red pepper, roughly chopped
1 red onion, roughly chopped
2 garlic cloves, minced
1 tsp dried basil
handful fresh basil
1 punnet cherry tomatoes
olive oil, for drizzling

Preheat the oven to 180°C/350°F/gas 4.

Cook the pasta as per packet instructions. Drain the pasta once cooked and run the cold tap over the pasta until completely cold, then leave to drain. You can drizzle a little olive oil over cold pasta to prevent it from sticking.

Chop the courgette into medium cubes (approx. 5 cm/2 in). Cut the butternut or sweet potato into similar-sized cubes. Place the courgettes and squash into a roasting tin and add the chopped pepper, onion and garlic. Drizzle olive oil over the vegetables, season and mix well. Add the dried basil and half the fresh basil, roughly torn. Combine with the vegetables. Roast in a medium-hot oven for 20 minutes or until vegetables are soft. Leave aside to cool. Don't overcook – check the vegetables after 10 minutes to see how they're doing. Once cooked, they should still have a bite in them. Leave them to cool slightly.

In a bowl, mix the cooked pasta and cooled vegetables and toss well.

Slice the cherry tomatoes in half. Roughly chop the spinach or Swiss chard (if using baby spinach, there's no need to chop). Add the tomatoes and spinach to the pasta. The heat from the warm vegetables will cause the spinach to wilt. Add the remainder of the torn basil and olive oil. Taste for seasoning and adjust if necessary. Serve warm, garnished with basil leaves.

Vegan. Dairy, sugar and yeast free.

Cook's Tips: Some of the butternut will break down while roasting. This is perfect, as it coats the pasta and gives it a lovely orange hue. This salad is also excellent served cold.

Nutritional Content: Carbohydrate, dietary fibre, lycopene, manganese, potassium and vitamins A, C and K.

Note to the Senses: This is a very appealing salad from a visual point of view. Lots of colour and warm roast vegetables make this a very appetising dish. The fresh basil has a wonderful aroma once combined with the warm vegetables, making the dish even more tantalising.

Summer Pasta with Basil Pesto

serves 4
ready in 25 minutes

100 g (4 oz) penne or farfalle
1 punnet cherry tomatoes
1 red pepper, deseeded
1 green pepper, deseeded
1 red onion
handful rocket, chopped

for the pesto:
handful fresh basil
2 tbsp olive oil
2 garlic cloves, minced
25 g (1 oz) pine nuts

Cook the pasta as per packet instructions. Drain the pasta once cooked and run the cold tap over the pasta until completely cold, then leave to drain. You can drizzle a little olive oil over cold pasta to prevent it from sticking.

Cut the cherry tomatoes in half and place in a bowl. Cut the peppers in thin strips approx 4 cm (1½ in) long and add to the tomatoes. Slice the red onion into half-moons and add to the vegetables.

Add the cold pasta to the vegetables and mix well. Add in the chopped rocket.

To make the pesto, place all the ingredients in a blender and blend to a smooth paste. Alternatively, you can use a pestle and mortar. The pesto shouldn't be too thick, as it's being used to coat the pasta. If you think it's too thick, just add a little more olive oil. Taste and season as required.

Pour half the pesto over the pasta and vegetables. Combine well. You can add more pesto if the salad is too dry. If you have pesto left over, it will keep in the fridge for up to 5 days.

Vegan. Dairy, sugar and yeast free. You can use wheat- and gluten-free pasta if desired.
Cook's Tips: This is a very easy salad and will keep for a few days in the fridge. If using again, you'll need to add a little more basil pesto or olive oil to moisten it, as it tends to dry out if left overnight.
Nutritional Content: Carbohydrate, lycopene, phosphorous, potassium, protein and vitamins A, B_6, C, E and K.
Note to the Senses: This is a crunchy, summery, fresh-flavoured salad.

couscous and bulghur wheat

Both of these grains are wonderful in salads. They are very quick-cooking food and much lighter than other carbohydrate-based salads. In most recipes that use these grains you're asked to boil the couscous or bulghur. This isn't necessary – all you need to do is rehydrate it, as it's already been cooked. Simply place the grain in a bowl and cover it with boiling water. The water should just cover the grain. Cover the bowl with a tea towel or lid of a saucepan and leave to stand.

Couscous and wheat are staples in North African cuisine. Couscous is yellow granules of semolina made from durum wheat, which are pre-cooked and then dried. As a result it merely needs to be rehydrated before inclusion in a recipe or meal. These grains are very useful for quick, easy solutions to meals.

Bulghur is a nutritious staple in the Middle East. Bulghur wheat consists of wheat kernels that have been steamed and dried. After some of the bran is removed, the remaining hard wheat kernels are crushed into small pieces. Bulghur has a tender, chewy texture and comes in coarse, medium and fine grinds. Because bulghur is pre-cooked it only needs a brief soaking before using, so it's a fast food!

Bulghur is often confused with, but isn't the same as, cracked wheat. Cracked wheat isn't boiled, steamed or dried. The whole berry is simply cracked, so you get all the bran in cracked wheat.

Taboulleh

serves 4
ready in 30 minutes

225 g (8 oz) bulghur wheat
475 ml (16 fl oz) boiling water
½ red pepper, finely diced
½ green pepper, finely diced
¼ cucumber, finely diced
1 tbsp chopped fresh mint
1½ tsp chopped fresh parsley

for the dressing:
1 garlic clove, finely chopped
juice of 1 lemon
75 ml (3 fl oz) sunflower oil

To rehydrate the bulghur wheat, place it in a medium-sized bowl and add half the boiling water. It should just cover the bulghur wheat. Add a little more if necessary. Leave to soak for 15 minutes. With a fork, mix the bulghur well, breaking up any lumps. After that time, if it's still a little too hard, add the rest of the water, cover and leave to stand for another 10 minutes. Mix well again, breaking up any lumps.

It should be light and fluffy. Leave to cool, then add the finely chopped vegetables and herbs.

Combine all the dressing ingredients together, making sure to season with salt and pepper.

Add two-thirds of the dressing to the salad and toss thoroughly. Taste and season further if necessary. Add the rest of the dressing if the salad seems a little dry.

You can leave the salad to chill until ready to serve. Before serving, taste and add remaining dressing if necessary.

Vegan. Dairy, sugar and yeast free.

Cook's Tips: I always add the dressing in stages, since if you add it all at once you may make the salad too moist and soggy. There's no going back – you then have a soggy couscous salad. I have learned from my mistakes! It's much safer to add the dressing in stages and you'll have a light, fluffy salad.

Nutritional Content: A complex carbohydrate-based dish with vitamins and minerals from the vegetables.

Note to the Senses: This salad should have an airy feeling to it, light and fluffy and very easy on the digestion. The trick here is getting the bulghur right. This takes a little bit of practice to ensure you have a well-hydrated bulghur that's just right.

Mediterranean Couscous

serves 4–6
ready in 30 minutes

175 g (6 oz) couscous
350 ml (12 fl oz) boiling water
1 red pepper
1 green pepper
½ cucumber
3 tomatoes
1½ tsp raisins or currants
handful fresh parsley, finely chopped
handful fresh coriander, finely chopped

for the dressing:

2 garlic cloves

juice of 1 lemon

½ tsp turmeric

½ tsp ground cumin

2 tbsp sunflower or olive oil

To rehydrate the couscous, place it in a medium-sized bowl and add half the boiling water. It should just cover the couscous. Add a little more if necessary. Leave to soak for 15 minutes. With a fork, mix the couscous well, breaking up any lumps. After that time, if it's still a little too hard, add the rest of the water, cover and leave to stand for another 10 minutes. Mix well again, breaking up any lumps. It should be light and fluffy. Leave to cool.

Meanwhile, finely dice the peppers and cucumber and place in a bowl. Cut the tomatoes in half, remove the seeds and leave to one side. Finely chop the remainder of the tomatoes and add to the peppers. Add the raisins to the vegetables.

Make the dressing by combining all the ingredients. Lightly season.

Combine the couscous and vegetables together. Add the freshly chopped parsley and coriander.

Gently pour half the dressing over the couscous. Combine well with a fork. Taste and add more dressing as required. Taste again and season a little more if required.

Vegan. Dairy, sugar and yeast free.

Cook's Tips: Replace lemon with lime juice for a more exotic flavour. By adding a protein to this, such as chickpeas, you'll have a full meal.

Nutritional Content: Carbohydrate-based meal, plus the addition of vitamins A and C (through its concentration of carotenoids such as beta carotene), two very powerful antioxidants and vitamin B$_6$ and folic acid from the vegetables.

Note to the Senses: The addition of turmeric gives this salad a deep yellow colour. This, together with the cumin, gives a delicate, exotic aroma to this salad, which is reflected in the subtle flavours that come through.

Marjoram-Infused Mushroom and Shallot Couscous Salad

serves 4–6
ready in 50 minutes

225 g (8 oz) couscous
450 ml (16 fl oz) boiling water
75 g (3 oz) field mushrooms
3 shallots
sea salt and freshly ground black pepper
4 sprigs fresh marjoram
1 tbsp balsamic vinegar
1 tbsp olive oil

To rehydrate the couscous, place it in a medium-sized bowl and add half the boiling water. It should just cover the couscous. Add a little more if necessary. Leave to soak for 15 minutes. With a fork, mix the couscous well, breaking up any lumps. After that time, if it's still a little too hard, add the rest of the water, cover and leave to stand for another 10 minutes. Mix well again, breaking up any lumps. It should be light and fluffy. Leave to cool.

Meanwhile, slice the mushrooms in half and place in a roasting tray. Slice the shallots in half and add the mushrooms. Season lightly, and add the fresh marjoram. Drizzle over with balsamic vinegar and toss well. Roast in a preheated oven for 20 minutes or until the vegetables are cooked through. Remove the stalks of marjoram. Allow the vegetables to cool slightly, then add them to the couscous and combine well. Drizzle over with olive oil. Taste and season as required.

Vegan. Dairy and sugar free.
Freezing: This is not suitable for freezing.
Cook's Tips: This salad is lovely served warm, but is very good cold also. If you have some left over for the next day, you may need to drizzle a little more balsamic vinegar and olive oil over the couscous and mix well.
Nutritional Content: Carbohydrate, chromium, dietary fibre, magnesium, phosphorus, potassium, selenium and vitamin B_2.

Note to the Senses: The aroma of the mushrooms and shallots roasting in the balsamic vinegar and marjoram is absolutely wonderful. The marjoram has an aromatic, sweet smell and combines perfectly with the sweetness of the balsamic vinegar.

soba noodles in salad

Soba noodles are native Japanese noodles made of buckwheat flour and wheat flour. The buckwheat flour gives the noodles their distinctive dark brownish-gray colour. They are about as thick as spaghetti, and prepared in various hot and cold dishes. Soba noodles are eaten as part of the Okinawa diet and by most health-conscious Japanese.

Buckwheat is a gluten-free grain that contains no wheat, so it's ideal for those sensitive or allergic to wheat and gluten. Because of their buckwheat content, soba noodles are a slow-releasing carbohydrate. They contain selenium and zinc.

Soba noodles and buckwheat pasta are both available from good health food stores. Soba noodles are available in 100 per cent buckwheat or as a mix of buckwheat and wheat flour. If you're allergic to wheat or gluten, read the packets carefully and check the buckwheat content.

When cooking 100 per cent buckwheat soba noodles, take care not to overcook, as they become very soggy.

Asian-Style Soba Noodle Salad

serves 4–6
ready in 60 minutes

100 g (4 oz) firm tofu
2 lemongrass stalks
1 tbsp soy sauce or tamari
2 tsp grated fresh ginger root
½ tsp miso

2 tsp sesame oil

150 g (5 oz) Japanese soba/buckwheat noodles

1 tsp sesame seeds

50 g (2 oz) fresh spinach, finely chopped

1 bunch spring onions, thinly sliced

freshly chopped coriander, to garnish

Cut the tofu into small cubes. Finely chop the lemongrass stalks. Make the marinade by mixing half the soy sauce with half the ginger, half the freshly chopped lemongrass, the miso and 1 teaspoon sesame oil. Toss the tofu in the marinade and leave to rest for 30 minutes.

Bring a large saucepan of salted water to the boil. Add the noodles to the boiling water and cook for 5 minutes, until al dente. Drain the noodles in a colander and run the cold tap over them until they're completely cold. Toss in a little sunflower oil to keep moist and stop the noodles from sticking together.

Make the dressing by combining the rest of the soy sauce, ginger, lemongrass, sesame oil and sesame seeds together.

Once the tofu has finished marinating, add the finely chopped fresh spinach and two-thirds of the spring onions. Combine the marinated tofu mixture with the noodles.

Just before serving, pour the dressing over the noodles and garnish with the remaining spring onions and some freshly chopped coriander.

Vegan. Dairy, gluten, sugar and wheat free. Omit the miso for a yeast-free dish.

Cook's Tips: The tofu can be marinated overnight for a more intense flavour. If you don't like coriander, replace it with freshly chopped flat-leaf parsley. You can add a little spice here by adding a pinch of chilli powder to the dressing.

Nutritional Content: Carbohydrate, dietary fibre, iron, manganese, protein, selenium and tryptophan.

Note to the Senses: The soba noodles have a tantalising nutty flavour. This is also a very enjoyable way to eat tofu. The tofu soaks up the wonderful flavour of the marinade and the result is a salad of clean Asian flavours.

soups

Introduction

Soup comes from the word 'sop' or 'sup', which means the slice of bread on which broth was poured. Apparently, until bread was invented, the only kind of thick soup was a 'concoction of grains, or of plants, or of meat cooked in a pot' (Maguelonne Toussaint-Samat, *History of Food*). What exactly is soup? Is it a meal, an appetiser, a snack, a lunchtime food, or is it all of these and much more?

Soup is one of those great Irish staples. You can go anywhere in Ireland and be sure to find a soup on the menu, and any small pub, café or restaurant will feature a soup of the day. Soup can be a thick, hearty, winter-warming dish, a meal in itself or a light, delicate, summery, flavour-filled dish. I love soup and I really love making soup. All the goodness of the ingredients are kept in the pot. It's such a basic, simple dish and by virtue of that fact I feel wholesome and full of goodness when making it.

Soup is a simple dish to make. Interestingly from a culinary point of view, it's one of the few dishes that isn't bound by the freshness of the ingredients. Indeed, making a soup is a great way of using up vegetables that aren't quite fresh. Vegetables that have been sitting around for a few days and are at a loss for a use are ideal for throwing into a soup.

A soup is simple dish to make, but this doesn't mean that you throw onions, vegetables, herbs and stock into a pot, cover it, boil it all up and hope for the best. It will taste okay, but it could taste better.

There are a few basic rules I apply when making soups. In my cookery classes, I always stress that a good soup is the result of a little bit of time dedicated to the flavour in the pot before you cover it and bring it to the boil. Firstly, the simplest process of sautéing the onions, garlic and herbs for a few minutes before anything else is added makes all the difference to a soup. Secondly, adding the vegetables and sweating for another 7–10 minutes ensures that the best flavours are extracted from the ingredients. Thirdly, I use a homemade vegetable stock or a very good-quality commercial brand. I find the best one is Marigold, which is available in all good health shops and delicatessens. If this is all you take from this section, I'll be happy, as you will have learned the secret to a good soup. Take time at the beginning and the end result will be infinitely superior!

An important consideration is that I never use flours, dairy or cream to make a soup thicker or creamy. I believe that if you use the three principles above, then you don't need any of these additions.

Soups are an ideal food to freeze. In the colder months, it's a good idea to make soup in bulk and freeze it so you have enough for a week or more.

miso

Miso is a fermented soy bean paste. There are three basic types – barley miso (mugi), rice miso (kome) and soybean miso (hatcho). They are developed by injecting cooked soy beans with a mould (koji), then cultivated in either a barley, rice or soy bean base. Additionally, the miso's colour, flavour and texture are affected by the amounts of soy beans, koji and salt used. It's further influenced by the length of time it's aged, which can range from 6 months to 3 years. It is thought to have originated in China around 2,500 years ago. (Paul Pritchford, *Healing with Whole Foods*, p. 519.) Miso is used in sauces, soups, marinades, dips, main dishes, salad dressings and as a table condiment. Miso can be found in Japanese markets and health food stores. It should be refrigerated in an airtight container. Miso soup is a daily feature on the Café Fresh menu. Some customers have miso soup every day.

Miso Soup

serves 4
ready in 15 minutes

1 small onion
1 small carrot, peeled
1 baby or ½ regular courgette
500 ml (17 oz) water
1 piece of kombu seaweed
1 spring onion
handful spinach
1 cube firm tofu
1 tbsp miso

Thinly slice the onion. Slice the carrot and courgette lengthwise and slice thinly again. Place the vegetables in a saucepan and add the water, then add the seaweed. Bring to the boil, reduce heat and simmer for about 15 minutes.

Finely chop the spring onion and spinach and add to the soup. Dice the tofu and add to the soup.

Remove some of the liquid from the soup and mix in a cup with the miso until dissolved. Add this to the soup, mix well and serve.

Vegan. Dairy, gluten, sugar and wheat free.
Freezing: Not suitable for freezing.
Cook's Tips: Add miso at the very end of the cooking process. If you add miso with the vegetables and boil everything together, the nutrients will be destroyed.
Nutritional Content: This soup is easily digested and extremely nutritious, having rich amounts of B vitamins, calcium, oestrogens and protein.
Note to the Senses: Miso soup has a broth-like consistency similar to consommé. Miso has a distinctive, almost meaty taste and can take a little getting used to at first. Add a little less miso at the start to get used to the flavour.

carrots

Carrots have been a feature of the European diet for centuries. The humble carrot has featured as a main ingredient in the Irish diet for many years. It grows easily in the Irish climate, and has many wonderful nutritional benefits.

Carrots have a vibrant orange colour as a result of their beta carotene content (beta carotene is the precursor of vitamin A). Carrots are also an excellent source of antioxidant compounds which help protect against cardiovascular disease.

Carrots have a high sugar content so their sweetness lends them to a child's palate. Here we have some easy soups with carrot as their main ingredient.

Carrot and Coriander Soup

serves 4–6
ready in 40 minutes

1 tbsp sunflower oil
1 medium onion, peeled and finely chopped
2 garlic cloves, finely chopped
10–12 carrots, peeled and roughly chopped
1 parsnip, peeled and roughly chopped
4 sticks of celery, sliced
1 litre (1¾ pints) vegetable stock
2 tbsp fresh coriander, finely chopped

Heat the oil in a saucepan and add the onions. Sauté for about 5 minutes. Add the garlic and continue sautéing for a further 2 minutes.

Add the chopped carrots, parsnip and celery, cover and sweat for 7 minutes. If you think the vegetables are sticking, add a tablespoon of water.

Add the stock, cover the pan and bring to the boil. Reduce the heat and simmer for 25–30 minutes, until the carrots are cooked. Allow to cool slightly, then blend to form a smooth soup.

Add the freshly chopped coriander and season with sea salt and pepper to taste. For a more piquant flavour, add a little lemon juice just before serving.

Vegan. Dairy, gluten, sugar, wheat and yeast free.

Freezing: This soup is ideal for freezing. Reheat on a medium temperature, but don't boil.

Cook's Tips: If using new carrots, they tend to be smaller, so add an extra 4 to the recipe. If you're unable to get fresh coriander, use 1 level teaspoon dried ground coriander and add with the garlic.

Nutritional Content: Vitamin A is derived from beta carotene, and carrots are full of beta carotene. Carrots are also a good source of disease-fighting flavonoids and contain a specific type of fibre, called calcium pectate, which may lower blood cholesterol. However, it's worth remembering that carrots contain more sugar than any other vegetable except beetroot. In fact, some of the nutrients in carrots are more easily absorbed when the vegetable has been cooked, even briefly.

Note to the Senses: This soup should have a vibrant orange colour. Of course, this will depend on the carrots, the season and quality. The green from the coriander gives a balance and makes it really enticing to eat.

Carrot and Orange Soup

serves 4–6
ready in 40 minutes

1 tbsp sunflower oil
1 medium onion, peeled and finely chopped
2 garlic cloves, finely chopped
10–12 carrots, peeled and roughly chopped
1 parsnip, peeled and roughly chopped
4 sticks of celery, sliced
1 litre (1¾ pints) vegetable stock
juice and grated rind of 1 orange

Fruit Fool

Tomato, Puy Lentil and Red Onion Soup

Courgette, Broccoli and Chilli Cashew Cream Soup

Asparagus

Puy Lentil Shepherd's Pie

Heat the oil in a saucepan and add the onions. Sauté for about 5 minutes. Add the garlic and continue sautéing for a further 2 minutes.

Add the chopped carrots, parsnip and celery, cover and sweat for 7 minutes. If you think the vegetables are sticking, add a tablespoon of water.

Add the stock, cover the pan and bring to the boil. Reduce the heat and simmer for 25–30 minutes, until the carrots are cooked.

Add the orange juice and rind and simmer for a further 5 minutes. Allow to cool slightly, then blend to form a smooth soup.

Vegan. Dairy, gluten, sugar, wheat and yeast free.
Freezing: Suitable for freezing.
Cook's Tips: It's actually the rind, not the juice, that gives the soup the citrus flavour, so if you think you can leave out the rind and add in extra juice, you won't get the desired flavour.
Nutritional Content: As for Carrot and Coriander Soup on p. 77.
Note to the Senses: The colour and the citrus aroma stimulate the sense of smell and sight simultaneously. The taste should reflect the expectation, with a subtle citrus aftertaste.

hearty winter warming soups

Lentil Soup

serves 6
ready in 30 minutes

Lentils are a fundamental source of protein for the vegetarian diet. This lentil soup recipe is a nutritious and hearty lunch. It can be accompanied with wholemeal bread, organic brown rice or a salad. The texture of this soup is smooth and dense. The soup is blended to give a more wholesome texture to it. There's no need to soak the lentils.

1½ tsp sunflower oil

1 small onion, chopped finely

2 garlic cloves, finely chopped

2 carrots, peeled and chopped

2 parsnips, peeled and chopped into small cubes

½ small turnip, peeled and chopped into small cubes

1 stick of celery, chopped

1 litre (1¾ pints) water or vegetable stock

2 tsp finely chopped thyme or rosemary

110 g (4 oz) red lentils

Heat the oil in a saucepan over a medium heat. Add the onions and sauté for 5 minutes. Add the garlic and sauté for a further 1 minute. Add the carrots, parsnips, turnip and celery, combining well with the onions and garlic. Lower the heat slightly and cover the pot for 5 minutes to allow the vegetables to sweat slightly. A tiny sprinkle of sea salt at this stage helps the flavour develop.

Add the vegetable stock or water and herbs and bring to the boil. Reduce the heat and allow to simmer for 15 minutes.

Add the lentils and combine well with the vegetable mix. The heat should be low at this stage. Red lentils stick to the pot and burn very quickly if the heat is too high. Cover and leave to simmer for 15–20 minutes, until the vegetables and the lentils are cooked. Lentils are cooked when they have changed colour from a deep orange to a pale orange or an almost yellow colour.

The lentils should sit on top of the other ingredients, as they have a tendency to burn very easily if allowed to sink to the bottom of the pan. The lentils will cook from the rising vapours.

Once cooked, remove from the heat and leave to cool slightly for about 5 minutes. Stir well.

Blend and season with sea salt and freshly ground black pepper. If the consistency is too thick, add some water. This keeps in the fridge for 3 days.

Vegan. Dairy, gluten, sugar, wheat and yeast free.
Freezing: Ideal for freezing.
Cook's Tips: Once lentil soup is left to stand, it thickens, so you may need to add

some water once reheating. This will depend on what consistency you like your-self. One tablespoon of water added when reheating will probably be sufficient. For a spicy lentil soup, add 1 tsp cumin and coriander and ¼ tsp ground chilli powder when sautéing the onions for North African flavours.

Nutritional Content: A good source of protein. This also contains amounts of calcium and vitamins A and B, and is a good source of iron and phosphorus as well.

Note to the Senses: Once cooked, the lentils will emit a wonderfully earthy aroma. This, together with the vegetables, herbs and thick consistency of the soup, makes a delicious lunchtime soup for any cold day.

Tomato, Puy Lentil and Red Onion Soup

serves 6
ready in 40 minutes

1½ tsp olive oil
3 medium red onions, sliced thinly into half-moons
3 garlic cloves, chopped
1½ tsp tomato purée
110 g (4 oz) Puy lentils, washed
2 × 400 g (14 oz) tins chopped tomatoes or equivalent in passata
750 ml (1¼ pints) vegetable stock
handful fresh basil (optional)

Heat the olive oil in a saucepan over a medium heat. Add the onions and sauté gently for 5 minutes. Add the garlic and sauté for a further 1 minute. Add the toma-to purée and sauté for 1 minute, until the colour has changed to a more orange tone. If you feel the purée is sticking, just add a tablespoon of water and stir well.

Add the Puy lentils and combine well. Add the chopped tomatoes and stock and a little seasoning at this stage. Cover and bring to the boil. Reduce the heat and simmer for 25–30 minutes, until the lentils are cooked. You may find that you need to add a little more liquid if the lentils are absorbing too much of the tomato. All you need to do is add a little more water. Don't worry, this won't adversely affect the flavour.

Once the lentils are cooked, they should be a dark brown colour. Remove from the heat and allow to cool slightly. Taste and season as required. Lastly, add in a little freshly chopped basil.

The consistency should be somewhat thick, with lots of red onions and Puy lentils visible.

Vegan. Dairy, gluten, sugar, wheat and yeast free.

Freezing: Suitable for freezing.

Cook's Tips: Puy lentils are very different to all other lentils. They hold their shape through the cooking process and have a wonderful texture and flavour. Through the cooking process they change from dark green to a brownish colour.

Nutritional Content: All the benefits of lentils as in the previous soup on p.81, with the added nutrients from tomatoes. Tomatoes are rich in vitamin C and contain amounts of vitamins A and B, potassium, iron, phosphorus and some fibre. They also contain a substance called lycopene which may have cancer-preventing qualities. Processed tomatoes (e.g. canned tomatoes, tomato sauce, ketchup) contain even more lycopene because cooking breaks down cell walls, releasing and concentrating carotenoids.

Note to the Senses: Visually, this soup appeals instantly. The thick consistency and earthiness of Puy lentils signals a very satisfying soup, perfect to eat in winter.

Curried Parsnip Soup

serves 4–6
ready in 30–40 minutes

Parsnips have been a staple vegetable in the Irish diet for the last century. As a result of being associated with an 'old-fashioned' diet, I think the parsnip has got a bit of a raw deal. It's a lovely, sweet root vegetable and is readily available from October to March. Adding some spices to parsnips adds depth to the flavour and makes it an ideal winter soup.

1 tbsp sunflower oil

1 medium Spanish onion, finely chopped

2 garlic cloves, finely chopped

½ tsp ground coriander

½ tsp mild or medium curry powder

¼ tsp ground cumin

¼ tsp turmeric

10 parsnips, peeled and chopped into 5 cm (2 in) pieces

2 carrots, peeled and chopped into 5 cm (2 in) pieces

750 ml (1¼ pints) vegetable stock

Heat the oil in a large saucepan over medium heat. Add the onion and sauté gently for 5 minutes. Add the garlic and spices and sauté for a further 1 minute. If the spices begin to stick, add a tablespoon of water. This will loosen the mixture and prevent it from burning.

Add the prepared vegetables and combine well with the onions and garlic. Lower the heat. Cover the pot for 5 minutes and allow the vegetables to sweat slightly. A tiny sprinkle of sea salt at this stage helps the flavour develop.

Add the stock, cover and bring to the boil. Lower the heat and simmer for 20–25 minutes, until the vegetables are cooked through.

Allow to cool slightly, then blend to a very smooth consistency. You should have a nice creamy texture. Taste and season as required – I use white pepper in this recipe. Garnish with freshly chopped parsley.

Vegan. Dairy, gluten, sugar, wheat and yeast free.

Freezing: Ideal for freezing.

Cook's Tips: Don't get too stressed about the size of the vegetables when cutting. Just remember that the smaller the chunk, the faster it will cook. The best advice is to decide what size is easy for you to cut, and cut all the vegetables more or less the same size. Always check the vegetables by removing a few from the pot and tasting. They should be soft and easy to mash with a fork. The root vegetables in this soup can be fibrous, particularly the parsnip, so make sure you blend really well to get a smooth texture.

Nutritional Content: Parsnips, like carrots, are a naturally sweet vegetable, which signals that it's a good source of complex carbohydrate and fibre. They also contain small amounts of iron and vitamin C. The addition of spices adds phytonutrients, which gives it strong antioxidant properties.

Note to the Senses: Parsnips haven't been the most popular vegetable recently. However, it's a very flavourful vegetable with a pleasantly sweet taste. The addition of the spices balances this sweetness wonderfully, giving it warmth and a delicate Indian flavour.

Split Pea Soup and Mint

serves 6
ready in 40 minutes

1 tbsp sunflower oil
1 large Spanish onion, finely chopped
2 garlic cloves, finely chopped
3 medium carrots, peeled and chopped
3 parsnips, peeled and chopped into bite-sized cubes
1 medium turnip, peeled and chopped into bite-sized cubes
110 g (4 oz) split peas – do not require soaking
1½ litres (3 pints) water
handful fresh mint

Heat the oil in a large saucepan over medium heat. Add the onions and sauté gently for 5 minutes. Add the garlic and sauté for a further 1 minute.

Add the chopped carrots, parsnips and turnip. Combine well with the onions and garlic. Lower the heat slightly. Cover the pot for 5 minutes and allow the vegetables to sweat slightly. A tiny sprinkle of sea salt at this stage helps the flavour develop.

Add the split peas and water, cover and bring to the boil. Lower the heat and simmer for 25–30 minutes, until the vegetables and peas are cooked through.

Allow to cool slightly, add the fresh mint and blend. Adjust the seasoning as required and add a little more freshly chopped mint if desired.

1 litre (1¾ pints) vegetable stock
110 g (4 oz) cooked cannellini beans or a 400 g (14 oz) tin, drained
freshly chopped parsley, to garnish

Heat the oil in a large saucepan over medium heat. Add the onions and sauté gently for 5 minutes. Add the garlic and sauté for a further 1 minute.

Add the cubed vegetables and herbs and combine well with the onions and garlic. Lower the heat slightly and cover the pot for 5 minutes to allow the vegetables to sweat slightly. A tiny sprinkle of sea salt at this stage helps the flavour develop.

Add the vegetable stock, cover and bring to the boil. Lower the heat and simmer for 20–25 minutes, until the vegetables are cooked through. Add the cooked cannellini beans. Combine well and allow to heat through. Remove the sprigs of thyme.

Taste and season as required. Garnish with freshly chopped parsley.

Vegan. Dairy, gluten, sugar, wheat and yeast free.
Freezing: Suitable for freezing.
Cook's Tips: To add richness to this soup, sprinkle a little cheese over each bowl of soup, such as Parmesan or Gruyère. Alternatively, you can add a few cubes of smoked tofu to make this a meal in itself! As the season moves to spring, you can change the vegetables accordingly and replace the cannellini beans with haricot beans.
Nutritional Content: This soup is full of vitamins and minerals from the vegetables and protein from the beans.
Note to the Senses: This winter soup is more of a broth with pieces of vegetables and beans throughout. The cannellini beans are interesting, as they tend to have a slightly smoky flavour. There is no hint of this in the cooking process – it's only revealed in the tasting, so it's a little surprise to the taste buds.

When cooking with tomatoes I tend to follow certain rules. I always use red onions because they are sweeter than others and therefore help to reduce the acidity of the tomatoes. I always use olive oil, as it marries perfectly with tomatoes, as we have learned from the Mediterranean diet. I tend to use a little tomato purée to intensify the flavour. When using the purée in cooking, I add it to the sautéed onion and garlic and allow it cook off for 3 minutes to intensify the flavour. If you have tomatoes left over that aren't good enough for salads, you can include them in a soup. You will need to immerse them in a bowl of boiling water for 5 minutes. Remove and run under the cold tap until cool enough to handle, then peel them and chop. Add in with tins of chopped tomatoes. Lastly, I never add sweeteners to tomatoes.

I use tins of tomatoes in tomato-based recipe. In general, tinned tomatoes have a much better flavour, are quicker to use and are more economical than fresh tomatoes for cooking. If you think about it, the tinned variety use tomatoes that are picked at the correct time and then canned so that the flavour is locked in. In a North European climate, we don't have the luxury of readily available Mediterranean tomatoes at an affordable price. There are excellent-quality tinned tomatoes available and there are now organic varieties as well.

Tomato and Basil Soup

serves 4
ready in 40 minutes

1½ tsp olive oil
2 medium red onions, peeled and finely chopped
3 garlic cloves, peeled and finely chopped
½ tsp dried basil
1 tsp tomato purée
2 × 400 g (14 oz) tins of chopped tomatoes or 900 g (32 oz) passata
500 ml (17 fl oz) vegetable stock
large handful fresh basil, chopped

Heat the oil in a large saucepan over medium heat. Add the onions and sauté gently for 5 minutes. Add the garlic and dried basil and sauté for a further 1 minute.

Add the tomato purée and cook off for 1 minute, until the colour changes from deep red to a light red or orangish colour. If the purée starts to stick to the base of the pan, simply add a little water (about 1½ tsp) and loosen the purée. This will allow it to continue to cook without burning.

Add the tomatoes and vegetable stock, season lightly, cover and bring to the boil. Once boiling, reduce the heat and simmer for 30 minutes. Garnish with the fresh basil.

Vegan. Dairy, gluten, sugar, wheat and yeast free.
Freezing: Ideal for freezing.
Cook's Tips: I use a little dried basil at the start to intensify the flavour of the basil. The fresh basil is added at the very last minute so that the flavour comes through and isn't lost through the cooking process. To vary this soup slightly, you can add a little Olive Tapenade (p. 10) or Basil Pesto (p. 3) to each bowl of soup before serving.
Nutritional Content: Tomatoes are rich in vitamin C and contain amounts of vitamins A and B, potassium, iron, phosphorus and some fibre. They also contain a substance called lycopene which may have cancer-preventing qualities. Processed tomatoes, such as canned tomatoes, tomato sauce or ketchup, contain even more lycopene because cooking breaks down the cell walls, releasing and concentrating carotenoids.
Note to the Senses: Tomato and basil soup should have the aroma of these two ingredients. The pepper aroma of the basil should waft from the bowl as you sit down to enjoy the soup.

Roast Aubergine and Tomato Soup

serves 4
ready in 30–40 minutes

2 medium aubergines

2 tbsp olive oil

250 g (9 oz) cherry tomatoes (optional)

2 medium red onions, finely chopped

4 garlic cloves, finely chopped

1 tbsp tomato purée

2 × 400 g (14 oz) tins chopped tomatoes + any leftover tomatoes you might have

750 ml (1¼ pints) vegetable stock

handful fresh basil

175 g (6 oz) Drumlin smoked cheese, cut into cubes (optional)

Preheat the oven to 180°C/350°F/gas 4.

Wash the aubergines and chop into cubes 5 cm (2 in) thick. Place on a baking tray, sprinkle over with a little salt and brush with 1 tbsp olive oil. Roast for 15 minutes, until the aubergines are cooked.

If you are using the cherry tomatoes, then in a separate tray, roast them with some olive oil and a little salt for 10 minutes.

Heat the remaining olive oil in a large pot. Add the onions and sauté until cooked, about 3 minutes. Add the garlic and continue cooking for a further 1 minute.

Add the tomato purée and combine with the onions and garlic. Allow to cook for a few minutes, until the paste has turned a dark red colour.

Add the tins of tomatoes and the cooked aubergine. Mix well and add the vegetable stock. Season lightly at this stage.

Cover, bring to the boil, reduce the heat and simmer for 25 minutes. Allow to cool slightly and then blend. Taste and season as required. If the soup is too thick, just add water to dilute slightly. Chop the fresh basil and mix into the soup.

Finally, if using, add the cherry tomatoes and some freshly ground black pepper.

Optional: Add a cube of Drumlin smoked cheese to each bowl as you serve.

Vegan. Dairy, gluten, sugar, wheat and yeast free.

Freezing: Ideal for freezing.

Cook's Tips: The cherry tomatoes and cubes of cheese aren't a requirement for this soup, but if you're making this soup for guests, I would definitely include them.

They make the soup a little more special. You don't need to peel the aubergine unless there are brown patches. Don't roast aubergine in aluminium, as it will discolour the vegetable.

Nutritional Content: Tomatoes are rich in vitamin C and contain amounts of iron, phosphorous, potassium, vitamins A and B and some fibre. They also contain a substance called lycopene, which may have cancer-preventing qualities. Processed tomatoes, such as canned tomatoes, tomato sauce or ketchup, contain even more lycopene because cooking breaks down the cell walls, releasing and concentrating carotenoids. Aubergine contains potassium and vitamin C. It also has anti-bacterial and diuretic effects, as well as flavonoids (cancer-fighting antioxidants). This soup is also low in calories.

Note to the Senses: When you combine the aubergine with the tomato, the soup becomes more robust. It also has a darker colour than the Tomato and Basil Soup (p. 88) and the flavour is richer.

Roast Red Pepper and Tomato Soup

serves 4
ready in 40 minutes

3 medium red peppers
1½ tsp olive oil
2 medium red onions, peeled and finely chopped
3 garlic cloves, peeled and finely chopped
1 tsp tomato purée
2 × 400 g (14 oz) tins chopped tomatoes or 900 g (32 oz) passata
250 ml (9 fl oz) vegetable stock
large handful fresh basil

Preheat the oven to 180°C/350°F/gas 4.

   Cut the peppers in half lengthwise, deseed them and remove the white vein running through the inside of the pepper. This vein is bitter and isn't good for a tomato-based soup. Brush lightly with a little olive oil and roast for 20 minutes, until the skin is soft. Alternatively, place under a hot grill to soften the skin. Once removed, place in a plastic bag for 15 minutes – this helps the skin to loosen. Remove from the bag and peel off the skin, then chop the pepper into small pieces.

Heat the oil in a large saucepan over medium heat. Add the onions and sauté gently for 5 minutes. Add the garlic and sauté for a further 1 minute.

Add the tomato purée and cook off for 1 minute, until the colour changes from deep red to a light red or orangish colour. If the purée starts to stick to the base of the pan, simply add a little water (1½ tsp) and loosen the purée. This will allow it to continue to cook without burning.

Add the tomatoes and vegetable stock, season lightly, cover and bring to the boil. Once boiling, reduce the heat and simmer for 20 minutes. Add the red peppers and simmer for a further 10 minutes.

Remove from the heat, allow to cool slightly, add the fresh basil and blend. Taste and season with sea salt and freshly ground black pepper as required.

Vegan. Dairy, gluten, sugar, wheat and yeast free.
Freezing: Ideal for freezing.
Cook's Tips: While the peppers are roasting, you can get started with the rest of the soup. The peppers will be just ready to add to the soup when required.
Nutritional Content: Tomatoes are rich in vitamin C and contain amounts of iron, phosphorous, potassium, vitamins A and B and some fibre. They also contain a substance called lycopene, which may have cancer-preventing qualities. Processed tomatoes, such as canned tomatoes, tomato sauce or ketchup, contain even more lycopene because cooking breaks down the cell walls, releasing and concentrating carotenoids. Peppers are an excellent source of vitamin C and contain some vitamin A and small amounts of calcium, iron, niacin, phosphorus, riboflavin and thiamine.
Note to the Senses: Red peppers should have a mild, sweet flavour and be crisp and exceedingly juicy. This is why they are a good complement to the tomato, balancing out the acidity. This soup is best made in the summer. When choosing peppers, make sure they are firm, have a richly coloured, shiny skin and are heavy for their size.

Minestrone

serves 4–6
ready in 40 minutes

'*Minestra*' is the Italian word for 'soup', most often a soup of medium thickness, frequently containing meat and vegetables. Minestrina ('little soup') is a thin broth, while minestrone ('big soup') refers to a thick vegetable soup that generally contains pasta and sometimes peas or beans. It's usually topped liberally with grated Parmesan cheese and is hearty enough to be considered a complete meal.

The vegetables used in this soup vary according to season and availability. I will typically use Mediterranean vegetables in the recipe below, but equally, root vegetables can be substituted in the winter.

1½ tsp olive oil
2 red onions, finely chopped
2 garlic cloves, finely chopped
1 tsp dried basil
1 tsp tomato purée
1 green pepper, deseeded and finely diced
1 red pepper, deseeded and finely diced
1 yellow pepper, deseeded and finely diced
1 aubergine, chopped into bite-sized pieces
1 carrot, chopped into bite-sized pieces
1 courgette, finely diced
400 g (14 oz) tin tomatoes
500 ml (17 fl oz) water
50 g (2 oz) spaghetti, broken into small pieces (approx. 4 cm/1½ in long)
sprinkle of freshly grated Parmesan (optional)

Heat the oil in a large saucepan over medium heat. Add the onions and sauté gently for 5 minutes. Add the garlic and dried basil and sauté for a further 1 minute.

Add the tomato purée and cook off for 1 minute, until the colour changes from deep red to a light red or orangish colour. If the purée starts to stick to the base of the pan, simply add a little water (1½ tsp) and loosen the purée. This will allow it to continue to cook without burning.

Add the vegetables, season lightly and combine well with the onions and garlic. Add the tomatoes and water, cover and bring to the boil. Once boiling, reduce the heat and simmer for 10 minutes. Add the spaghetti and continue simmering for another 15 minutes.

Remove from the heat and allow to cool slightly. Taste and season with sea salt and freshly ground black pepper. Sprinkle each bowl of soup with a little freshly grated Parmesan, if using.

Vegan. Dairy, sugar and yeast free.
Freezing: Ideal for freezing.
Cook's Tips: If you have leftover cooked pasta shells or any other suitable leftover pasta, you can use it here. Add the leftover cooked pasta at the very end of the cooking process, as it only needs to be heated through.
Nutritional Content: This soup is full of the goodness of the tomatoes (see p. 89) and the added vitamins and minerals from the vegetables. The addition of the pasta makes the soup a carbohydrate-rich dish.
Note to the Senses: This is a good all-in-one soup. A bowl of minestrone soup should be full of visible vegetables and pasta. The visible pasta should alert your tummy to the fact that you don't need bread with this soup, as there are plenty of carbs in the soup already.

celeriac

Celeriac is a large, unattractive, knobby brown root vegetable. Celeriac is the root of a special celery cultivated specifically for its root. The taste is a cross between celery, parsley and parsnip, with a nutty flavour, if you can imagine such a thing. It's becoming more readily available in supermarkets in Ireland now and is easily found in food markets when in season from mid-September to the end of April.

Creamy Celeriac Soup

serves 4
ready in 50 minutes

1 tbsp sunflower oil
2 medium Spanish onions, peeled and chopped
3 garlic cloves, crushed
¼–½-inch piece of ginger, peeled and finely grated (just a hint)
3 medium celeriacs, peeled and roughly chopped (see Cook's Tips below)
2 parsnips, peeled and roughly chopped
750 ml (1¼ pints) vegetable stock
handful freshly chopped parsley, to garnish

Heat the oil in a large saucepan over medium heat. Add the onions and sauté gently for 5 minutes. Add the garlic and ginger and sauté for a further 1 minute.

Add the prepared vegetables and combine well with the onions and garlic. Lower the heat. Cover the pot for 5 minutes and allow the vegetables to sweat slightly. A tiny sprinkle of sea salt at this stage helps the flavour develop.

Add the stock, cover and bring to the boil. Lower the heat and simmer for 20–25 minutes, until the vegetables are cooked through.

Allow to cool slightly, then blend to a very smooth consistency. You should have a nice creamy texture. Taste and season as required – I use white pepper in this recipe, as I feel it works well with this vegetable. Garnish with freshly chopped parsley.

Vegan. Dairy, gluten, sugar, wheat and yeast free.
Freezing: Ideal for freezing.
Cook's Tips: Preparing celeriac can seem a bit of a challenge. For me, the best way to tackle this strange vegetable is to slice off the ends and then slice the vegetable into about 4 circles. I then peel it with a small knife, then cut into small chunks. Make sure to get all the rough skin off – sometimes it tends to be quite thick. It's easier to handle this way and you can see the thickness of the skin more easily. If preparing the celeriac in advance, you need to place it in a bowl of water with a squeeze of lemon juice to prevent browning. You can have a richer version

of this soup for the Christmas table by adding 25 g (1 oz) chestnuts with the vegetable stock.

Nutritional Content: Celeriac contains small amounts of vitamin B, calcium and iron and is a good source of fibre. It's also very low in calories.

Note to the Senses: The soup has an attractive appearance, as it has a cream colour and a rich, thick texture. There is no guilt eating such a rich-looking soup, as it's low in calories. The texture should be smooth and velvety and has a distinctive nutty flavour.

courgettes

Courgettes are from the squash family. The off-white flesh has a very pale green cast and the flavour is light and delicate. The great advantage of courgettes is that they are light and very low in calories. There is need for a little care when using courgettes. The danger in using them in soups is that you can get a watery, bland soup. To counter this and get a better flavour, I find it's best to combine them with other vegetables or a nut cream. Below I have given a few options which result in delicious, delicate-flavoured courgette-based soups.

Courgette and Almond Soup

serves 4
ready in 25 minutes

¼ tbsp olive oil
1 medium Spanish onion, finely chopped
2 leeks, thinly sliced
3 garlic cloves, finely chopped
10 medium courgettes, cut into chunks
500 ml vegetable stock
50 g (2 oz) blanched almonds

Heat the oil in a large saucepan over medium heat. Add the onions and leeks and gently sauté for 5 minutes. Add the garlic and sauté for a further 1 minute.

Add the courgettes and combine well with the onions and garlic. Lower the heat. Cover the pot for 5 minutes and allow the vegetables to sweat slightly.

Add the stock, cover and bring to the boil. Lower the heat and simmer for 15 minutes, until the vegetables are cooked through. Add the blanched almonds and continue to simmer for another 5 minutes.

Allow to cool slightly, then blend to a very smooth consistency. You should have a nice creamy texture. Taste and season as required and garnish with freshly chopped parsley.

Vegan. Dairy, gluten, sugar, wheat and yeast free.
Freezing: Suitable for freezing.
Cook's Tips: Courgettes cook very quickly, so it's easy to overcook them and lose the flavour. Many people think that courgettes have no flavour, but I beg to differ. If handled with care, you'll bring out the delicate flavour and have a lovely soup.
Nutritional Content: Courgettes are lacking on the nutritional front in general. On the other hand, they are low in calories. The combination with the almonds helps to increase the nutritional value, adding protein and vitamin E. Most of the fat in almonds is monounsaturated, also known as the 'good' fat. It also contains lots of minerals, like magnesium, phosphorus and zinc, as well as lots of healthy fibre, calcium and folic acid.
Note to the Senses: The smooth, silky texture of the courgette is broken up by the tiny almond bits that are blended through the soup, making it an interesting and pleasurable experience for the palate.

Courgette, Broccoli and Chilli Cashew Cream

serves 4–6
ready in 40 minutes

This soup is a good combination of vegetables. Once combined with broccoli, they take on a much more luxurious flavour while still maintaining their lightness. When cooking courgettes, remember that they're a very soft, watery vegetable and require less cooking time than other, more fibrous vegetables.

2 heads of broccoli, including the stalks

1 tsp olive oil

1 medium Spanish onion, finely chopped

2 garlic cloves, finely chopped

8 medium courgettes, roughly chopped

1 litre (1¾ pints) vegetable stock

handful fresh coriander leaves

for the cashew cream (optional):

1 tbsp cashew nuts

3 tbsp water

¼ green or red chilli, deseeded and roughly chopped

tiny pinch of sea salt

Remove the florets from the broccoli stalks, then finely chop the stalks so that they resemble the size of the chopped onion. Roughly chop the florets and keep them separate from the stalks.

Heat the oil in a medium-sized saucepan. Add the onions and chopped broccoli stalks and gently sauté for 5 minutes, until soft. Add the garlic and sauté for a further 2 minutes. Add the broccoli florets and combine well, then add the chopped courgettes. Mix all the ingredients well together, cover the pan and steam for 5 minutes.

Add the vegetable stock, cover and bring to the boil. Reduce the heat and simmer for 15–20 minutes. The vegetables should be soft, ready for blending. Allow to cool slightly and blend to a smooth consistency.

While the soup is simmering, make the cashew cream. Place all the ingredients in a blender and blend to a smooth paste. Refrigerate and use within 4 days.

Once the soup is cooked, taste and add seasoning as desired – I use white pepper in this recipe. Before serving, garnish with a teaspoon of cashew cream and freshly chopped coriander on each bowl of soup.

Vegan. Dairy, gluten, sugar, wheat and yeast free.

Freezing: Suitable for freezing.

Cook's Tips: Broccoli stalks have a wonderful flavour, but don't use any dried-up stalks. They are quite hard and fibrous, so you need to sauté them for a little while to soften them. They really add flavour to the soup.

Nutritional Content: Without the cashew cream, this soup is low in calories. Broccoli gives the soup most of its nutrients, adding beta carotene and vitamin C (though a lot is lost through cooking), as well as calcium, iron and riboflavin. If adding the cashew cream, you're adding B vitamins, copper, fibre, folate, magnesium, phosphorous, potassium, protein and selenium, as well as some unsaturated fat, which may help protect the heart. Cashew nuts are high in calories, but this is balanced by the soup, which is very low in calories. You only need a very little of the cream. Of course, this can be kept for special occasions if you're concerned about the calories.

Note to the Senses: When cooking, the aroma from the broccoli stalks and broccoli are quite strong. However, the courgettes tame this and the flavour is much more subtle and balanced. The courgettes add silkiness to the soup.

Roast Fennel and Courgette Soup

serves 4–6
ready in 35–40 minutes

Fennel is a mild, slightly sweet, aniseed-flavoured bulbous vegetable. It's closely related to carrots, dill, parsley and coriander. It's crunchy and fibrous and is refreshing on the palate. The flavour of the fennel is softened and lightened by adding courgettes. This soup is a little more work, as I roast the fennel before adding it to the soup mix. I guarantee you the extra work is well worth the end result.

3 fennel bulbs
1 tbsp olive oil
½ tsp fennel seeds
1 medium Spanish onion, finely chopped
2 garlic cloves, finely chopped
4 medium courgettes, washed and roughly chopped
570 ml (1 pint) vegetable stock
handful freshly chopped flat-leaf parsley

Preheat the oven to 180°C/350°F/gas 4.

Slice the fennel lengthwise. At the base of each half there is a core which is inedible – cut this core out and discard. Roughly slice the remaining fennel. There may be some dirt lodged in between the fennel layers, so wash the chopped fennel thoroughly to ensure all the gritty bits are removed.

Place the chopped fennel in a baking tray, drizzle over with half the oil, sprinkle the fennel seeds over and season lightly. Mix well, and roast for 15–20 minutes.

Meanwhile, heat the remaining oil in a pan and sauté the onion for 5 minutes over a medium heat. Add the garlic and continue sautéing for another 1 minute.

Add the chopped courgettes and combine well. Courgettes have a high water content, so they don't take long to cook. However, you need to treat them with care, as they're a delicate vegetable. With this in mind, keep the heat medium and allow them to sweat in the pan for 5 minutes.

Add the stock, bring to the boil, reduce the heat and simmer for 15 minutes. Add the roast fennel, combine well and simmer for a further 5 minutes.

Allow to cool slightly before blending to a smooth texture. Garnish with freshly chopped flat-leaf parsley, if available.

Vegan. Dairy, gluten, sugar, wheat and yeast free.
Freezing: Ideal for freezing.
Cook's Tips: Adding the fennel seeds when roasting the fennel intensifies the flavour of the fennel. You can replace the parsley with some chopped fresh coriander if available.
Nutritional Content: This is another low-calorie soup. The fennel adds vitamin A and some calcium, fibre, phosphorus and potassium. The great nutritional benefit of fennel is that it contains its own unique combination of phytonutrients, including flavonoids, and various kaempferol glycosides that give it its strong antioxidant properties.
Note to the Senses: The smell of fennel roasting is wonderful. It really awakens the taste buds. Once you remove the roast fennel from the oven, you're immediately excited about how the soup will taste. The roasting adds a real depth to the flavour of the soup.

mushrooms

Mushrooms, a fungus, are a wonderful earthy ingredient. Mushroom soup is such a delight if it's a *good* mushroom soup. Too often it disappoints, with lots of cream added and a weak mushroom flavour coming through. My friend and chef DK makes the best mushroom soup I've ever tasted, with no cream or dairy added. It's a simple process of sweating the mushrooms in some herbs before adding the stock. Here are a few options and some helpful hints to guide you on your way to making a really good mushroom soup.

Wonderfully Earthy Mushroom and Rosemary Soup

serves 4
ready in 30 minutes

1½ tsp sunflower or olive oil
3 shallots, finely chopped
3 garlic cloves, finely chopped
3 sprigs fresh rosemary, leaves removed and finely chopped
300 g (11 oz) garden mushrooms, sliced
1 litre (1¾ pints) vegetable stock
truffle oil, to garnish (if available)

Heat the oil in a large saucepan over medium heat. Add the shallots and sauté gently for 5 minutes. Add the garlic and chopped rosemary and sauté for a further 1 minute. Add the mushrooms and a tiny pinch of sea salt and combine well. Cover the pot for 5 minutes to allow the mushrooms to sweat.

Add the stock, cover and bring to the boil. Lower the heat and simmer for 20–25 minutes, until the vegetables are cooked through.

Allow to cool slightly, then blend to a very smooth consistency. You should have a nice creamy texture. Taste and season as required and garnish with a little truffle oil, if available.

Vegan. Dairy, gluten, sugar and wheat free.

Freezing: Suitable for freezing.

Cook's Tips: Using olive oil in this recipe will enhance the flavour. If you have mastered the basic recipe above, you can add a little dried mushroom for a richer, more luxurious flavour. All you need to do is rehydrate the dried mushrooms in cold water for 30 minutes, then add to the soup with the stock. I think shallots work particularly well when combined with mushrooms. They complement each other perfectly.

Nutritional Content: Mushrooms are full of essential minerals and B-complex vitamins not easily found in produce. In addition, the presence of phytonutrients may prove useful in the treatment and prevention of serious diseases. They are low in calories and fat and are sodium free.

Note to the Senses: Using your sense of smell here will guide you through the cooking process. As the mushrooms sweat off with the shallots, garlic and herbs, they emit their distinctive aroma. As they cook they reduce in size, release their juices and become shiny. Once they are cooked enough to eat, you then add the vegetable stock. When I cook this soup my nose is immediately awakened to something pleasing. The aromas given off during the sweating process allow me to anticipate how the soup should taste. Your taste buds should be happily satiated if you have taken the time at the sautéing process.

Mushroom and Fennel Soup

serves 4–6
ready in 40 minutes

Two earthy vegetables are combined here to give a rich-flavoured soup.

2 fennel bulbs
1 tbsp olive oil
1 medium Spanish onion, finely chopped
2 garlic cloves, finely chopped
½ tsp fennel seeds

200 g (7 oz) garden mushrooms
570 ml (1 pint) vegetable stock
handful fresh parsley, chopped, to garnish
truffle oil, to garnish (if available)

Slice the fennel lengthwise. At the base of each half there is a core which is inedible – cut this core out and discard. Roughly slice the remaining fennel. There may be some dirt lodged in between the fennel layers, so wash the chopped fennel thoroughly to ensure all the gritty bits are removed.

Heat the oil in a pan and sauté the onions for 5 minutes over a medium heat. Add the garlic and fennel seeds and continue sautéing for a further 1 minute. Add the sliced fennel and mushrooms and combine well. Cover the saucepan and allow everything to sweat in the pan for 5 minutes.

Add the stock, cover and bring to the boil. Lower the heat and simmer for 20–25 minutes, until the vegetables are cooked through.

Allow to cool slightly, then blend to a very smooth consistency. Taste and season as required and garnish with freshly chopped parsley or truffle oil, if available.

Vegan. Dairy, gluten, sugar and wheat free.
Freezing: Suitable for freezing.
Cook's Tips: I visited Nice in the south of France on my honeymoon in 2004. On that trip I visited the famous truffle restaurant in the city. It was a wonderful fungus-infused experience, if a little expensive. I brought back a little jar of truffles, which cost a lot, and grated the truffles into different dishes, including mushroom soups, for the next few weeks. If you ever get the chance to pick up a jar, grate a little into this soup for extra flavour – yummy!
Nutritional Content: The fennel adds vitamin A and some calcium, fibre, phosphorus, potassium and phytonutrients, including the flavonoids and various kaempferol glycosides that give it its strong antioxidant properties. Mushrooms are full of essential minerals and B-complex vitamins not easily found in produce. In addition, the presence of phytonutrients may prove useful in the treatment and prevention of serious diseases. They are low in calories and fat and are sodium free.
Note to the Senses: This is an elegant soup, simply exquisite.

pumpkin and butternut soups

I've always associated pumpkins with the US. We never had pumpkins when I was growing up, and certainly not in cooking. However, they're becoming ever more popular in Ireland during the autumn months. It's important to note that there are many varieties of pumpkin and many aren't suitable for cooking. I suggest you seek out the best ones for cooking, such as the Australian/New Zealand blue pumpkin or the organic orange pumpkin. If you choose a lesser-quality pumpkin, you'll be very disappointed with your end result. The standard Halloween pumpkins aren't suitable for cooking in any real sense. I have to say I'm not a big fan of pumpkins in cakes or pies; I prefer to use them for savoury dishes. The traditional American pumpkin pie is frequently made from canned pumpkin purée, and to be honest, I think it tastes very poor indeed. I feel it's best to stick with the natural product. If you can get a good-quality pumpkin, you'll have an excellent soup. Just follow the recipe below.

Butternut squash is also widely available during the autumn and winter months and makes a wonderful soup. If you're finding it hard to get a good-quality pumpkin, I advise you to stick with the butternut squash.

Ginger works wonderfully with any squash or pumpkin.

Pumpkin Soup

serves 4–6
ready in 40 minutes

1½ tsp olive oil
2 shallots, finely chopped
3 garlic cloves, finely chopped
3 sprigs fresh thyme, leaves removed and finely chopped or ½ tsp dried thyme

1 red chilli, finely chopped

5 cm (2 in) piece of ginger, peeled and finely chopped or grated

1 large pumpkin, deseeded and chopped into 5 cm (2 in) chunks

750 ml (1¼ pints) vegetable stock

Heat the olive oil in a pan and sauté the shallots for 5 minutes over a medium heat. Add the garlic, thyme, chilli and ginger and continue sautéing for a further 1 minute. Add the chopped pumpkin and combine well. Cover the saucepan and allow everything to sweat in the pan for 5 minutes.

Add the stock, cover and bring to the boil. Lower the heat and simmer for 20 minutes, until the vegetables are cooked through.

Blend the soup to a smooth consistency. Taste and season as required and garnish with freshly chopped coriander leaves.

Vegan. Dairy, gluten, sugar, wheat and yeast free.

Freezing: Ideal for freezing for up to 2 months.

Cook's Tips: The blue pumpkin is very hard to chop. You may need to ask the help of someone strong to help with the initial chopping. To make a richer, Asian-flavoured soup, add an extra chilli and add half a can of coconut milk with the vegetable stock (use light coconut milk if you're concerned with fat content). You will then have Coconut, Pumpkin and Chilli Soup.

Nutritional Content: This is a starchy and therefore carbohydrate-based food. As their rich colour suggests, pumpkin and butternut squash contain beta carotene, which is the precursor to vitamin A. They also contain copper, niacin and vitamins B_1, B_3, B_5 (pantothenic acid), B_6 and C. It's a very nutritious food. Adding the ginger increases the levels of phytonutrients.

Note to the Senses: This soup is a reminder that Halloween is either approaching or not long past, and that winter is well and truly on the way!

Butternut Soup

serves 4–6

ready in 40 minutes

1½ tsp olive oil

1 medium onion, finely chopped

2 garlic cloves, finely chopped

5 cm (2 in) piece of ginger, peeled and finely chopped or grated

3 butternut squash, peeled, deseeded and chopped into 5 cm (2 in) cubes

1 sweet potato, peeled and chopped into 5 cm (2 in) cubes

750 ml (1¼ pints) vegetable stock

handful fresh coriander, to garnish (optional)

Heat the olive oil in a pan and sauté the onions for 5 minutes over a medium heat. Add the garlic and ginger and continue sautéing for a further 1 minute. Add the chopped butternut squash and sweet potato and combine well. Cover the saucepan and allow everything to sweat in the pan for 5 minutes.

Add the stock, cover and bring to the boil. Lower the heat and simmer for 20–25 minutes, until the vegetables are cooked through.

Blend the soup to a smooth consistency. Taste and season as required and garnish with freshly chopped coriander leaves.

Vegan. Dairy, gluten, sugar, wheat and yeast free.

Freezing: Ideal for freezing for up to 2 months.

Cook's Tips: Preparing butternut isn't difficult once you know how to do it. The easiest way is to peel it with a good peeler, or slice it and then peel it. Remember that the bulbous end has a hollow with seeds in it. Remove these before cutting into pieces.

Nutritional Content: This is a starchy and therefore carbohydrate-based food. As their rich colour suggests, pumpkin and butternut squash contain beta carotene, which is the precursor to vitamin A. They also contain copper, niacin and vitamins B_1, B_3, B_5 (pantothenic acid), B_6 and C. It's a very nutritious food. Adding the ginger increases the levels of phytonutrients.

Note to the Senses: This soup cries out to be eaten. It has a deep orange colour and velvety texture with a slight edge to it from the starchy composition of the butternut, which also gives it a wonderfully thick consistency. But the soup never feels heavy – quite the opposite, actually.

frittatas, tarts and quiches

frittatas

Everyone recognises the term 'omelette' and has an idea of what an omelette is. It is, of course, an egg-based dish. In Europe, the Italians, French and Spanish have their own interpretations of the omelette.

A frittata is an Italian egg-based dish. The traditional Italian recipe is just a simple egg omelette. Adding different vegetables and herbs give different variations. An Italian frittata usually has the ingredients mixed with the eggs. A frittata is firm because it's cooked very slowly over a low heat, and round because it isn't folded.

With the French omelette, the vegetables are folded inside. It can be flipped or the top can be finished under a broiler. An omelette is cooked quickly over moderately high heat and, after folding, has a flat-sided, half-oval shape. The centre remains quite soft, unlike the frittata.

Then there's the Spanish tortilla. A Spanish omelette is traditionally a potato and onion omelette. In Spain, the dish goes by two names: *tortilla de patatas* or *tortilla española*. The Spanish omelette is more about the potato than the eggs. It's firm and dense, with a thick layer of potato held together with eggs. This is a wonderfully satisfying dish served in most tapas bars. It tastes great whether served warm, cool or at room temperature. It makes an excellent breakfast, lunch, dinner, snack or crowd-pleasing tapa. My Spanish friend Sylvia made the traditional recipe for me. It consists of cooking the very thinly sliced potatoes in lots of olive oil. It took a long time to make and the amount of oil used was phenomenal, but it tasted amazing.

I loved this dish so much I have devised a potato and onion frittata recipe that tastes equally delicious but uses oil very sparingly! I have combined the idea of the frittata and tortilla together to make a really tasty, healthy dish. The Café Fresh frittata is all about the vegetables in the dish. The eggs bind the vegetables together but don't take over the dish. It's wonderfully easy.

Good cheese is a great combination with eggs. In Café Fresh we use the Corleggy Farmhouse Cheeses for the more robust flavours. These cheeses go very well with the autumn and winter flavours and with the potato and onion frittata. You can choose a similar cheese of your liking if you can't source the Corleggy option. For the summer frittatas or lighter flavours, it's good to go with Parmesan or something similar. However, Parmesan cheese with vegetarian rennet in it is very hard to locate. Check out the Irish Farm hard cheese varieties for good alternatives.

I have given two alternatives for cooking frittatas. They can be baked in the oven or cooked on a hot plate. When I'm oven roasting the vegetables, I bake the dish, as the oven is already on. Personally, I prefer the frittatas baked in the oven.

You will need a frying pan or a cast iron pan. For 2–3 people, the size should be 20 cm (8 in) in diameter. A 26 cm pot should suffice for 6 people. Below I give smaller-sized recipes, as they can't successfully be frozen. You can use these recipes if you're cooking for one and the cold frittata will be just as good the next day for lunch.

Eggs: For years we've been advised to limit our egg consumption because of the high cholesterol levels of egg yolks. Dietary cholesterol was originally thought to increase blood cholesterol levels and the risk of heart disease. The US has been influenced by this belief to the extent that in restaurants, diners can have an egg dish with egg whites only, such as an egg white omelette! Happily, research has dispelled this theory and we can now eat eggs guilt free. Many scientific studies now focus on saturated fat and transfats, not cholesterol, as the major dietary culprits behind heart disease.

Eggs are a highly nutritious food source. They're a good source of low-cost, high-quality protein, providing 5.5 grams of protein (11.1 per cent of the daily value for protein) in one egg for a caloric cost of only 68 calories. The egg white is an excellent source of protein and riboflavin. This protein is of very high quality and is easily absorbed by the digestive system. Egg yolks contain all of the fat in an egg and are a good source of choline, iron, phosphorous, protein and vitamins A and D. Our bodies can produce some choline, but we can't make enough to make up for an inadequate supply in our diets. Choline deficiency can also cause deficiency of another B vitamin critically important for health. Lutein, a carotenoid thought to help prevent age-related macular degeneration and cataracts, may be found in even higher amounts in eggs than in green vegetables such as spinach, which have been considered its major dietary sources.

Eggs can be a quick and easy way of making a nutritious meal. A poached egg on wholegrain brown toast is my Sunday brunch treat. It's important to get free-range and organic eggs if possible for better quality. In Café Fresh we use eggs to make frittatas and egg-based tarts and quiches. These recipes can be varied as you like. Some methods of making these dishes are quicker than others. It will depend on your catering needs. For a quick frittata, instead of baking it in the oven (as in the following recipes) you can cook the mix in a pan on the hotplate and finish it off under the grill to brown.

Potato and Onion Frittata with Mature Traditional Drumlin Cheese

serves 2–3
ready in 50 minutes

250 g (9 oz) waxy potatoes (baby potatoes, roosters or similar)
1½ tsp extra virgin olive oil
1 Spanish onion, thinly sliced into half-moons
1 garlic clove, finely chopped
4 eggs
handful chives or parsley, chopped
25 g (1 oz) mature Drumlin cheese or mature Cheddar, grated

Scrub the potatoes. If using large potatoes, cut into quarters. If using baby potatoes, leave whole. Boil until almost tender (slightly undercooked). Remember, we'll be slicing the potatoes once cooled, so we want them to hold their shape. They'll finish cooking in the egg mix.

Heat half the oil in a pan and gently sauté the onions until soft but not coloured, about 5–7 minutes. Add the garlic and gently sauté for another 2 minutes. Remove from the pan and leave to cool.

Drain the potatoes, return to the pot and allow to cool. Once cool enough to handle, thinly slice them.

Lightly beat the eggs in a large bowl, add the chopped chives/parsley and season well. Stir the cooled onion and potato into the eggs. Return the egg mixture to the pan and cook over a very low heat until cooked through. Test by touching the top – it should be firm with no sign of give.

Sprinkle the grated Drumlin cheese on top and place under a medium grill until evenly browned.

Gluten, sugar and wheat free.

Cook's Tips: If serving this for guests, I suggest you serve it with Salsa Verde on the side (see p. 9). If you want to do this dish completely in the oven, then you can slice the uncooked potatoes and oven roast them together with the onions and garlic for about 20 minutes. Combine the eggs, vegetables and herbs and place the egg mixture into a ovenproof round dish and bake for 20 minutes. Top with cheese and return to the oven to brown. This is worth doing if you're having guests and is delicious.

Nutritional Content: This dish is a good source of protein from the eggs and cheese. The potatoes supply the carbohydrate. This dish is rich in the essential amino acids and a good source of calcium, choline, copper, dietary fibre, lutein, manganese, phosphorus, potassium, riboflavin and vitamins A, B_6, C and D.

Note to the Senses: This dish appeals immediately on a visual basis. When you cut a slice you should have a 6–7 cm-thick slice of firm frittata. The dish shouldn't taste eggy – the eggs are simply holding everything together.

Chickpea, Roast Butternut, Spinach and Pinenut Salad

Chicory, Beetroot and Fennel Salad

Date and Oat Slice

Vegan Chocolate Cake

Summer Vegetable Frittata with Herbs

serves 2–3
ready in 35 minutes

1½ tsp olive oil
1 red onion, thinly sliced
½ red pepper, cut into 5 cm (2 in) pieces
½ yellow pepper, cut into 5 cm (2 in) pieces
½ small courgette, cut into bite-sized chunks
1 garlic clove, chopped
25 g (1 oz) young peas or frozen peas
4 large eggs
1½ tsp fresh basil, chopped
1½ tsp fresh mint, chopped
25 g (1 oz) Parmesan

Heat the oil in a pan and sauté the sliced onion over a medium heat for 5 minutes. Add the peppers and continue sautéing for a further 5 minutes. Add the courgettes and garlic and sauté for a further 5–7 minutes. Set aside.

Cook the fresh peas in boiling water until tender or defrost frozen peas.

Lightly beat the eggs in a large bowl with a fork until the whites and yolks are well blended. Add the peas and cooked vegetables to the eggs. Add the freshly chopped basil and mint and season well.

Pour the egg mixture back into the pan, stirring with a fork while pouring so that the vegetables don't sink to the bottom.

Return the pan to the heat, lower the heat and cook for 15–20 minutes. There's no need to stir. The important thing is to keep the heat at its lowest possible point, otherwise the eggs will burn. You can cover the dish with a saucepan lid to help the dish cook faster.

Sprinkle the Parmesan over the frittata. Set the pan under the grill and cook for another 1–2 minutes to set the top and allow the cheese to brown evenly.

Leave in the pan for a few minutes to settle and cool slightly before slipping onto a plate. Serve warm, cut into wedges like a cake.

Gluten, sugar and wheat free.

Cook's Tips: You can experiment with other summer vegetables such as French beans or mangetout (you will need to blanch them). You can also use asparagus spears or fennel. You can sauté them as with the red peppers.

Nutritional Content: This is a protein-based dish and a good source of vitamins A, C and K. This dish contains some calcium and phosphorus and is a good source of copper, folic acid, lutein, manganese, phosphorus, potassium, riboflavin and vitamin B_6.

Note to the Senses: This is a summer dish so it should have a light, airy freshness about it and should look colourful and bright.

Roasted Red Pepper and Tomato Frittata with Basil and Parmesan

serves 2–3
ready in 50 minutes

2 red peppers
1 tbsp olive oil
2 garlic cloves, peeled and left whole
1 punnet cherry tomatoes
4 large eggs
2 spring onions, thinly sliced
handful basil leaves, torn
25 g (1 oz) Parmesan, finely grated

Preheat the oven to 220°C/425°F/gas 7.

Slice the peppers in half lengthwise and remove the seeds. Lay on a roasting tray and lightly brush over with olive oil. Add the whole garlic cloves. Roast for 15 minutes.

Cut the tomatoes in half around the widest part. Add to the roast peppers in a single layer and return to the oven for a further 5 minutes. Remove from the oven and cool, then remove the skins from the peppers and cut the flesh into thin strips.

Remove the garlic cloves; they should be very soft. Squash the garlic with the back of a knife.

Lightly beat the eggs in a large bowl. Stir in the peppers, sliced spring onions, garlic and basil. Gently place the roast tomatoes on the top. They are soft and delicate, so be careful. Place the egg mix in a lightly oiled ovenproof round (20 cm/9 in) baking dish.

Reduce the oven to 180°C/350°F/gas 4. Return the baking dish to the oven and bake for 15–20 minutes. Remove the dish from the oven and sprinkle over with fresh Parmesan. Return to the oven and continue cooking for a further 5–7 minutes, or until the dish is browned evenly. Remove from oven and allow to cool slightly before cutting and serving.

Gluten, sugar and wheat free.

Cook's Tips: Roasting gives a deeper flavour to the peppers. It takes more time than the Summer Vegetable Frittata, but the flavour is more intense. Both are good, so it really depends on your time. If you're making this for guests or a summer party, I think it's definitely worth roasting the vegetables. Once the oven is on for roasting, we cook the entire dish in the oven.

Nutritional Content: A protein-based dish with all the added nutrients eggs provide. The red-coloured vegetables signal the presence of beta carotene, the precursor to vitamin A, and there's lots of vitamin K here as well. Tomatoes contain lycopene, a powerful antioxidant. Smaller amount of minerals are present too.

Note to the Senses: This is another good summer option. This frittata has a slightly less firm texture from the juice of the tomatoes.

Roast Autumn Vegetable Frittata with Smoked Drumlin Cheese

serves 2–3
ready in 50 minutes

1 small sweet potato or butternut squash
1 shallot
1 leek
1–2 garlic cloves, sliced
2 tbsp fresh marjoram, chopped
2 tbsp olive oil
200 g (7 oz) spinach, washed and chopped
4 large eggs
3 tbsp fresh parsley, chopped
50 g (2 oz) smoked Drumlin cheese or other cheese of choice

Preheat the oven to 220°C/425°F/gas 7.

Peel the sweet potato or butternut and cut into bite-sized chunks. Place in a medium-sized roasting tin. Slice the shallot into half-moons and add to the roasting tin. Wash the leeks and slice into thin rounds, then add to the vegetables. Add the sliced garlic and half the chopped marjoram. Drizzle with olive oil and combine well. Roast for 20 minutes, remove and allow to cool slightly. Add the chopped spinach to the vegetables. The heat of the vegetables will wilt the spinach.

Lightly beat the eggs in a large bowl. Add the vegetables and remaining herbs to the beaten eggs. Place the egg mix in a lightly oiled ovenproof round (20 cm/9 in) baking dish.

Reduce the oven to 180°C/350°F/gas 4. Return the baking dish to the oven and bake for a further 15–20 minutes.

Remove the dish from the oven. Cut the cheese into 3 or 4 pieces and divide evenly on top of the frittata – each person should get a piece of cheese. Return to the oven and continue cooking for a further 5–7 minutes, or until the cheese has melted. Remove from oven and allow to cool slightly before cutting and serving.

Gluten, sugar and wheat free.

Cook's Tips: To get the best flavours here, you need to roast the sweet potato. I wouldn't be in favour of boiling the vegetables – the roasting really brings out their sweetness. As the flesh of sweet potatoes will darken upon contact with the air, you should cook them immediately after peeling and/or cutting them. If this isn't possible, then to prevent oxidation, keep them in a bowl covered completely with water until you're ready to cook them.

Nutritional Content: This is a protein-based dish with carbohydrate from the sweet potato. Sweet potato is a very popular food in the Okinawa diet. It has a high content of a particular flavonoid which stimulates the 'sirtuin pathway', a way of producing a protein that puts the body into preservation mode rather than the usual reproductive mode. Apparently this may help us to live longer! It also contains copper, dietary fibre, manganese and vitamins A and C. The cheese adds essential amino acids, calcium, phosphorus and other minerals.

Note to the Senses: The smoked Drumlin cheese is wonderful with this combination of vegetables. When buying sweet potatoes, choose ones that are firm and don't have any cracks, bruises or soft spots. Avoid those that are displayed in the refrigerated section of the produce department, since cold temperature negatively alters their taste.

Roast Winter Vegetable Frittata with Drumlin Cumin Cheese

serves 3–4
ready in 55 minutes

1 carrot, peeled and cut into bite-sized chunks
1 parsnip, peeled and cut into bite-sized chunks
½ small sweet potato or butternut squash, peeled and cut into bite-sized chunks
¼ small turnip, peeled and cut into bite-sized chunks
1 small Spanish onion, roughly chopped
1–2 garlic cloves, sliced
1½ tsp chopped fresh rosemary
1½ tsp chopped fresh thyme
2 tbsp olive oil
4 large eggs
50 g (2 oz) Drumlin cumin cheese or other cheese of choice

Preheat the oven to 220°C/425°F/gas 7.

Place the carrot, parsnip, sweet potato and turnip in a medium-sized roasting tin. Add the chopped onion, garlic and fresh rosemary and thyme. Drizzle over with olive oil. Roast for 20 minutes, remove and allow to cool slightly.

Lightly beat the eggs in a large bowl. Add the vegetables to the beaten eggs. Place the egg mix in a lightly oiled ovenproof round (20 cm/9 in) baking dish.

Reduce the oven to 180°C/350°F/gas 4. Return the dish to the oven and bake for a further 15–20 minutes.

Remove the dish from the oven. Cut the cumin cheese into 3 or 4 pieces and divide evenly on top of the frittata – each person should get a piece of cheese. Return to the oven and continue cooking for a further 5–7 minutes, or until the cheese has melted. Remove from oven and allow to cool slightly before cutting and serving.

Gluten, sugar and wheat free.
Cook's Tips: You can use any winter vegetables (celeriac, fennel, etc.) available. One the vegetables are roasted, you can finish the dish on the hob, as in the Potato and Onion Frittata (p. 109).

Nutritional Content: A protein-based dish with lots of carbohydrate from the root vegetables, which also give you lots of B vitamins and minerals.

Note to the Senses: Root vegetables aren't always the best sellers on a menu. People seem to have bad memories of them. However, roasting the vegetables brings out their sweetness, and combining them with eggs, fresh herbs and a good cheese is definitely a winner during the winter months.

egg tarts and quiche

Very simply, a tart is a pastry crust with shallow sides, a filling and no top crust. The filling can be savoury or sweet. Depending on the type of tart, the pastry shell can be baked and then filled, or filled and then baked.

A quiche is the French term for a savoury, open-top pie made of eggs, milk or cream, and anything else within reach. The most famous of these is the quiche Lorraine of Alsace.

The following recipes are all suitable for 4–6 people using a 23 cm (9 in) diameter tart/quiche dish/tin. For presentation, ideally you should use one with a removable base, but this isn't necessary.

Asparagus and Cherry Tomato Tart

serves 4–6
ready in 45–60 minutes

23 cm (9 in) diameter fluted quiche tin, removable base preferable but not necessary
1 quantity shortcrust pastry (see p. 222)
1 punnet cherry tomatoes
½ red onion, finely chopped
125 g (4 oz) asparagus, trimmed and washed
8 large eggs
1 tbsp milk
50 g (2 oz) grated Parmesan

Preheat the oven to 240°C/475°F/gas 9.

Blind bake the prepared pastry for 15 minutes by covering the pastry with foil and then covering the foil with dried beans or peas. Remove the beans and foil, return to the oven and bake for a further 5 minutes, until the pastry is dry.

Reduce the oven to 180°C/350°F/gas 4.

Cut the cherry tomatoes lengthwise in half. Place in an oven roasting tray or dish. Add the finely chopped red onion. Drizzle over very lightly with olive oil. Roast for 5–7 minutes. The tray can be placed on the lower level in the oven while the pastry is baking on the top level.

Trim away the woody part of the asparagus, then cook in a small amount of boiling water until tender. Fresh asparagus will be crisp-tender in 5–8 minutes. Drain and run under the cold water tap until the asparagus is cold.

Whisk the eggs, milk and Parmesan together and season lightly.

Place the asparagus and tomatoes evenly on the base of the pastry so that when 6 slices are cut, each person will get some of each vegetable. You can use your artistic skills to make a nice design. Gradually add the egg mix. It's a good idea to put the egg mix in a jug and pour into the pastry case.

Bake for 30 minutes, or until the egg is firm and cooked through. Allow to cool slightly before cutting. Remove from the loose-based baking tin if using and garnish with freshly chopped parsley.

Sugar free.

Cook's Tips: When adding egg mix to a pastry base, you may feel that if you over-fill it, it will spill as you put it into the oven or may spill in the oven. The solution here is to fill the pastry with the egg mix to a comfortable level, place in the oven and then pour the remainder of the egg mix into the pastry case. This will ensure that there are no spills and the pastry case will be filled to the top.

Nutritional Content: A protein-based dish high in nutrients, including fibre, folic acid, potassium, thiamin and vitamins A, B_6, C and K. Lycopene and antioxidants are also present.

Note to the Senses: This dish is a wonderful summer tart. Asparagus is such a beautiful, elegant vegetable – the Audrey Hepburn of the vegetables. This is a simple tart that will impress. You don't need to say anything, just place in the centre of a summer buffet table and everyone will ooh and aah! Tasting will only confirm their expectations.

Caramelised Onion and Blue Cheese Tart

serves 4–6
ready in 1 hour

23 cm (9 in) diameter fluted quiche tin, removable base preferable but not
necessary
1 quantity shortcrust pastry (see p. 222)
1 tbsp olive oil
4 medium Spanish onions, thinly sliced
175 g (6 oz) Cashel Blue or Crozier Blue cheese, roughly chopped or crumbled
8–10 eggs
1 tbsp milk

Preheat the oven to 240°C/475°F/gas 9.

Blind bake the prepared pastry for 15 minutes by covering the pastry with foil
and then covering the foil with dried beans or peas. Remove the beans and foil,
return to the oven and bake for a further 5 minutes, until the pastry is dry.

Reduce the oven to 180°C/350°F/gas 4.

Heat the olive oil in a medium/large frying pan over a medium heat. Add the
sliced onions. Cook over a gentle heat covered with a lid until they collapse and
are very soft and meltingly tender. This can take 15–20 minutes. Check every 5
minutes to ensure the onions aren't burning. Remove the lid, increase the heat and
continue to fry to caramelise the onions.

Spread the onions over the pre-cooked pastry case and scatter over half the
cheese.

Beat the eggs, milk and some salt and pepper together. Pour the egg mix over
the onions and sprinkle the remaining cheese over, making sure the tart is filled to
the top. (See Cook's Tips on p. 118.) Bake for 25–30 minutes, until the egg mixture is fully cooked through and is firm to touch.

Sugar free.
Cook's Tips: If you like blue cheese, you can add a little more.
Nutritional Content: Choline, chromium, dietary fibre, flavonoids, lutein, protein,

selenium, tryptophan and vitamins C and K. Onions also contain several anti-inflammatory agents.

Note to the Senses: The sharpness of blue cheese is balanced out by the natural sweetness of the caramelised onions.

Leek, Pine Nut and Organic Feta Tart

serves 4–6

ready in 40 minutes

23 cm (9 in) diameter fluted quiche tin, removable base preferable but not necessary

1 quantity shortcrust pastry (see p. 222)

1½ tsp olive or sunflower oil

1 Spanish onion, finely chopped

4 leeks (approx 300 g/11 oz), thinly sliced and thoroughly washed

1½ tsp chopped fresh rosemary

2 garlic cloves, finely chopped

50 g (2 oz) toasted pine nuts

8 eggs

1 tbsp milk

pinch of nutmeg

100 g (4 oz) crumbled feta cheese, such as Abbey organic feta

Preheat the oven to 240°C/475°F/gas 9.

Blind bake the prepared pastry for 15 minutes by covering the pastry with foil and then covering the foil with dried beans or peas. Remove the beans and foil, return to the oven and bake for a further 5 minutes, until the pastry is dry.

Meanwhile, heat the oil in a pan over a medium heat. Add the onion, leeks and chopped rosemary and sauté for 10 minutes. Add the garlic and sauté for another 2 minutes.

Lightly toast the pine nuts by placing on a baking tray and oven roasting for 2–3 minutes. Be careful not to let them burn.

Beat the eggs lightly. Stir in the milk, a pinch of nutmeg and salt and pepper.

Spread the onion and leek mixture over the pastry and top with crumbled feta cheese. Pour over the egg mixture, making sure the tart is filled to the top. (See Cook's Tips on p. 118.) Bake for 25–30 minutes, until golden on top and firm to touch. Cool in the tin for 5 minutes, then remove and slice as required.

Sugar free.

Cook's Tips: This is a lovely late winter and spring tart. There are good-quality Irish farmhouse feta-like cheeses available and are really good with this tart. In Café Fresh we use Paddy Jack organic feta cheese.

Nutritional Content: A protein-filled egg-based dish with all the nutrients of eggs. As leeks are a member of the onion family, the nutritional content is similar to the Caramelised Onion and Blue Cheese Tart (p. 119), but there are less amounts of nutrients in leeks.

Note to the Senses: The French are big fans of the leek. While being a member of the onion family, it has a more delicate, sweeter flavour and is complimented by a well-flavoured feta cheese. I use organic feta from Abbey Cheese Co., available at farmers' markets.

Roast Mediterranean Vegetable, Basil Pesto and Organic Brie Tart

serves 4–6

ready in 1 hour

23 cm (9 in) diameter fluted quiche tin, removable base preferable but not necessary

1 quantity shortcrust pastry (see p. 222)

1 courgette, cut into bite-sized pieces

1 red pepper, cut into bite-sized pieces

1 yellow pepper, cut into bite-sized pieces

½ aubergine, cut into bite-sized pieces

1 small red onion, roughly chopped

2–4 garlic cloves, roughly chopped

2–3 tbsp olive oil (or less if you prefer)

50 g (2 oz) cherry tomatoes

40 g (1½ oz) pitted black olives, roughly chopped

1–2 tsp capers, roughly chopped

a few sprigs fresh basil leaves, torn into pieces

6–8 large eggs

1 tbsp Basil Pesto (see p. 3)

1 tbsp milk (use light milk or unsweetened soy milk if preferred)

100 g (4 oz) brie cheese (I use organic Abbey brie cheese)

Preheat the oven to 240°C/475°F/gas 9.

Blind bake the prepared pastry for 15 minutes by covering the pastry with foil and then covering the foil with dried beans or peas. Remove the beans and foil, return to the oven and bake for a further 5 minutes, until the pastry is dry.

Reduce the oven to 180°C/350°F/gas 4.

Place the vegetables, onion and garlic in a roasting dish. Drizzle over with the olive oil. Season lightly, mix together well and roast for 15 minutes.

Meanwhile, cut the cherry tomatoes in half lengthwise. Add to the cooked vegetables and return to the oven for another 5 minutes.

Add the olives, capers and fresh basil to the vegetables, then place the roast vegetable mixture into the pre-baked pastry case.

Whisk the eggs, pesto and milk together and season. Gently pour the egg mix over the vegetables, making sure to fill it to the top (see Cook's Tips on p. 118).

Cut the brie into 6 slices and gently lay on top of the egg and vegetable tart. Bake for 30–35 minutes. Touch the centre to make sure the tart is cooked in the centre. Remove from the oven and allow to settle for about 10 minutes before removing from the tin.

Sugar free.

Cook's Tips: When you have prepared your pastry and it's chilling in the fridge, you should then prepare your vegetables. This will save time, as you can then blind bake your pastry on the top shelf and roast your vegetables on the lower shelf. Both are then ready at more or less the same time.

Nutritional Content: A protein-based egg and cheese tart with choline, chromium, dietary fibre, flavonoids, lutein, protein, selenium, tryptophan and vitamins C and K.

Note to the Senses: This is a lovely summer tart. The addition of the Basil Pesto adds a wonderful green colour to the vegetable mix and identifies the fresh flavours that are about to be experienced.

Roast Fennel, Swiss Chard and Goat's Cheese Tart

serves 4–6

ready in 1 hour

23 cm (9 in) diameter fluted quiche tin, removeable base preferable, but not necesssary

1 quantity shortcrust pastry (see p. 222)

2 large fennel bulbs

1½ tsp sunflower or olive oil

400 g (14 oz) Swiss chard or spinach, finely chopped (if using baby spinach, there's no need to chop)

6 large eggs

1 tbsp milk or soy milk

110 g (4 oz) goat's cheese (I use Paddy Jack Organic Goat's Cheese)

Preheat the oven to 240°C/475°F/gas 9.

Blind bake the prepared pastry for 15 minutes by covering the pastry with foil and then covering the foil with dried beans or peas. Remove the beans and foil, return to the oven and bake for a further 5 minutes, until the pastry is dry.

Meanwhile, prepare the fennel by slicing in half lengthwise. Remove the core at the base of the fennel, then cut into slices about 1 cm (½ in) thick.

Place the prepared fennel and the oil in a roasting pan. Roast the fennel until tender, stirring occasionally, about 20 minutes.

Reduce the oven to 180°C/350°F/gas 4.

Add the chopped Swiss chard or spinach to the fennel. The heat of the fennel will wilt the spinach.

Whisk the eggs and milk together in a small bowl. Line the pre-baked pastry with the vegetables. Gently pour in the egg mix, making sure to fill it to the top (see Cook's Tips on p. 118).

Crumble the goat's cheese on top. Bake for 30 minutes, until cooked through. The centre of the dish should be firm to touch. Allow to cool slightly before serving.

Sugar free.

Cook's Tips: When you have prepared your pastry and it's chilling in the fridge, you should then prepare your vegetables. This will save time, as you can then blind bake your pastry on the top shelf and roast your vegetables on the lower shelf. Both are then ready at more or less the same time. Adding ½ tsp fennel seeds to the fennel before roasting intensifies the flavour of the fennel. Rocket is a very good alternative to Swiss chard or spinach when you can get it.

Nutritional Content: A protein-based egg and cheese tart with choline, dietary fibre, flavonoids, lutein, magnesium, manganese, phosphorous, protein and selenium. Swiss chard is a nutritious green leafy vegetable.

Note to the Senses: This is a summer tart of robust flavours. The Swiss chard has a pungent, bitter flavour and the aniseed flavour of the fennel combines very well here. The goat's cheese is an ideal cheese here.

grain-based dishes

In this section I concentrate on the grain, the base of the dish to which we add vegetables, stock, wine, pulses and sometimes cheese. Here we will look at risotto recipes and rice, bulghur and quinoa pilafs. These delicious dishes are a relatively simple way to take the natural goodness of the grain to truly great heights by making it the vehicle for all sorts of exceptional ingredients. The resulting dishes are a combination of down-to-earth goodness and deep, rich flavours. All the recipes given are interchangeable. Once you get the basics right, you can experiment with the various recipes and flavours. They have the added advantage of being one-pot wonders!

In the north of Italy, up around Piedmont, Milan, Lombardy and the area around Venice, rice rules the day. **Risotto** is a rice dish using risotto rice. Arboria rice is the most popular and readily available, but **arborio** is very well regarded. Less popular risotto rices are carnaroli, roma, balso, padona and vialone nano. This pearly-looking, round, fat Italian white rice is quick and easy to cook. What distinguishes it is a higher than normal amount of soluble starch that's released during cooking, which is what makes a risotto creamy. It takes about 18 minutes to cook. When cooked, it should be al dente, tender on the outside and firm in the centre. Like pasta, risotto is pure comfort food. A hot, creamy bowl of risotto is a great way to get through a cold winter night.

Brown rice risotto: You can sometimes find brown risotto rice, which has more fibre and nutrients, but it isn't nearly as creamy as white risotto rice. To compensate for this, though, you get a nutty flavour and added nutrients.

You can use regular short grain or long grain brown rice as substitutes in these dishes. This isn't risotto in the true sense of the word, as risotto must be made with risotto rice in true Italian fashion. As I'm not Italian, I can live with this. If you use brown rice, just remember that it takes longer to cook. In Café Fresh, we make organic short grain brown rice risotto very successfully. Remember, the cooking time is increased from 18 minutes to 40 minutes, though there are ways of speeding up the cooking time. For example, you can pre-soak the brown rice – put the rice in a bowl and cover with cold water. The water should just cover the rice. Leave to soak overnight. This will reduce the cooking time by about 15 minutes. However, it's important not to drain the rice, as valuable nutrients will be lost. There's really no point in using brown rice for its nutritional value if you drain off the goodness.

There are a few simple principles when making risotto. Let's have a look at these rules before we look at recipes.

Basic Risotto (1 portion)

300 ml (10 fl oz) vegetable stock
knob of butter or 1 tsp olive oil
¼ finely chopped Spanish onion
½ garlic clove
85 g (3 oz) Arborio rice
¼ glass white wine (optional)

Place the vegetable stock in a pot and heat slowly. While it's heating, sauté a bit of chopped onion and garlic in a little butter and/or olive oil. When the onion is soft, add the rice and start stirring. Sauté for a few minutes, until the rice is well coated with the oil or butter.

Now start adding liquid. Many people choose to begin by adding a glass of wine, after which comes the broth. The wine is optional. The key to adding the liquid is to add a little at a time and to keep stirring while the rice absorbs it. Once you add the stock, a puff of steam should go up from the pan. If not, then the stock isn't hot enough.

When the stock is absorbed, add a little more. Stir. Add a little more. Stir, stop, stir. Add a little more. Stir, stop, stir. The dish is done in about 18 minutes, when the rice is al dente (cooked through, but still a bit firm in the middle). You can then add your cheese and any other ingredients you like. Stir well.

Risotto recipes are best when you add 2 or at most 3 ingredients to the rice dish. Too many added ingredients tend to cloud the flavour of the finished dish. Less is more here.

Courgette and Mushroom Risotto

serves 4–6
30 minutes

1 litre vegetable stock
1 tbsp olive oil
1 Spanish onion, finely chopped
2 garlic cloves, finely chopped
1 courgette, cut into small cubes
350 g (12 oz) mushrooms, sliced – cremini are best
350 g (12 oz) arborio or other risotto rice
1 glass white wine (optional)
75 g (3 oz) Parmesan cheese, half grated, half shaved

Place the vegetable stock in a pot and heat slowly. Meanwhile, heat 1 tbsp olive oil in a large, heavy pan over a low heat. Add the chopped onions and garlic and cook gently, until soft and transparent but not coloured, about 5 minutes. Add the courgettes and mushrooms and cook for a few minutes more. Stir in the dry, washed rice, stirring constantly until the rice becomes opaque and is completely coated with olive oil and onions.

If using the wine, add it now, before the stock, and allow it to cook for 5 minutes. Add a ladleful of hot stock and stir until it's absorbed. Keep stirring and adding ladlefuls of stock until nearly all the stock has been absorbed and the rice is almost cooked – this will take about 18 minutes (see p. 127). The rice should now have a creamy texture.

Remove from the heat and add the grated Parmesan and seasoning. Stir gently but well. This will make the risotto rich and creamy. Cover with a lid and leave to rest for 1 minute. Scatter Parmesan shavings on top when serving.

Gluten, sugar and wheat free.
Freezing: Not great for freezing.
Cook's Tips: You can swap the courgette for 450 g (1 lb) frozen peas, defrosted. See the brown rice recipe on p. 130 for an equally good alternative on any of the other combinations listed.
Nutritional Content: Carbohydrate-based dish with added protein and nutrients from the various vegetables you add to the dish, including B vitamins, copper, dietary fibre and selenium.
Note to the Senses: Risotto should be creamy. Some recipes add cream, but I never do. The cheese is added at the end so you get the full impact of its flavour.

Saffron and Leek Risotto

Once the onion is cooked, add 4 leeks, finely sliced, and sauté for 5 minutes before adding the broth. After the rice has been cooking for 5 minutes and has turned opaque, add ½ tsp powdered saffron before adding the stock.

Asparagus Risotto

Once the onion is cooked, add 500 g (1 lb 2 oz) chopped asparagus and sauté for 2 minutes before adding the rice. (This is my favourite risotto.)

Sweet Potato/Butternut/Pumpkin Risotto

Once the onion is cooked, add 500 g (1 lb 2 oz) sweet potato, butternut squash or pumpkin (peeled, deseeded and chopped) and sauté until cooked but not too soft. Then add the rice, wine and stock, as in the main recipe. This turns a lovely orange colour when some of the sweet potato breaks down.

Spinach/Swiss Chard Risotto

Steam 1 kg (2 lbs) young spinach or Swiss chard until it collapses. Drain and squeeze to remove as much water as possible. (This water can be used in the vegetable stock.) Add to the rice and onion mixture after the rice has been cooking for 5 minutes and has turned opaque and before adding the wine and stock. Season before serving with a little grated nutmeg and a handful of toasted pine nuts.

Mushroom, Blue Cheese and Pea Brown Rice Risotto

serves 4–6
ready in 1 hour

1 litre vegetable stock
1 tbsp olive oil
1 red onion, finely chopped
2 garlic cloves, finely chopped
350 g (12 oz) mushrooms, sliced – cremini are best
350 g (12 oz) organic short grain brown rice, pre-soaked
1 glass white wine (optional)
450 g (1 lb) frozen peas, defrosted
100 g (4 oz) blue cheese
50 g (2 oz) Parmesan cheese, half grated, half shaved

Place the vegetable stock in a pot and heat slowly. Meanwhile, heat the olive oil in a large, heavy pan over a low heat. Add the chopped red onion and garlic and cook gently, until soft and transparent but not coloured, about 5 minutes. Add the mushrooms and cook for a few minutes more. Stir in the pre-soaked brown rice and stir constantly until the rice becomes opaque and is completely coated with the oil and onion. Because the brown rice is wet from pre-soaking, you may find that it sticks to the pan. Just add 1 tbsp of vegetable stock to loosen the rice from the bottom.

If using the wine, add it now, before the stock, and allow it to cook for 5 minutes. Add a ladleful of hot stock and stir until it's absorbed. Keep stirring and adding ladlefuls of stock until nearly all the stock has been absorbed and the rice is almost cooked – this will take about 20 minutes (see p. 127). If you feel the rice is still too hard, add a little more stock and cook for a little longer.

Add the peas and allow to heat through. Remove from the heat and add the blue cheese and seasoning. Stir gently but well. This will help to make the brown rice risotto creamy. Cover with a lid and leave to rest for 1 minute. Scatter Parmesan shavings on top when serving.

Gluten, sugar and wheat free.
Freezing: Not great for freezing.
Cook's Tips: The ingredients can be changed for any of the alternatives on p. 129 and any other combinations you like.
Nutritional Content: Carbohydrate, copper, dietary fibre, folic acid, magnesium, manganese, protein, selenium, tryptophan, and vitamins B_6, C and K.
Note to the Senses: This is a great way of getting people to eat brown rice who otherwise would shy away from it. It is not easily discernable that it is brown rice, so you can fool family members very successfully with this. I have done it with the most anti-brown rice person I know!

pilaf

This rice- or bulghur-based dish (also called pilau) originated in the Near East. Traditionally it always begins by first browning the rice in butter or oil before cooking it in stock. Pilafs can be variously seasoned and usually contain other ingredients. We will add chopped cooked vegetables, pulses and nuts. In India they're highly spiced with curry. In these dishes, lots of vegetables and Middle Eastern spices are added, together with some dried fruit.

Spicy Chickpea Pilaf

serves 4–6
ready in 30 minutes

850 ml (1½ pints) vegetable stock
200 g (7 oz) whole bulghur wheat, uncooked
1 tbsp olive oil
1 red onion, thinly sliced
2 garlic cloves, crushed
5 cm (2 in) piece root ginger, finely grated
1 red chilli, trimmed and finely chopped
1 tsp cumin seeds
1 tsp turmeric
2 red peppers, cut into thin strips
1 courgette, cut into 5 cm (2 in) pieces
300 g (11 oz) chickpeas, cooked, or 400 g (14 oz) tin chickpeas
50 g (2 oz) raisins or dried apricots
500 g (1 lb 2 oz) fresh spinach, chopped
1 tbsp sesame seeds, toasted
large handful fresh coriander, chopped
crème fraîche or Tofu Mayonnaise (see p. 29), to serve

Heat half the vegetable stock to boiling point. Place the bulghur in a large bowl and cover with the boiling vegetable stock. Cover and leave to stand for 20 minutes.

Meanwhile, heat the oil and sauté the onion over a low heat for 5 minutes, until softened. Stir in the garlic, ginger, chilli, cumin and turmeric and sauté for a further 2–3 minutes. Add half a tablespoon of vegetable stock if the spices start to stick.

Add the peppers and sauté for 5 minutes. Add the courgettes and sauté for 5 minutes. Add the chickpeas, raisins and the remaining vegetable stock and cook for 3 minutes more. The raisins should plump up.

Add the bulghur and stir thoroughly. Add the chopped spinach and combine well. It will wilt in the heat of the dish in a few minutes. Add the toasted sesame seeds and fresh coriander and mix through (leave some sesame seeds and chopped coriander aside for serving). Taste and season as required.

Serve immediately, sprinkled with coriander and sesame seeds and a spoonful of crème fraîche or Tofu Mayonnaise.

Vegan. Dairy and sugar free. Omit dried fruit for a yeast-free dish.

Freezing: This can be frozen for up to 1 month. However, it's not ideal for freezing; it's best made fresh.

Cook's Tips: This dish should be moist but not too wet. Like all grains, it will dry out if left for a while. You can add a little water or stock to bring it back to the right consistency.

Nutritional Content: A complex carbohydrate-based dish with a range of B vitamins. The grains provide calcium, iron, magnesium, phosphorous, potassium and zinc.

Note to the Senses: The turmeric gives the dish a wonderful Middle Eastern hue and flavour, having both an aromatic spiciness and sweetness that combine perfectly to give a very satisfactory dish.

quinoa pilaf

Quinoa is an ancient grain-like product which is native to the Andes. It sustained the ancient Incas and has been cultivated continuously for more than 5,000 years. It's not actually a grain, but the seed of a leafy plant that's distantly related to spinach.

Quinoa is now considered a 'supergrain' because of its nutritional content. It has excellent reserves of protein, and unlike other grains, it's not missing the amino acid lysine, so the protein is more complete. Quinoa offers more iron than other grains and contains high levels of potassium and riboflavin, as well as other B vitamins (B_6, niacin and thiamin). It's also a good source of copper, magnesium, manganese and zinc, and has some folate (folic acid).

Quinoa grains are about the same size as couscous, but flattened with a pointed, oval shape. The colour ranges from pale yellow through red and brown to black. Quinoa cooks quickly to a light, fluffy texture. As it cooks, the external germ, which forms a band around each grain, spirals out, forming a tiny crescent-shaped 'tail', similar to a bean sprout. Although the grain itself is soft and creamy, the tail is crunchy, providing a unique texture to complement quinoa's delicate flavour. It has a light, subtle taste and can be substituted for almost any other grain.

Cooking quinoa: You can see that quinoa is a good food to include in your diet. But how do you cook it? Like everything, you need to know how to cook it properly. From teaching I have found that people simply boil it as per the cooking instructions on the packet and are very unhappy with the end result. If you boil quinoa, you end up with something that resembles wallpaper paste and tastes equally as bad. No matter how good it is for you, are you really going to eat anything that looks and tastes like wallpaper paste? I wouldn't. The secret to cooking quinoa is toasting. Before you cook quinoa, you need to toast it in a dry pot over a medium heat for 5 minutes, as if you're toasting seeds. It will pop just like popcorn and the resulting roasted flavour will completely transform the end product. Always wash quinoa before using to remove any powdery residue of saponin.

Moroccan Spiced Vegetable Quinoa Pilaf

serves 6
ready in 40 minutes

200 g (7 oz) quinoa, rinsed
650 ml (22 fl oz) vegetable stock
2 tbsp olive oil
1 medium onion, finely chopped
2 garlic cloves, finely chopped
2 cm (¾ in) piece root ginger, finely grated
2 red chillies, deseeded and finely chopped
4 tsp cumin seeds
1 tsp turmeric
1 carrot, peeled and thinly sliced
1 parsnip, peeled and thinly sliced
250 g (9 oz) cooked chickpeas or 400 g (14 oz) tin organic chickpeas/kidney

beans or cooked bean of preference
50 g (2 oz) green beans
1 medium head broccoli
400 g (14 oz) baby spinach
1 tbsp sesame seeds, toasted
handful fresh coriander, chopped

Toast the quinoa in a dry pan for 5 minutes, until the grain starts to pop (like pop-corn) and gives off a smoky aroma. Once this is done, add the vegetable stock, bring to the boil and simmer for 15 minutes.

Meanwhile, heat the oil and sauté the onion over a low heat for 5 minutes, until softened. Stir in the garlic, ginger, chillies, cumin and turmeric and sauté for a further 2–3 minutes. Add the carrot and parsnip and combine well. Cover and allow to sweat for 7–10 minutes over a medium heat, until the vegetables are cooked. If sticking, add 1–2 tablespoons of water. Add the chickpeas or kidney beans and combine well. Add the vegetable mix to the cooked quinoa.

Blanch the green beans and broccoli and add to the quinoa. Add the spinach and combine well – this will wilt in the heat of the quinoa. Season to taste and serve garnished with the toasted sesame seeds and freshly chopped coriander.

Vegan. Dairy, gluten, sugar, wheat and yeast free.
Freezing: Freezes well for up to 2 months.
Cook's Tips: The quinoa has a tendency to dry out if left. You can add a little more stock to moisten it.
Nutritional Content: B vitamins (B_6, niacin and thiamin), copper, iron, lysine, magnesium, manganese, potassium, protein, riboflavin and zinc, as well as some folate (folic acid).
Note to the Senses: When cooked, quinoa looks like couscous sprinkled with little spirals or crescent moons. It has a similar texture and lightness to couscous, but with a lovely nutty flavour.

Sabzi Pulao – An Indian Pilaf

serves 6

ready in 1 hour

This is an Indian pilaf recipe using basmati rice. If using brown basmati, soaking will reduce your cooking time considerably.

350 g (12 oz) organic brown (pre-soaked) or white basmati rice

1 tbsp vegetable oil

1 Spanish onion, halved and thinly sliced

2 garlic cloves, finely chopped

4 cardamom pods

3 green chillies, deseeded and finely chopped

1 tsp turmeric

1 cinnamon stick

300 g (11 oz) mushrooms, roughly chopped

2 carrots, peeled and cut into cubes

1 red pepper, seeded and roughly chopped

125 g (4 oz) green beans, topped and tailed

75 g (3 oz) cashew nuts

10 curry leaves

750 ml (1¼ pints) vegetable stock

handful fresh mint leaves, chopped

Rinse the rice in a large sieve with cold running water, then drain. Meanwhile, heat the oil in a heavy-based saucepan and sauté the onion until lightly browned. Add the garlic, cardamom pods, chillies, turmeric and cinnamon stick. Stir-fry for 1 minute. Add the rice and fry, stirring for a further 1 minute. Add the vegetables, cashew nuts and curry leaves and stir well.

Add the vegetable stock, cover and bring to the boil. Lower the heat and simmer for about 20 minutes (for brown basmati) or 15 minutes (for white basmati), until the rice is cooked. Season to taste.

Leave to stand, covered, for 10 minutes, then fluff up the rice with a fork. Serve garnished with the fresh mint leaves.

Vegan. Dairy, gluten, sugar and wheat free.

Freezing: Can be frozen for up to 2 months.

Cook's Tips: Curry leaves are available in Asian and ethnic food stores. They really make this dish. You can buy them fresh or dried. The leaves are inedible (like bay leaves), so remove them before serving or else warn the diners to leave them aside.

Nutritional Content: This is a carbohydrate-based dish with added protein and nutrients from the various vegetables you add, including B vitamins, copper, dietary fibre, selenium, lots of antioxidants and anti-inflammatory agents.

Note to the Senses: This dish exudes Indian flavours. If you like your food spicy, add extra chillies and serve Cucumber Raita (p. 12) on the side.

jambalaya

What a great word to describe a food dish! Jambalaya is one of Creole cookery's hallmarks. Similar to pilaf, it's a versatile dish that traditionally combines cooked rice with a variety of ingredients, including tomatoes, onion, green peppers and almost any kind of meat, poultry or shellfish. The dish varies widely from cook to cook. It's thought that the name derives from the French *jambon*, meaning 'ham', the main ingredient in many of the first jambalayas. At Café Fresh we've adapted this dish to suit ourselves. We use rice, beans and vegetables with a spicy tomato base to make a fantastic vegetarian jambalaya.

Kidney Bean and Vegetable Jambalaya

serves 4–6
ready in 40 minutes

1 tbsp sunflower oil
1 Spanish onion, finely chopped
2 garlic cloves, finely chopped
1 green pepper, chopped
1 red or yellow pepper, roughly chopped
2 sticks of celery, roughly chopped
1 tsp dried oregano
1 tsp dried thyme
1 tsp chilli powder or ½ tsp cayenne pepper
1 tsp tomato purée
⅛ tsp allspice
400 ml (14 fl oz) vegetable stock
400 g (14 oz) tin chopped tomatoes
175 g (6 oz) organic brown rice, pre-soaked
1 tsp sea salt
2 bay leaves
400 g (14 oz) tin organic kidney beans, drained
1 bag frozen peas
250 g (9 oz) tin sweetcorn, drained
3 spring onions, thinly sliced
handful fresh parsley, chopped

Heat the oil in a large pot, then add the onions and garlic and sauté until soft, about 5 minutes. Add the peppers and celery and sauté for another 5–10 minutes. Add the oregano, thyme, chilli, tomato purée and allspice and combine well. Sauté for 1 minute. Add 1½ tsp water if it's sticking.

Add the stock, tomatoes, rice, sea salt and bay leaves, cover and bring to the boil. Reduce the heat and simmer for about 40 minutes.

About 5 minutes before the rice is done, add the beans, peas and sweetcorn.

Simmer until the rice is done and the peas are heated through. Serve garnished with sliced spring onions and freshly chopped parsley.

Vegan. Dairy, gluten, sugar, wheat and yeast free.
Freezing: Can be frozen for up to 2 months.
Cook's Tips: You can use a different bean, as preferred.
Nutritional Content: This is a carbohydrate-based dish with added protein and nutrients from the various vegetables you add, including B vitamins, copper, dietary fibre, selenium, lots of antioxidants and anti-inflammatory agents.
Note to the Senses: This dish has a rich, deep red colour and should have a slightly soupy consistency. It has spice and is very different from the Indian pilaf.

layers

This section is dedicated to Café Fresh layers. These dishes were devised so that they have a visual impact – layers or stacks always make an impression. In Café Fresh, we need the visual impact, but we also need relatively quick dishes, so we devised the dishes below.

These dishes are ideal for a family dinner and also make an impressive party dish. The rice-filled pies are the perfect way to use up leftover rice, and the vegetable layers are an interesting way of serving vegetables for a dinner party. These layers always look impressive, but aren't that much hard work at all.

I use filo pastry for two of the recipes. The great advantage of this is that you can buy this guilt-free, as it's very difficult to make. In Café Fresh this is the only pastry we don't make ourselves, and for very good reasons. I tried making it once, and let's just say I never tried again! We buy filo pastry in the Asian markets, and it's also available in most supermarkets.

If the filo recipes are too large for your needs, you can make filo wraps with the fillings instead. Remember, the filling for the layers is for 8 servings. You can adjust the measurements to suit your needs when making wraps.

For these dishes you will need a 31.5 cm (12 in) round springform tin.

Middle Eastern Filo Rice Torte

serves 8
ready in 1 hour 15 minutes

Don't forget to take the pastry out of the freezer, or buy in the shop, the day before.

150 g (5 oz) basmati rice, washed (400 g/14 oz cooked)

25 g (1 oz) wild rice, washed (65 g/2½ oz cooked)

325 ml (11 fl oz) water

1 red onion, finely chopped

2 garlic cloves, finely chopped

1 tbsp cinnamon

1 tbsp garam masala

400 g (14 oz) field mushrooms, thinly sliced

4 carrots, peeled and finely diced

1 tbsp semi-sun-dried tomatoes

handful raisins

handful toasted flaked almonds, roughly chopped

1½ tsp chopped apricots

1½ tsp fresh parsley, chopped

1½ tsp fresh coriander, chopped

1 tbsp Basil Pesto (p. 3)

3 large free-range eggs or 100 g (3½ oz) silken tofu

1 packet filo pastry (approx. 12 sheets)

sunflower oil

Cucumber Raita (p. 12) or Sun-Dried Tomato Pesto (p. 4), to serve

31.5 cm (12 in) round springform tin, greased

Preheat the oven to 180°C/350°F/gas 4.

Cook the rice by bringing the water to boil in a medium pot. Add the rice and cook for 15 minutes. (If using brown basmati rice, it takes 30 minutes to cook, so you need to add the wild rice 10 minutes into the cooking time.) Once the rice is cooked, drain and rinse under the cold tap to remove the starch. Leave aside to dry.

Meanwhile, sauté the onion and garlic together for 5 minutes over a medium heat. Add the spices and cook for 2 more minutes. If the spices are sticking, just add a little water.

Add the mushrooms and sauté for a further 5 minutes. Add the carrots and 1 tbsp water, cover the pot and sweat for 5–7 minutes. Remove the lid and add the semi-sun-dried tomatoes, raisins, flaked almonds and apricots. Combine the rice with the vegetables.

In a large mixing bowl, add the fresh parsley, coriander and pesto to the eggs or tofu. Add the egg and tofu mix to the rice mixture.

Open the filo pastry and lay it out. Lightly brush the first sheet of pastry with sunflower oil and lay in the prepared tin. Continue this with 5 more sheets of filo, overlapping the sheets so that the tin is covered with pastry 2 sheets thick. Some of the filo pastry sheets should hang out over the edge of the tin.

Place the rice filling inside and cover with 4 overlapping oiled filo sheets. There will be pastry hanging over the edge. Grease 4 more sheets of filo pastry and overlap over the top to cover the filling. Gather the pastry that lies over the edges and neatly roll it up to form an edge on the top of the tin.

Cover with foil and bake for 25 minutes. Remove the foil and brown for a further 5 minutes. Be careful, as the filo browns very quickly.

Remove from the oven and allow to cool slightly before removing from the tin. Garnish with fresh coriander and serve with Cucumber Raita (p. 12) or Sun-Dried Tomato Pesto (p. 4).

Vegan option. Dairy and sugar free.

Freezing: Not suitable for freezing. The filling is good for freezing, though, so you can make double the amount and freeze half for the following week.

Cook's Tips: Add 100 g of crumbled feta cheese to the rice mix before cooking. You can use short grain rice in this recipe also. If you'd like to have a little spice, add ½ tsp chilli powder with the other spices. You can make individual wraps with this recipe if you prefer.

For a party, it's a good idea to use white basmati rice, as not everyone is a fan of brown rice. The dish will also look much better when sliced.

Nutritional Content: If using brown rice, the nutritional benefits are higher with the benefits of fibre, flavonoids, lycopene, magnesium, manganese, selenium, tryptophan and some vitamin A, B_2 (riboflavin), B_5 and K.

Note to the Senses: Filo pastry is visually very pleasing. When you're working with filo pastry, it tends to be delicate, so a little care is needed. Once you've used it a few times, you'll get a feel for it.

Lebanese Courgette Filo Pie

serves 8

ready in 1 hour

Don't forget to take the pastry out of the freezer, or buy in the shop, the day before.

2 tbsp sunflower oil, plus extra for pastry

½ large onion, finely chopped

1 tsp cumin seeds

1 tsp turmeric

1 tsp ground coriander

3 plump courgettes, diced

200 g (7 oz) basmati rice

400 ml (14 fl oz) vegetable stock (Marigold organic is best quality)

425 g (15 oz) cooked chickpeas

1 tbsp freshly chopped coriander

200 g (7 oz) filo pastry (approx. 8 sheets)

sprinkle of paprika and freshly chopped coriander, to garnish

Tomato and Coriander Salsa (p. 18), to serve

31.5 cm (12 in) round springform tin, greased

Preheat the oven to 180°C/350°F/gas 4.

Heat the oil in a pan and sauté the onions and spices together until soft, about 3–5 minutes. Add the courgettes and cook on a high heat to avoid the courgettes watering.

When the courgettes are soft but still holding their shape, add the rice and mix well to ensure the rice is coated with the oil and vegetables. Reduce the heat and add in one-third of the stock. Allow the rice to absorb the liquid, stirring occasionally. Repeat twice until the stock is gone and the rice is cooked.

When all of the stock is absorbed, add the chickpeas and check the seasoning. It's important at this stage not to over-season, as the stock will have a good flavour. Finally, add in the fresh coriander.

Open the filo pastry and lay it out. Lightly brush the first sheet of pastry with sunflower oil and lay in the prepared tin. Continue this with 5 more sheets of filo, overlapping the sheets so that the tin is covered with pastry 2 sheets thick. Place the filling inside and press down evenly.

Grease 4 more sheets of filo and overlap over the top to cover the filling. Gather the pastry that lies over the edges and neatly roll up to form an edge on the top of the tin.

Cover with foil and bake for 25 minutes. Remove the foil and brown for a further 5 minutes. Be careful, as the filo browns very quickly.

Remove from the oven and leave to rest for 5 minutes before cutting to serve. Garnish with a sprinkle of ground paprika and freshly chopped coriander. Serve with Tomato and Coriander Salsa (p. 18).

Vegan. Dairy and sugar free.
Freezing: Not suitable for freezing. This is only good when made fresh.
Cook's Tips: This is a variation of a wonderful recipe I found in Nigella Lawson's *How to be a Domestic Goddess* cookbook. It's actually a really quick dish. If you have leftover basmati rice, you can use it up here. All you need to do is reduce the amount of stock by half and follow the recipe as normal.

For a party, it's a good idea to use white basmati rice, as not everyone is a fan of brown rice. The dish will also look much better when sliced.
Nutritional Content: If using brown rice, the nutritional benefits are higher with the benefits of fibre, flavonoids, lycopene, magnesium, manganese, selenium, tryptophan and some vitamin A, B_2 (riboflavin), B_5 and K.
Note to the Senses: Filo pastry is visually very pleasing. When you're working with filo pastry, it tends to be delicate, so a little care is needed. Once you've used it a few times, you'll get a feel for it.

Mushroom, Leek, Tofu and Cashew Stack

serves 8
ready in 60 minutes

for the crumble base:

1 tbsp sunflower oil

1 Spanish onion, finely chopped

1 garlic clove, finely chopped

250 g (9 oz) fine breadcrumbs (brown is preferable)

50 g (2 oz) roasted cashew nuts, finely chopped

1 tbsp chopped fresh chives

1 tbsp chopped fresh parsley

sea salt and ground white pepper

for the topping:

1½ tsp sunflower oil

1 white onion, finely chopped

1 garlic clove, finely chopped

4 leeks, trimmed, washed and thinly sliced

750 g (1 lb 10 oz) mushrooms

1 tbsp red wine

1 tsp soy sauce or tamari

300 g (10½ oz) silken tofu

sea salt and ground white pepper

1 tbsp fresh thyme

1 tbsp fresh parsley

handful of toasted sesame seeds, for garnish

31.5 cm (12 in) round springform tin, greased and lined

Preheat the oven to 200°C/400°F/gas 6.

To make the crumble base, heat the oil in a pan and sauté the onions and garlic for 5 minutes, until soft.

Combine the breadcrumbs, cashew nuts, chives and parsley together in a bowl. Season lightly with sea salt and ground white pepper.

Add the onions, garlic and oil to the breadcrumbs and mix well. You may need to add some more sunflower oil to bind, as if you were making stuffing. The mix should be moist but not soggy. Place the crumble on the base of the greased and lined springform tin and press down evenly.

To make the topping, sauté the onions and garlic in the sunflower oil until soft, about 3–5 minutes. Add the leeks and continue cooking for 5 more minutes. Add the mushrooms and sauté for another 8 minutes. Add the wine and soy sauce and allow the juices to evaporate. Remove from the heat, add the tofu and mix well. Season with salt and white pepper and add the fresh chopped thyme and parsley.

Place the leek topping over the crumble base. Cover with foil and bake for 35 minutes. Remove from the oven and allow to cool slightly before removing from the tin. Garnish with toasted sesame seeds.

This dish looks better if you invert it. With a knife, loosen the layer from around the sides of the tin. Place a large plate over the tin (the bottom of the plate facing out). Gently turn the tin upside down so that the plate is now on the bottom. Open the sides of the springform tin. You will now have the crumble on top. Garnish with toasted sesame seeds.

Vegan. Dairy and sugar free.

Freezing: Suitable for freezing. Any leftover slices can be frozen for up to 2 months.

Cook's Tips: You can replace the breadcrumbs with an equal quantity of toasted and boiled quinoa for a wheat-free base. Alternatively, you can use equal quantities of rehydrated bulghar wheat for a nutty-flavoured version.

Nutritional Content: Carbohydrate from breadcrumbs, copper, iron, magnesium, potassium, protein, riboflavin, selenium, tryptophan and vitamins B_3 and B_5.

Note to the Senses: This is a great way of using tofu imaginatively, as no one will know it's in the dish. It will look like a vegetable layer. There are good flavours from the mushrooms and leeks and the tofu is really a binder in the dish, so it's not visible!

Mexican Bean Stack

serves 8
ready in 45 minutes

This is meant to be a quick and easy recipe. A New Zealand girl, Jackie, shared this recipe with us a few years ago and it has been a winner ever since.

1½ tsp olive oil

1 Spanish onion, finely chopped

2 garlic cloves, finely chopped

2 chillies, deseeded and finely chopped

1 red pepper, deseeded and finely chopped

1 yellow pepper, deseeded and finely chopped

1 green pepper, deseeded and finely chopped

3 carrots, peeled and finely diced

1¼ kg (2¾ lb) cooked kidney beans

5 large tortillas

2 tbsp Greek-style yoghurt

50 g (2 oz) grated Cheddar

handful fresh coriander, to garnish

Salsa Verde (see p. 9), to serve

31.5 cm (12 in) round springform tin, greased and lined

Preheat the oven to 200°C/400°F/gas 6.

Heat the olive oil in a pan and sauté the onions until soft, 3–5 minutes. Add the garlic and chillies and gently sauté for 1 minute more.

Add the peppers and carrots and cover, allowing to sweat over a low heat for 10 minutes. Add 1 tablespoon of water after 5 minutes to prevent the vegetables from burning.

When cooked, place in a large bowl. Add the cooked kidney beans, season well and blend the mixture roughly. You don't want the beans totally blended; you should be able to see bits of kidney beans and vegetables. Taste for seasoning. You'll probably find you need to season this dish a little more than normal, as the kidney beans absorb a lot of flavour. If you think you need a little more spice, add a pinch of ground chilli powder.

Place 1 tortilla in the base of the greased and lined springform tin. Place one-third of the bean mixture on top of the tortilla. Place a second tortilla on top of the bean mixture, then spread a thin layer of yoghurt on top of the tortilla. Repeat these 2 steps again, ending with yoghurt.

Cover with foil and bake for 25 minutes. Remove the cover and sprinkle with the grated Cheddar cheese. Return to the oven, uncovered, to brown, 5–10 minutes. Allow to cool before removing from the tin.

Garnish with fresh coriander leaves and serve with Salsa Verde (p. 9).

Sugar free.

Freezing: Suitable for freezing. Any leftover pieces can be frozen for up to 2 months. If you're making the dish for a small number, you can bake it, use half, and when the other half is cold, freeze and reuse for another dinner.

Cook's Tips: This recipe is designed to be made in a short space of time. If you don't have fresh chillies, then use 1 tsp ground chilli powder. If you don't have kidney beans, you can use pinto beans, though mind you, kidney beans look the best. The vegetables can also be changed to whatever you like.

Nutritional Content: A protein-based dish with smaller amounts of carbohydrate. This dish is a good source of cholesterol-lowering dietary fibre, folate, iron, magnesium, manganese and smaller amounts of other minerals.

Note to the Senses: This is quite a substantial dish. It's a puréed bean and vegetable dish, so it's a good idea to have something light with it, such as a green salad or chicory salad.

Beetroot, Fennel and Kale Stack

serves 8
ready in 50 minutes

1 tbsp sunflower oil
1 Spanish onion, finely chopped
2 garlic cloves, finely chopped
1 tsp fennel seeds
5 fennel bulbs, halved, decored and chopped into small pieces
1 tbsp white wine
3 heads curly kale
3 large tortillas
100 g (4 oz) organic feta
3 large beetroot, grated
1 tbsp sesame oil

toasted sesame seeds, to garnish

31.5 cm (12 in) round springform tin, greased and lined

Preheat the oven to 200°C/400°F/gas 6.

Heat the oil in a pan and sauté the onion over a medium heat until soft, 3–5 minutes. Add the garlic and fennel seeds and sauté for a further 2 minutes. Add the fennel bulbs and white wine and sauté for 10 minutes, until the fennel is soft.

Meanwhile, boil the curly kale in a small amount of salted boiling water. Drain and allow to cool, then chop finely.

Assemble the dish by placing 1 tortilla on the bottom of the greased and lined springform tin. Place half the cooked fennel mixture on top. Crumble one-third of the feta over the fennel and place a layer of kale on top of the cheese. Cover with a tortilla.

Repeat by layering the fennel, crumbled feta and kale and ending with a tortilla. Place the grated beetroot over the tortilla and then crumble feta cheese over the dish. Drizzle the sesame oil over the beetroot and feta.

Cover with foil and bake for 30 minutes. Garnish with toasted sesame seeds.

Vegan option. Gluten, sugar, wheat and yeast free. Dairy free if you use tofu instead of cheese.

Freezing: Not suitable for freezing.

Cook's Tips: You can substitute the feta with goat's cheese or with grated tofu if you prefer. The kale can be substituted with spinach or other green leafy vegetables. If you can't get large tortillas, use smaller ones and overlap them to cover each layer.

Nutritional Content: Some carbohydrate, dietary fibre, folate, manganese, potassium, some protein from cheese, vitamin A and smaller amounts of other minerals.

Note to the Senses: This is a perfect winter dish. It's an interesting way of presenting a vegetable dish. You'll be curious from the presentation and delighted with the taste.

lasagne and comfort food

Lasagne is probably the best-known Italian pasta dish. This baked pasta dish is varied from region to region: Tuscans and Emilia-Romagnans make it with béchamel sauce, sugo alla bolognese and grated Parmigiano; Ligurians make it with pesto sauce and serve it up as a refreshing summer dish; Calabrians (among others) use ricotta salata (salted ricotta); and Neapolitans make an extraordinarily sumptuous Carnival lasagne with ricotta and a variety of other ingredients. As you can see, there are many wonderful variations. This allows for the most robust and flavourful sauces and the most sumptuous and creative fillings.

If you can't eat wheat, there are still options. You can now buy a corn-based lasagne in good health food stores. This is ideal for the recipes below. It tends to be a little more brittle, but don't worry about that − just lay the pasta sheets or pieces of pasta sheets together. Once they're baked, they'll be perfect.

The sauce for lasagne is a béchamel sauce. It's basically flour, butter and milk. You can substitute maize flour for the regular flour if on a wheat-free diet. The consistency is a little different, but it tastes great. People tend to panic when they hear 'béchamel sauce', but there's no need for alarm. When making béchamel sauce, it's convenient to use a hand whisk. As you're making the sauce, lumps may appear. Don't panic! This is remedied by beating with the hand whisk. If all else fails, you can put the sauce through a sieve. The best advice is to start slowly and don't panic.

I'm always amazed at how the lasagne sheets never fit perfectly into baking dishes − there are always a few pieces that need to be broken. It doesn't really matter, though, as once cooked it will hold together perfectly.

You will need a 13" × 9" × 2" ovenproof dish or one of similar size for the recipes in this chapter.

Roast Mediterranean Vegetable Lasagne

serves 4–6
ready in 1 hour 30 minutes

1 large carrot, roughly diced
2 medium courgettes, roughly diced
2 small aubergines, roughly chopped
3 mixed peppers, cored and cut into medium-sized pieces
1 red onion, roughly chopped
4 garlic cloves, crushed
2 tbsp chopped basil or 2 tsp dried basil
1–2 tbsp olive oil
10–12 strips lasagne
50 g (2 oz) grated Parmesan

for the béchamel sauce:
1 tbsp butter or vegan margarine
50 g (2 oz) white flour or maize flour
570 ml (1 pint) milk or soy milk
1 tsp Dijon mustard
pinch ground nutmeg
2 bay leaves
1½ tsp Basil Pesto (see p. 3) (optional)

Preheat the oven to 180°C/350°F/gas 4.

Roast the vegetables by placing all the chopped vegetables, onion and garlic into a medium-sized baking tray. Lightly season and add the basil. Drizzle over with olive oil and toss the vegetables well. Roast for 20–25 minutes, until soft but not overcooked! Remember, the vegetables will be going back into the oven to bake once the lasagne is assembled.

Meanwhile, make the sauce. In a medium saucepan, melt the butter, add the flour and combine to form a ball at the side of the pan. Lower the heat and allow this roux to cook for 5 minutes. Add the milk slowly, stirring/whisking constantly until all the milk has gone. Add the mustard, nutmeg and bay leaves. Combine well. Stir constantly so that the sauce doesn't form lumps – a good whisk will help to prevent this. Bring the sauce gently to the boil, stirring all the time. The sauce should now have a smooth, thick, creamy consistency. Remove from the heat, season and add the pesto, if using. Leave to infuse for 15 minutes. Cover the pot so a skin doesn't form on the sauce. Remove the bay leaves from the sauce and discard.

Once the vegetables are roasted, assemble the lasagne. In a 13" × 9" × 2" ovenproof dish, coat the bottom with a little sauce, then place a layer of lasagne sheets on top of the sauce and half the vegetables on top of the lasagne. Place a layer of lasagne sheets over the vegetables and generously coat with sauce. Add the remaining vegetables and top with lasagne sheets and the rest of the sauce. Cover with foil and bake for 35 minutes. Remove the cover, sprinkle grated Parmesan on top and return to the oven for 10 minutes to brown. Serve with salad on the side.

Vegan if using soy milk. Sugar free. Wheat free if using wheat-free lasagne sheets and maize flour.
Freezing: Ideal for freezing.
Cook's Tips: Add a touch of luxury to this by adding 25 g (1 oz) chopped semi-sun-dried tomatoes and 25 g (1 oz) chopped olives.
Nutritional Content: A carbohydrate-based dish with protein from the milk and full of vitamins and minerals from the summer vegetables, such as dietary fibre and vitamins A, B_6, C and K, as well as smaller amounts of manganese and potassium.
Note to the Senses: Plenty of comfort food here. This is a pleasant alternative to the tomato-based lasagnes available everywhere. It has wonderful flavour from the roasting process. When buying summer vegetables, ensure they have a bright colour and are firm to touch. Don't buy peppers with soft spots. Make sure the courgettes are firm by pressing the courgette firmly between you hands. If it's soft, the inside is stringy and flavourless.

Roast Root Vegetable Lasagne

To vary this vegetable lasagne seasonally, use root vegetables and Cheddar cheese as an alternative. Simply roast a selection of roots, e.g. chopped butternut squash, carrot, celeriac, celery, turnip and sweet potato, with some rosemary sprigs, onion and garlic. Use Parsley Pesto (see p. 5) instead of Basil Pesto if desired.

Spinach, Leek and Organic Feta Cheese Lasagne

serves 4–6
ready in 1 hour 30 minutes

1½ tsp sunflower oil
1 Spanish onion, finely chopped
2 garlic cloves
6 leeks, washed and thinly sliced
450 g (1 lb) fresh spinach, chopped
100 g (4 oz) organic feta cheese
50 g (2 oz) grated Parmesan

for the béchamel sauce:
1 tbsp butter or vegan margarine
50 g (2 oz) white flour or maize flour
570 ml (1 pint) milk or soy milk
1 tsp Dijon mustard
pinch ground nutmeg
2 bay leaves

Preheat the oven to 180°C/350°F/gas 4.

Heat the oil in a pan over a medium heat and sauté the onions and garlic for 5 minutes. Add the leeks and cook for 10 minutes more, until the leeks are soft. Add the spinach and allow to wilt. This will only take about 3 minutes. Once the spinach has wilted, remove the pan from the heat.

Meanwhile, make the sauce. In a medium saucepan, melt the butter, add the flour and combine to form a ball at the side of the pan. Lower the heat and allow this roux to cook for 5 minutes. Add the milk slowly, stirring/whisking constantly until all the milk has gone. Add the mustard, nutmeg and bay leaves. Combine well. Stir constantly so that the sauce doesn't form lumps – a good whisk will help to prevent this. Bring the sauce gently to the boil, stirring all the time. The sauce should now have a smooth, thick, creamy consistency. Remove from the heat and season. Leave to infuse for 15 minutes. Cover the pot so a skin doesn't form on the sauce. Remove the bay leaves from the sauce and discard.

To assemble the lasagne, place a layer of lasagne sheets on the bottom of a 13" X 9" X 2" ovenproof dish and lightly cover with sauce. Place half the spinach and leek mix over the sauce, then another layer of lasagne and sauce. Crumble the organic feta cheese over the sauce. Next place the remaining spinach and leek mix over the feta cheese. Finish with a layer of lasagne and sauce.

Wipe the edges of the baking dish and cover with tin foil. Bake for 35 minutes. Remove the cover and sprinkle Parmesan on top. Return to the oven to brown. Remove from the oven and allow to cool slightly and settle before cutting.

Sugar free. Wheat free if using wheat-free lasagne sheets and maize flour.

Freezing: Ideal for freezing.

Cook's Tips: When using leeks, wash them thoroughly. I find the best way to do this is to chop the leeks first, then fill a sink with cold water and wash thoroughly. I suggest you change the water at least twice. Lots of dirt get lodged in between the layers, so it's best to be thorough.

Nutritional Content: Calcium, carbohydrate, folate, iron, manganese, protein and vitamins A, B_2 and K.

Note to the Senses: When cooking spinach, you'll find that it releases a lot of juices. In most recipes you're asked to discard this, but if you do this, a lot of the nutrients are lost. The main reason for doing this is to ensure a good consistency in your dish so that when you cut a slice it holds its shape. This is never done in Café Fresh and I never do this at home either unless I'm making spinach lasagne for guests, but even then I generally avoid doing that. The juice can be added to a vegetable stock. The best solution is to just use the spinach, juice and all, in the dish. You can use a little less milk in your sauce so it's thicker. Once the lasagne is cooked, I leave it to stand for 10 minutes to settle. Alternatively, this can be made a day in advance.

Spinach, Fennel and Organic Goat's Cheese Lasagne

serves 4–6

ready in 1 hour 30 minutes

3–4 medium fennel bulbs, peeled and cut into quarters

1 tsp fennel seeds

1 onion, finely chopped

4 garlic cloves

3 tbsp olive oil

1 tbsp white wine (optional)

450 g (1 lb) fresh spinach

100 g (4 oz) organic goat's cheese

50 g (2 oz) grated Parmesan

for the béchamel sauce:

1 tbsp butter or vegan margarine

50 g (2 oz) white flour or maize flour

570 ml (1 pint) milk or soy milk

1 tsp Dijon mustard

pinch ground nutmeg

2 bay leaves

Preheat the oven to 180°C/350°F/gas 4.

Roast the vegetables by placing the fennel, fennel seeds, onion and garlic into a medium-sized baking tray. Lightly season and drizzle over with the oil and toss the vegetables well. Add the white wine (if using) and roast for 20–25 minutes.

Mix the spinach into the hot fennel mix. It will wilt very quickly. This is a simple and time-efficient way of cooking the spinach.

Meanwhile, make the sauce. In a medium saucepan, melt the butter, add the flour and combine to form a ball at the side of the pan. Lower the heat and allow this roux to cook for 5 minutes. Add the milk slowly, stirring/whisking constantly until all the milk has gone. Add the mustard, nutmeg and bay leaves. Combine well. Stir constantly so that the sauce doesn't form lumps – a good whisk will help to prevent this. Bring the sauce gently to the boil, stirring all the time. The sauce should now have a smooth, thick, creamy consistency. Remove from the heat and season. Leave to infuse for 15 minutes. Cover the pot so a skin doesn't form on the sauce. Remove the bay leaves from the sauce and discard.

To assemble the lasagne, place a layer of lasagne sheets on the bottom of a 13" × 9" × 2" ovenproof dish and lightly cover with sauce. Place half the fennel and spinach mix over the sauce, then another layer of lasagne and sauce. Crumble the goat's cheese over the sauce. Next, place the remaining vegetables over the goat's cheese. Finish with a layer of lasagne and sauce.

Wipe the edges of the dish and cover with tin foil. Bake for 35 minutes. Remove the cover and sprinkle the Parmesan on top. Return to the oven to brown. Remove from the oven and allow to cool slightly and settle before cutting.

Sugar free. Wheat free if using wheat-free lasagne sheets and maize flour.

Freezing: Ideal for freezing.

Cook's Tips: When buying goat's cheese, choose a good flavour for cooking. If it's too mild, the flavour will be overwhelmed by the strong fennel aniseed flavours.

Nutritional Content: Calcium, carbohydrate, folate, iron, manganese, protein and vitamins A, B$_2$ and K, as well as flavonoids from the fennel with anti-cancer effects.

Note to the Senses: Goat's cheese and fennel is a classic combination. The tang of the goat's cheese works perfectly with the aniseed flavour of the fennel. If you like robust flavour, this lasagne is perfect for you.

Roast Butternut/Pumpkin, Spinach and Hazelnut Lasagne

An alternative to fennel in the recipe above is butternut squash, pumpkin or sweet potato. Substitute 1 large butternut or 3 sweet potatoes for the fennel. Cut into 5 cm (2 in) chunks and roast as above. Add 50 g (2 oz) chopped toasted hazelnuts to the butternut and spinach mix. Substitute the goat's cheese with 100 g (4 oz) ricotta. Assemble as usual, with the ricotta cheese in the centre. Bake as normal.

cannelloni

Cannelloni shells are 3–4 inches long and an inch in diameter. The cooking time for traditionally made ones that must be boiled before they're stuffed will depend on the manufacturer. There are cannelloni shells that don't require pre-boiling – you stuff them while still stiff, then bake smothered in a very liquid sauce, a runny béchamel sauce or watery tomato sauce, which will provide the liquid the pasta needs to absorb as it cooks. These are the quickest and easiest to use.

This dish is more labour intensive than the lasagne recipes, so it's more suitable for a dinner party, as it looks very impressive and you probably wouldn't go to all this trouble unless to impress!

Asparagus, Red Pepper, Aubergine and Ricotta/Tofu Cannelloni

serves 4
ready in 1 hour 30 minutes

2 large aubergines, sliced lengthways
olive oil
12 asparagus spears
12 cannelloni shells (3 per person) or 12 sheets of lasagne
1 red pepper, thinly sliced
750 g (1½ lbs) cooked spinach
225 g (8 oz) ricotta cheese or silken tofu

for the tomato béchamel sauce:
1 tbsp butter or vegan margarine
50 g (2 oz) white flour or maize flour
500 ml (17 fl oz) milk or soy milk
1 tsp tomato purée
1 tsp dried oregano
400 g (14 oz) tin chopped tomatoes
handful fresh oregano, to garnish (optional)

You will need a deep dish, approximately 20 cm (9 in) square.

Preheat the oven to 200°C/400°F/gas 6.

Lay the aubergine slices on a tray and brush with olive oil and a little sea salt. Roast for 15 minutes, remove and allow to cool a little.

Blanch the asparagus spears by placing them in pot of boiling water for 5 minutes. Drain and immerse in cold water until completely cold.

To make the béchamel sauce, in a medium saucepan, melt the butter, add the flour and combine to form a ball at the side of the pan. Lower the heat and allow to cook for 5 minutes. Add the milk, tomato purée and dried oregano and combine well. Once the sauce begins to thicken, add the tin of chopped tomatoes. Stir constantly so that the sauce doesn't form lumps – a good whisk will help to prevent this. Bring to the boil, stirring all the time. Remove from the heat, season and leave to infuse for 15 minutes. Cover the pot so a skin doesn't form on the sauce.

In a bowl, combine the spinach and ricotta cheese together.

To prepare the pasta, immerse the cannelloni shells or lasagne sheets in a pot of boiling water for 1 minute, until soft and easy to bend.

Once the aubergines have cooled, assemble the dish by laying a slice of aubergine diagonally on a board. Place a cannelloni shell lengthwise on top of each aubergine. Place an asparagus spear and pepper strip inside a cannelloni shell, then place a spoonful of ricotta and spinach mix on top of the cannelloni.

Roll up the aubergine around the cannelloni, cheese and spinach to form an oblong roll. Once rolled, the aubergine is on the outside and the cannelloni and cheese are wrapped inside. The strips of pepper and asparagus stick out each side of the roll. Repeat until all the aubergine and vegetables are used up.

Lay each roll in a lightly greased baking tray and pour the béchamel tomato sauce on top. Cover with tin foil and bake for 25 minutes.

Remove the foil and sprinkle the cannelloni with the grated Parmesan and return to the oven to brown, about 10 minutes. Serve 3 cannelloni per person, sprinkled with fresh oregano.

Can be made vegan. Sugar free.
Freezing: Ideal for freezing.

Cook's Tips: Yes, this sounds complicated, but it's not once you try it. You can make life a little easier by omitting the aubergine.

Nutritional Content: Carbohydrate, dietary fibre, protein and vitamins A, B$_6$, C and K, as well as smaller amounts of manganese and potassium.

Note to the Senses: This is a very pleasing dish to the eye. Once cooked, the cannelloni is smothered in a lovely creamy tomato sauce. I don't blend the chopped tomatoes, as I like the texture of the tomato pieces through the sauce. If you like, though, you can blend them for a smooth sauce.

comfort pies

Comfort food absolutely satisfies, evokes memories of childhood and reminds us of the simpler things in life. As we enter the cooler autumn months, we're alerted to the approaching winter and the longing for comfort, warmth, nourishment and second helpings. These foods are very functional during the colder months – they're warm, nourishing, filling, and make you feel better.

Puy lentils are used as a meat substitute in the more traditional recipes. Everyone will eat these delicious dishes, meat eaters or not. The Puy lentil is the king of lentils. It holds its shape and tastes wonderful. They are widely used in French cuisine and everyone loves them.

These dishes are easy to make, with the guarantee that everyone will really enjoy them. One helping is never enough!

Puy Lentil Shepherd's Pie with Celeriac Mash

serves 6
ready in 1 hour

for the mash topping:
350 g (12 oz) floury potatoes, peeled and cut into small chunks
350 g (12 oz) celeriac, peeled and cut into small chunks
25 g (1 oz) vegan margarine
1 tbsp organic soy milk
handful fresh chives, chopped
handful fresh parsley, chopped

for the base filling:
1 tbsp vegetable oil
1 Spanish onion, finely chopped
1 garlic clove, crushed
1 tsp dried mixed herbs
3 carrots, peeled and diced
2 leeks, halved and sliced
1 stick of celery, chopped
200 g (7 oz) Puy lentils, washed, or 400 g (14 oz) canned cooked Puy lentils, drained
450 ml (15 fl oz) vegetable stock
1 tsp miso

Preheat the oven to 180°C/350°F/gas 4.

Cook the potatoes and celeriac in a pot of lightly salted boiling water until tender.

Meanwhile, heat the oil. Add the onion, garlic and herbs and sauté for 5 minutes. Add the carrots, leeks and celery and sauté gently for 5 minutes more. Add the Puy lentils and combine well with the vegetables. Add the stock and miso, stir well, cover, bring to the boil and simmer for 20 minutes, until the lentils are cooked. Stir occasionally. You may need to add a little more stock or water, as lentils absorb a lot of liquid. Season as required.

When the potatoes and celeriac are cooked, drain and mash. Add the margarine and milk to the potatoes and mash until smooth. Season to taste and add in the fresh parsley and chives.

Spoon the lentil and tomato mixture into a 13" × 9" × 2" ovenproof dish and top with the mash. Use a fork to smooth over. Cook for 20 minutes, until the topping is golden brown. The juice of the lentil base should bubble up over the sides.

Remove from the oven and allow to cool for 5 minutes before serving. Garnish with fresh parsley.

Vegan. Dairy, gluten, sugar and wheat free.
Freezing: Ideal for freezing for up to 2 months.
Cook's Tips: You can add mushrooms to this recipe if you like.
Nutritional Content: A protein- and carbohydrate-rich dish with copper, dietary fibre, folate, iron, molybdenum, phosphorous and tryptophan.
Note to the Senses: This dish is a complete meal. The celeriac doesn't brown as well as the potatoes, but don't worry – once the juices bubble up around the edges, everyone will want some. Place the dish in the centre of the table and dig in. All you need is a leafy salad if you're feeling generous.

Puy Lentil and Vegetable Moussaka

serves 6
ready in 1 hour 15 minutes

for the topping:
4 aubergines, peeled and sliced into slices 2 cm (¾ in) thick
olive oil
pinch sea salt

for the vegetables:
1 tbsp vegetable oil
2 onions, finely chopped
2 garlic cloves, crushed
1 tsp dried basil
1 tsp dried oregano
1 tsp tomato purée
1 red pepper
1 green pepper
1 courgette
1 carrot
200 g (7 oz) Puy lentils, washed, or 400 g (14 oz) canned cooked Puy lentils, drained
400 g (14 oz) tin chopped tomatoes
250 ml (9 fl oz) vegetable stock
1½ tsp soy sauce or tamari
1 tbsp red wine (optional)
50 g (2 oz) grated Parmesan (optional)

for the béchamel sauce:
1½ tsp vegan margarine
25 g (1 oz) white flour or maize flour
250 ml (9 fl oz) milk or soy milk
½ tsp Dijon mustard

1 bay leaf

pinch ground nutmeg

Preheat the oven to 180°C/350°F/gas 4.

Brush the aubergines with olive oil and sprinkle with sea salt, place on a lightly greased baking tray and bake for 20 minutes.

Meanwhile, heat the oil and add the onions, garlic and herbs and sauté for 5 minutes. Add the tomato purée and sauté for 2 minutes more. Add a little stock if sticking. Add the vegetables and sauté for 10 more minutes. Add the Puy lentils and combine well with the vegetables. Add the tomatoes, season to taste and simmer for 5 minutes. Add the stock, soy sauce and red wine if using, cover, bring to the boil and simmer for 25 minutes, or until the lentils are cooked. Stir occasionally. You may need to add more stock or a little water, as lentils absorb a lot of liquid. Season as required. Taste and add a little more soy sauce/tamari if needed.

Meanwhile, make the sauce. In a medium saucepan, melt the margarine, add the flour and combine to form a ball at the side of the pan. Lower the heat and allow to cook for 5 minutes. Add the milk slowly, stirring/whisking constantly until all the milk has been used. Add the mustard, bay leaf and nutmeg. Combine well. Stir constantly so that the sauce doesn't form lumps – a good whisk will help to prevent this. Bring the sauce gently to the boil, stirring all the time. The sauce should now have a smooth, thick, creamy consistency. Remove from the heat and season. Leave to infuse for 15 minutes, covering the pot so a skin doesn't form on the sauce. Remove bay leaves from sauce and discard.

To assemble the dish, place the lentil filling in a lightly greased baking dish. Lay the roast aubergines on top of the lentils so that they completely cover the filling. Spread the sauce over the aubergines. Cover with tin foil and bake for 35 minutes. Remove the cover and allow to cool for 5 minutes before serving.

Vegan. Dairy free (if using soy milk) and sugar free. Gluten and wheat free if using maize flour and tamari. Yeast free if not using wine.

Freezing: Ideal for freezing.

Cook's Tips: You can top with grated Parmesan 10 minutes from the end of the cooking time and return to the oven to brown if desired.

Nutritional Content: A protein- and carbohydrate-rich dish with copper, dietary fibre, folate, iron, molybdenum, phosphorous and tryptophan.

Note to the Senses: This Greek-inspired dish will satisfy vegetarians and non-vegetarians alike. The Puy lentil base has a rich and satisfying texture when combined with the béchemal sauce and baked aubergine.

Broccoli, Mushroom and Tofu Cashew Nut Bake

serves 6

ready in 1 hour

1½ tsp sesame oil

1 medium onion, finely chopped

2 garlic cloves, finely chopped

1¼ cm (½ in) piece of ginger, peeled and finely chopped or grated

500 g (1 lb 2 oz) mushrooms, sliced

1 tbsp maize flour

750 ml (1½ pints) soy milk

1 tbsp soy sauce or tamari

3–4 heads broccoli, broken into small florets

2 tbsp margarine

400 g (14 oz) breadcrumbs or spelt flakes

150 g (5 oz) cashew nuts, toasted and chopped

1 tbsp freshly chopped herbs, such as rosemary, thyme, parsley

250–350 g (4 cubes) firm tofu, chopped into small pieces

Preheat the oven to 180°C/350°F/gas 4.

Heat the sesame oil in a pan and sauté half the chopped onions for 3 minutes. Add the garlic and ginger and sauté for another 3–4 minutes. Add the mushrooms and combine well. Allow to cook for 5 minutes. Add the maize flour and combine well, then add the soy milk and mix well. Some lumps may appear, but as the mixture cooks and continues to be mixed, they will disappear. Add the soy sauce or tamari and cook on a low heat for 10 minutes.

Meanwhile, blanch the broccoli by placing the florets in a bowl of boiling water for 5 minutes. Drain and run under the cold tap until completely cold. Allow to drain and set aside.

In a separate pan, melt the margarine and add the remainder of the finely chopped onions. Sauté gently until cooked.

In a large bowl, mix the breadcrumbs and cashew nuts together. Add the fresh herbs and mix well. Add the sautéed onions and combine well. Season as required. The mixture should be moist but not sticky – you may need to add a little more melted margarine.

Once the mushroom sauce is cooked, add the broccoli and tofu and combine well. Place the mushroom mix into an ovenproof dish and top with the breadcrumb mix. Bake for 15–20 minutes, until the top is brown.

Vegan. Dairy and sugar free. Gluten and wheat free if using maize flour and tamari.
Freezing: Suitable for freezing.
Cook's Tips: If you have a particularly hot oven, cover the dish for 15 minutes, then remove the cover and brown.
Nutritional Content: Folate, iron, manganese, protein**,** selenium, tryptophan and vitamins A, B_2, B_3 and C and rich in flavonoids.
Note to the Senses: This dish is a good tofu-based dish. The ginger, sesame and soy sauce/tamari add Asian flavours that are absorbed by the tofu.

Winter Vegetable Hotpot

serves 6
ready in 1 hour 15 minutes

This is a warm and filling winter or early spring dish. It's full of nutritious ingredients, all cooked in their own juices so that the full flavours of all the vegetables are retained. None of the nutrients are lost, as all the juices form part of the meal. The dish is simply prepared and then put into the oven to cook. You can go away and forget about it for an hour. Adding miso has a threefold benefit – it adds wonderful flavour, is easily digested and is extremely nutritious.

1 onion, roughly chopped

2 potatoes, peeled

1 small turnip, scrubbed, peeled and cut into chunks

2 medium carrots, peeled and cut into slices 5 cm (2 in) thick

2 parsnips, peeled and cut into slices 5 cm (2 in) thick

4 sticks of celery, cut into slices 5 cm (2 in) thick

100 g (4 oz) mushrooms (if yeast is okay)

25 g (1 oz) wakame seaweed, or another seaweed of your choice

1 tsp finely chopped fresh rosemary

1 tsp finely chopped thyme

1 tsp finely chopped fresh parsley

1 tbsp miso

190 ml (⅓ pint) of water

Preheat the oven to 180°C/350°F/gas 4.

If the mushrooms are big, then cut them into halves, otherwise leave whole. Place all the prepared vegetables in an ovenproof dish and add the seaweed. Add the fresh herbs to the vegetables.

Add the miso to the water and mix well, then pour over the vegetables. Season as required. Cover the dish and bake for 1 hour. Serve with organic brown rice or roast potatoes.

Vegan. Dairy, gluten, sugar and wheat free.

Freezing: This dish can be frozen for up to 1 month.

Cook's Tips: Use a good-quality miso with a dark colour to enhance the look and taste. Hatcho miso is a good choice, available in health food stores.

Nutritional Content: B vitamins, calcium, carbohydrates, dietary fibre, folate, iodine, magnesium and protein.

Note to the Senses: This hotpot is a real favourite for Café Fresh customers. There is oodles of flavour from the herbs, seaweed and miso. The taste of the seaweed is indistinguishable in the dish once cooked, but the goodness still remains.

Cheesy Winter Vegetable Crumble

serves 6
ready in 1 hour

This is a great way of getting seeds into your diet and is a tasty winter dish full of nutrition.

1½ tsp sunflower oil
1 Spanish onion, finely chopped
2 garlic cloves, finely chopped
2 carrots, peeled and cut into 5 cm (2 in) chunks
1 small turnip, peeled and cut into 5 cm (2 in) chunks
1 parsnip, peeled and cut into 5 cm (2 in) chunks
1 potato, peeled and cut into 5 cm (2 in) chunks
1 stick of celery, cut into 5 cm (2 in) chunks
50 g (2 oz) white/wholemeal flour
500 ml (17 fl oz) soy milk
2 bay leaves

for the topping:
150 g (5 oz) breadcrumbs
150 g (5 oz) rolled oats, oat flakes or porridge oats
100 g (4 oz) Cheddar cheese, grated
100 g (4 oz) mix of sesame, sunflower and pumpkin seeds
2 tsp dried mixed herbs
100 g (4 oz) butter or vegan margarine

Preheat the oven to 180°C/350°F/gas 4.

Heat the sunflower oil and sauté the onions and garlic for 3 minutes. Add all the chopped vegetables and combine well. Add 1 tbsp water, cover the pan and cook for 10 minutes over a medium heat. This sweats the vegetables and allows them to cook in their own juices. Remove the lid, add the flour and combine well. Cook over a low heat for 5 minutes. Add the soy milk and mix well. Some lumps may appear, but as the mixture cooks and continues to be mixed, they will disappear. Add the bay leaves. Slowly bring to the boil and allow to simmer for 10 minutes.

Make the topping by placing the breadcrumbs, oats, grated cheese and seeds in a bowl. Add the herbs and season with salt and ground white pepper. Rub the margarine into the oat mix as if making pastry, making sure it's evenly distributed. If the mixture seems very dry, rub in a little more margarine.

Place the vegetable mix in an ovenproof dish and top with the oat topping. Bake for 20 minutes, or until evenly browned. Allow to cool slightly before serving.

Vegan. Dairy and sugar free.
Freezing: I don't think this freezes well, as the crumble tends to get soggy.
Cook's Tips: You can vary the vegetable selection to your taste. Add sweet potato, leeks, butternut, celeriac, etc.
Nutritional Content: Calcium, carbohydrate, copper, dietary fibre, iron, magnesium, manganese, phosphorous, tryptophan, zinc and vitamins B_1 and E.
Note to the Senses: This dish works very well with a broccoli and cauliflower salad with tahini dressing. The colours make the entire dinner very appetising.

stews and curries

Introduction

A stew is a dish that's prepared by cooking the ingredients in a pot which is barely covered with liquid and simmered slowly for a period of time in a tightly covered pot. Stewing allows the flavours of the ingredients to blend deliciously and retain all the goodness of the ingredients in the cooking juices.

In Café Fresh, stew comes in many guises. All around the world, countries have their own interpretations of a stew to suit their own cuisine. In Café Fresh, our stews are the result of adapting the national stew dishes from around the world to suit ourselves.

Herby Chickpea and Vegetable Stew

serves 4–6
ready in 40 minutes

This stew is the mainstay of the Café Fresh menu. It's very simple to prepare and highly nutritious. It has the added advantage of catering to a vast array of food allergies.

1 tbsp sunflower oil
1 medium onion, chopped
2 garlic cloves, crushed
3 sticks of celery, chopped into 5 cm (2 in) cubes
½ tsp dried mixed herbs
2 carrots, peeled and chopped into 5 cm (2 in) cubes
2 parsnips, peeled and chopped into 5 cm (2 in) cubes
1 small turnip, peeled and chopped into 5 cm (2 in) cubes
1 litre (1¾ pints) vegetable stock
1 small head of broccoli, broken into small florets
½ small head of cauliflower, broken into small florets
250 g (9 oz) cooked chickpeas or 400 g (14 oz) tin cooked chickpeas
1 tbsp fresh tarragon, chopped

Heat the oil in a medium saucepan and add the onion and garlic. Sauté for 5 minutes. Add the celery and dried herbs and sauté for another 2 minutes. Add the rest of the root vegetables and coat with the oil. Add 1 tbsp of the vegetable stock, cover the saucepan and allow the vegetables to sweat for 7 minutes. Add the rest of the stock and season lightly. Cover the saucepan and allow to simmer for 20 minutes, until the vegetables are cooked.

Meanwhile, blanch the broccoli and cauliflower florets by placing them in a bowl of boiling water for 5–7 minutes. Drain and run under a cold tap until completely cold.

Once the vegetables are cooked, remove the cover, add the chickpeas, broccoli and cauliflower and heat through. Taste and season as required. Add the chopped tarragon and mix through. Serve with organic brown rice.

Vegan. Dairy, gluten, sugar, wheat and yeast free.

Freezing: Suitable for freezing.

Cook's Tips: You can choose a different pulse here if you like. I like cannellini beans in the spring, in which case I like to use marjoram or sage, as they work very well here. Substitute the turnip for sweet potato or butternut and add in a little leek for a delicious variation.

Nutritional Content: This is a virtually fat-free, high-protein dish with minerals such as dietary fibre, folate, manganese, molybdenum, tryptophan and vitamins A, C and K, and smaller amounts of other vitamins and minerals.

Note to the Senses: This stew completely satisfies the senses. The smells that emanate from this dish are heart warming and it looks wholesome with the chunky vegetables and seasoned stock. The dish has a surprisingly sweet flavour from the roots and the herbs give a clean finish to the dish.

Miso, Tofu, Ginger and Bean Stew

serves 4–6
ready in 40 minutes

This stew is a variation of the Herby Chickpea and Vegetable Stew and is equally as easy to prepare. It's a really good winter stew, so it's on the menu for the cold, miserable winter months.

1 tbsp sunflower oil
1 medium onion, chopped
2 garlic cloves, crushed
1¼ cm (½ inch) piece of ginger, finely chopped
3 sticks of celery, chopped into 5 cm (2 in) cubes
2 carrots, peeled and chopped into 5 cm (2 in) cubes
2 parsnips, peeled and chopped into 5 cm (2 in) cubes
1 small turnip, peeled and chopped into 5 cm (2 in) cubes
1 small celeriac, peeled and chopped into 5 cm (2 in) cubes
1 litre (1¾ pints) vegetable stock
½ tbsp mugi miso or other dark-coloured miso
3 cubes tofu, chopped into small cubes
250 g (9 oz) cooked aduki beans or 400 g (14 oz) tin cooked aduki beans
2 tbsp fresh coriander, chopped

Heat the oil in a medium saucepan. Add the onion and sauté for 5 minutes. Add the garlic and ginger and sauté for 5 more minutes. Add the vegetables and coat with the oil. Add 1 tbsp of the vegetable stock, cover the pot and allow the vegetables to sweat for 7 minutes. Add the remaining stock, cover the saucepan and simmer for 25–30 minutes, until the vegetables are cooked. Add the miso and mix well into the stew, making sure it dissolves properly. Add the tofu and beans and heat through.

To give it extra flavour, finely chop the coriander and add to the stew. Adjust the seasoning if necessary.

Vegan. Dairy, gluten, sugar and wheat free.
Freezing: Suitable for freezing.
Cook's Tips: You can dissolve the miso in a spoonful of vegetable stock before adding to the stew to ensure it's fully blended. I like to add some mushrooms to this sometimes. Add them after the garlic and ginger and before you add the rest of the vegetables. Sauté for 5 minutes.
Nutritional Content: A high-fibre, protein-based dish with low fat content. Folate, zinc and vitamins A, B_{12}, C and K are present, as well as smaller amounts of other vitamins and minerals.
Note to the Senses: The miso gives this dish a rich, dark colour. It has a very distinctive taste, but when combined with the vegetable stock, it's very subtle, giving a richness and depth to the stew.

New Orleans Okra and Butterbean Succotash

serves 4–6
ready in 30 minutes

Succotash is a southern US favourite. It's a stew consisting of butterbeans, corn and some vegetables. The name is taken from the Naragansett Indian word 'misickquatash' which means ' boiled whole kernels of corn'. In this recipe, we use sweetcorn. Okra is available in ethnic stores such as Asian markets or African shops.

1 tbsp sunflower oil

1 Spanish onion, finely chopped

2 large garlic cloves, minced

1 tsp tomato purée and 1 tsp chilli powder

1 tsp dried thyme

½ tsp ground allspice

2 sweet potatoes or 1 pumpkin, cut into thick cubes

3 carrots, peeled and cut into thick cubes

400 g (14 oz) tin chopped tomatoes

2 large bay leaves

300 g (11 oz) okra, trimmed

250 g (9 oz) tin sweetcorn

400 g (14 oz) tin butterbeans

juice of ½ lemon

Heat the oil in a medium saucepan. Add the onion and sauté for 5 minutes. Add the garlic and sauté for a further 5 minutes. Add the tomato purée and spices and sauté for a further 1 minute.

Add the sweet potatoes and carrots and mix well. Add the tomatoes and bay leaves and season with sea salt. Cover the pan, bring to the boil, reduce the heat to medium-low and simmer until the vegetable are tender but still holding their shape, about 20 minutes.

Add the okra, corn and beans and simmer until tender, about 10 minutes. Add the lemon juice and season to taste. If you like a little more spice, add a little hot pepper sauce.

Vegan. Dairy, gluten, sugar, wheat and yeast free.

Freezing: Suitable for freezing.

Cook's Tips: When trimming okra, just cut the top and tail off. When cut, it releases a sticky substance with thickening properties, very useful for soups and stews.

Nutritional Content: A high-fibre, protein-filled, low-fat dish with folic acid, lycopene, potassium and vitamin B_6 and other antioxidants.

Note to the Senses: Okra adds another dimension to a dish. Its subtle flavour can be compared to aubergines, though the texture is somewhat unusual. It's definitely worth a try.

Spanish-Style Spinach, Potato and Chickpea Stew

serves 4–6

ready in 50 minutes

900 g (2 lbs) baby potatoes, cut in half

1 large onion, roughly chopped

1 tsp tomato purée

1 tbsp olive oil

3 garlic cloves, finely chopped

2 tsp paprika

1 tsp turmeric

¼ tsp cayenne pepper

400 g (14 oz) tin chopped tomatoes

250 g (9 oz) cooked chickpeas or 400 g (14 oz) tin cooked chickpeas

500 g (1 lb 2 oz) chopped spinach

2 hardboiled eggs

Preheat the oven to 190°C/375°F/gas 5.

Place the potatoes, onion and tomato purée in a medium-sized roasting tin and drizzle with a little olive oil and sea salt. Combine well and roast for 10 minutes. Add the garlic and spices, mix well and return to the oven for a further 10 minutes.

Add the tinned tomatoes and a little more salt and mix through the potatoes. Return to the oven and roast for a further 20 minutes, or until the potatoes are cooked.

Add the chickpeas and return to the oven to allow the chickpeas to heat through, about 5 minutes.

Remove the dish from the oven and stir the spinach through the dish. It will wilt in the heat of the sauce. The sauce should be thick. Serve topped with halved hardboiled eggs and a sprinkle of paprika.

Leave out the hardboiled eggs at the end to make this vegan. Dairy, gluten, sugar, wheat and yeast free.

Potato and Onion Frittata

Roast Beetroot, Shallot and Mushroom Salad

Thai Green Vegetable Curry

Asparagus Cannelloni

Freezing: Suitable for freezing.

Cook's Tips: Be careful adding the cayenne pepper. When the dish is cooked and if you feel it isn't spicy enough, then you can add a little more cayenne pepper and mix it through. Paprika adds a depth to the colour and a very subtle flavour. If you can find smoked paprika, all the better.

Nutritional Content: Carbohydrate, dietary fibre, folate, lycopene, manganese, molybdenum, protein, vitamins A and K and other antioxidants.

Note to the Senses: A rich Spanish stew should have a thick consistency and some olive oil visible on top. This doesn't look greasy, but rather appetising, as it signifies the richness of the sauce.

Classic Ratatouille

serves 4
ready in 1 hour

Ratatouille is a classic Niçoise dish from the south of France. It's been a vegetarian option on so many menus for so many years that it has become clichéd. This has never diminished my love for this dish when summer comes along and I long for that holiday feeling.

2 aubergines, cut into 2 cm cubes (¾ in)
3 courgettes, roughly chopped
1 tbsp olive oil
2 red onions, chopped
4 garlic cloves, chopped
2 red peppers, deseeded and roughly chopped
1 yellow pepper, deseeded and roughly chopped
1 green pepper, deseeded and roughly chopped
1 sprig fresh rosemary
lots of fresh basil leaves
fresh parsley, finely chopped
fresh thyme, chopped
10 tomatoes, skinned, deseeded and chopped or 400 g (14 oz) tin chopped tomatoes

Prepare the aubergine and courgettes first. Sprinkle them with salt and leave them to sweat for 30 minutes, then wash and dry with kitchen paper.

Heat the olive oil in a large frying pan and sauté the onions until soft, about 5–7 minutes. Add the garlic and cook for a further 2 minutes. Add the dry aubergines and courgettes together with the peppers to the pan. Increase the heat and sauté until the peppers are just turning brown. Reduce the heat. Add the herbs, cover the pan and cook gently for 25 minutes. Add the tomatoes and season. Cook uncovered for a further 10 minutes, until the vegetables are soft but not too mushy. Remove the sprigs of herbs, leave to cool slightly and garnish with the remaining basil leaves.

Vegan. Dairy, gluten, sugar, wheat and yeast free.
Freezing: If freezing, don't cook the vegetables right down. Freeze and reheat slowly and the vegetables will soften some more.
Cook's Tips: It's a good idea to prepare the aubergines and courgettes in advance. If you buy the smaller aubergines, it's not necessary to salt them.
Nutritional Content: Carbohydrate, dietary fibre, folate, lycopene, manganese, molybdenum, protein, vitamins A and K and other antioxidants.
Note to the Senses: This dish shouldn't be just another tomato-based vegetable stew. This is a rich vegetable stew that brings out the sweetness of the vegetables by cooking them right down. In this recipe the vegetables are cooked so that they are very soft; all the goodness is retained and the flavours are intensified as a result.

Hungarian-Style Butterbean Goulash

serves 4–6
ready in 1 hour

Hungary gives us their own version of stew under the name goulash. Traditionally this is a meat dish flavoured with paprika and sometimes served with sour cream. Café Fresh goulash is meatless, of course. The wonderful flavours of paprika and a rich natural yoghurt combine to give a delicious Hungarian-style goulash.

1 tbsp sunflower oil

1 medium onion, finely chopped

1 garlic clove, finely chopped

1 red pepper, deseeded and cut into strips

1 green pepper, deseeded and cut into strips

2 tbsp tomato purée

1 tbsp paprika

1 carrot, peeled and cut into chunks

400 g (14 oz) tin chopped tomatoes

120 ml (4 fl oz) water

150 ml (5 fl oz) vegetable stock

1 tsp salt

1 medium head of cauliflower, broken into florets

1 head of broccoli, broken into florets

50 g (2 oz) green beans (or mangetout)

200 g (7 oz) dried butterbeans, soaked overnight and boiled for 1–1 ½ hours,
or 400 g (14 oz) tin butterbeans

2 tbsp Greek-style yoghurt (the thickest one you can find)

1 tbsp fresh coriander, finely chopped

sprigs of coriander, to garnish

Heat the oil in a heavy saucepan and sauté the onion and garlic for about 5 minutes. Add the peppers, tomato purée and paprika and sauté for another 5 minutes. Add the carrot and mix well.

Pour in the tinned tomatoes, water, vegetable stock and salt and mix well. Cover and bring to the boil, then reduce the heat and simmer for 20 minutes.

Add the cauliflowers and broccoli florets, green beans and butterbeans, mixing well with the other ingredients, and simmer for another 10–15 minutes, until all the vegetables are cooked.

Remove from the heat, add the yoghurt and incorporate well into the goulash. If you like a very creamy sauce, add a little more yoghurt. You can also omit the yoghurt if you have an allergy or are vegan.

Place the goulash back on the heat and heat gently for a further 5 minutes. Add in two-thirds of the coriander and season. Garnish with sprigs of coriander over the goulash. Serve with rice.

Gluten, sugar, wheat and yeast free.
Freezing: Suitable for freezing before you add the yoghurt.
Cook's Tips: When adding the yoghurt, add it just at the end. It has a tendency to split, but if you mix it through well, it will go unnoticed. You can also let the goulash cool slightly before adding the yoghurt, which can help avoid splitting.
Nutritional Content: Antioxidants, carbohydrate, dietary fibre, folate, lycopene, manganese, molybdenum, protein, tryptophan and vitamins A, B_2, B_6 and C.
Note to the Senses: Butterbeans are a starchy bean with a creamy texture, which is complemented by the creamy tomato sauce. It's warming, inviting and rich tasting, with the paprika adding a subtle flavour.

Moroccan Chickpea Tagine with Herb Couscous

serves 4–6
ready in 1 hour

In North Africa and particularly in Morocco, the traditional stew is called tagine. In actual fact, the word 'tagine' refers both to the cooking pot and the stew itself. This stew is distinctive because dried fruit is added to give a sweetness to the dish.

1 tbsp sunflower or olive oil
1 large Spanish onion, finely chopped
2 garlic cloves
1 tsp freshly chopped ginger
1 tsp turmeric
1 tsp sea salt
½ tsp each of black pepper and cayenne, combined
2 cinnamon sticks, cut into 2 cm (1 in) lengths
1 tbsp tomato purée
3 medium carrots, peeled, cut in half and sliced into batons

½ butternut squash, peeled and cubed

400 g (14 oz) tin chopped tomatoes

350 ml (12 fl oz) water

125 g (4 oz) chopped dates

125 g (4 oz) dried apricots

400 g (14 oz) tin chickpeas, drained

1 tbsp fresh coriander, finely chopped

parsley, to garnish

for the couscous:

175 g (6 oz) couscous

275–350 ml (10–12 fl oz) boiling water

½ red onion, very finely chopped

1 garlic clove, minced

2 tbsp extra virgin olive oil

1 tbsp fresh lemon juice, or to taste

25 g (1 oz) fresh parsley, finely chopped

25 g (1 oz) fresh basil, finely chopped

25 g (1 oz) fresh mint, finely chopped

To make the couscous, place the couscous in a bowl and pour over with boiling water. Cover and allow to rest for 30 minutes. Fluff with a fork and stir in the onion, garlic, olive oil, lemon juice and herbs.

Heat the oil in a large pan. Add the onions, garlic and spices and sauté until the onions are tender, stirring occasionally. Add the tomato purée and sauté for another 1 minute. Add the carrots and squash and mix well. Add the tomatoes and water, cover, bring to the boil and simmer for 20 minutes.

Add the dates, apricots and chickpeas and cook uncovered for 15 minutes more, until the fruit is softened and the liquid has reduced to give a rich sauce.

Remove from the heat and add the fresh coriander. Taste and season as required. Serve with the herb couscous and garnish with parsley or coriander.

Vegan, Dairy, gluten and wheat free.

Freezing: Suitable for freezing.

Cook's Tips: Leaving the lid off the pot for the last 15 minutes allows the liquid to evaporate, creating a thicker, richer sauce, as a tagine should be.

Nutritional Content: Dietary fibre, folate, lycopene, potassium, protein, manganese, molybdenum, tryptophan and vitamins A and C.

Note to the Senses: There's a sweetness to this dish that's unmistakeable from the dried fruit. They plump up when allowed to simmer and release their sweetness into the sauce.

Thea's Californian Vegetable and Chickpea Chilli

serves 4
ready in 1 hour

I've never met anyone who can tolerate hot, spicy food like my Californian friend Thea. She has regaled us with stories of the wonderful chillies that are available in her much-cherished Napa Valley. California has a large Mexican community, with Mexican restaurants everywhere, and needless to say, plenty of chilli to be had with varying degrees of temperature! Thea has shared her recipe with me and I now share it with you – with slight adjustments to the quantity of chilli pepper!

1 tbsp sunflower oil
1 medium-sized onion, chopped
1 garlic clove, finely chopped or minced
1 tsp tomato purée
1 red chilli, deseeded and finely chopped, or 1 tsp chilli powder
1 stick of celery, chopped
1 small green pepper, deseeded and chopped
1 red pepper, deseeded and chopped
2 medium courgettes, scrubbed, ends trimmed and chopped
250 g (9 oz) cooked chickpeas or 400 g (14 oz) tin cooked chickpeas, drained
400 g (14 oz) tin chopped tomatoes
1 large handful or 1 tbsp freshly chopped coriander

1½ tsp chopped fresh oregano leaves, or ½ tsp dried

1½ tsp chopped fresh basil leaves, or ½ tsp dried

1 tsp ground cumin

cayenne pepper, to taste

In a medium-sized pot, heat the oil over a moderate heat, add the onion and sauté for 3 minutes. Add the garlic, tomato purée and the chilli or chilli powder and sauté for a further 2 minutes. If using dried herbs, add them with the chilli. Add the celery and peppers and cook, stirring, until softened, about 2 minutes. Add the courgette and cook, stirring, 3 minutes longer to soften. Add the tomatoes and remaining spices and stir well.

Reduce the heat to a low simmer, cover and cook for 30 minutes, adding a little water if the stew begins to get too thick.

Add the cooked chickpeas, combine well and allow to heat through, approximately 5 minutes. Finally, add in fresh coriander (and fresh basil and oregano, if using) and combine with the chilli. Taste and season, if required.

Vegan. Dairy, gluten, sugar, wheat and yeast free.

Freezing: This chilli freezes well for 2 months.

Cook's Tips: All I can say here is be careful with the chillies. You don't want to blow someone's head off. Serve Cucumber Raita (p. 12) on the side if you've gone overboard with the chillies for some people's taste. Of course, if you've added far too much, then all you can do is throw it out and start again.

Nutritional Content: Antioxidants, dietary fibre, folate, lycopene, manganese, molybdenum, omega 3s, protein and vitamins A, B_1 and C.

Note to the Senses: This is a chilli for those who like a touch of sweetness in their savoury dishes.

Vegetable and Kidney Bean Chilli

serves 4

ready in 30 minutes

1 tbsp olive oil

2 large onions, coarsely chopped

3 large garlic cloves, finely chopped

1 green pepper, cut into 4 cm (1½ in) pieces

1 red pepper, cut into 4 cm (1½ in) pieces

2 jalapeños, finely diced

1–2 red chillies, deseeded and finely chopped, or 1 tsp chilli powder

1 tsp ground cumin

2 tsp salt

400 g (14 oz) tin chopped tomatoes

2 courgettes, cut into 4 cm (1½ in) pieces

½ medium aubergine, cut into 4 cm (1½ in) pieces

250 g (9 oz) cooked kidney beans or 400 g (14 oz) tin cooked kidney beans, drained and rinsed

50 g (2 oz) dark chocolate (preferably Green & Black's vegan)

1 tbsp chopped fresh coriander

Sauté the onions, garlic, peppers and jalapeño in oil in a heavy pot over a moderately high heat, stirring until softened, about 5 minutes. Add the chopped chilli, cumin and salt and cook, stirring, for 1 minute. Add the tomatoes, courgettes and aubergines and simmer, stirring occasionally, for 15 minutes. Stir in the beans and chocolate and simmer until the beans are heated through and the chocolate has melted. Stir in the chopped coriander and serve.

Vegan. Dairy, gluten, wheat and yeast free.

Freezing: Suitable for freezing.

Cook's Tips: This is a simple, no-fuss chilli. Serve with pitta for a simple, delicious meal.

Nutritional Content: Antioxidants, dietary fibre, folate, iron, manganese, molybdenum, tryptophan and vitamins A, B_6, C and K.

Note to the Senses: You wouldn't know there's chocolate in the recipe, but it adds a subtle depth of flavour to the dish and is certainly worth a try at least once.

Cajun-Style Black-Eyed Bean Chilli

serves 4
ready in 30 minutes

1 tbsp sunflower oil
1 large onion, finely chopped
3 garlic cloves, finely chopped
2 red chillies, deseeded and finely chopped
1 tbsp ground cumin
2 tsp dried thyme
2 carrots, peeled and chopped into 4 cm (1½ in) pieces
1 green pepper, cored, deseeded and cut into 4 cm (1½ in) pieces
1 red pepper, cored, deseeded and cut into 4 cm (1½ in) pieces
1 aubergine, chopped into 4 cm (1½ in) pieces
400 g (14 oz) tin chopped tomatoes
250 g (9 oz) cooked black-eyed beans or 400 g (14 oz) tin black-eyed beans, drained
250 g tin sweetcorn, drained
500 g (1 lb 2 oz) spinach, well washed and coarsely chopped
1½ tsp fresh lemon juice
2 spring onions (with the green part left on), thinly sliced on the diagonal

Heat the oil in a medium pot and sauté the onions for 3 minutes. Add the garlic, chillies, cumin and dried thyme and sauté for a further 2 minutes. Add the carrots and peppers, cover and cook, stirring occasionally, for 7 minutes, or until the vegetables are very soft. If sticking, add 1 tbsp water. Add the aubergine and cook for a further 5 minutes, until it begins to get soft. Add the tomatoes and combine well. Add the black-eyed beans and corn and cook, stirring occasionally, for 10 minutes longer.

Remove from the heat. Add the spinach and stir until it's well combined and wilted. Season generously with sea salt and pepper and stir in the lemon juice. Serve over rice, garnished with sliced spring onions.

Vegan. Dairy, gluten, sugar, wheat and yeast free.
Freezing: Ideal for freezing up to 2 months.
Cook's Tips: If using sweetcorn, it's better to use frozen rather than canned.
Nutritional Content: Antioxidants, beta carotene, copper, dietary fibre, folate, manganese, phosphorous, potassium, protein and vitamins B_6 and C.
Note to the Senses: There are interesting flavours here. Black-eyed beans aren't a particularly popular bean, which is a pity. In their dried state, they cook more quickly than other pulses and they taste wonderful without any spices. The addition of cumin, thyme and chilli complements them surprisingly well. They're a refreshing change from the usual beans.

curries

The word 'curry' comes from the southern Indian word 'kari', meaning 'sauce'. The word 'curry' has become a catch-all word to describe any number of hot, spicy, sauce-based dishes of East Indian origin. Indeed, for many people, 'curry' means almost any dish from India. In actual fact, most people in India don't even use the word 'curry'.

In general, a curry consists of a dish made with dried and fresh spices cooked in oil, with a sauce made from puréed onions, garlic and ginger. The variety of spices used can be extensive, but the most common are chilli, coriander, cumin and turmeric. Other typical ingredients are cream, ground nuts and yoghurt.

In Café Fresh, we have many curry recipes. We've been lucky to have some Indian chefs working with us who have shared their curry secrets with us. I've given a selection of the recipes to show the different styles and flavours in curries from various parts of the world.

Sri Lankan Butterbean and Cashew Nut Curry

serves 4–6
ready in 1 hour

Sri Lankan cuisine is made distinctive by its indigenous spices, such as cloves and cinnamon. People arrived in Sri Lanka to trade in spices and left some of their culinary practices as well. Sri Lankan cooking has evolved by combining the culinary practices of many of these cultures. The most noticeable impacts have been the Portuguese, Dutch, Moor and Malay influences. As a result of their influences, coconut milk is central to Sri Lankan cooking. This recipe combines cinnamon and coconut milk for a rich flavour.

1 tbsp sunflower oil
1 large onion, finely chopped
2 garlic cloves, finely chopped
2 green chillies, finely chopped
1 tbsp finely chopped fresh ginger
1 tsp turmeric
½ tsp ground cinnamon
2 sweet potatoes, cut into cubes 5 cm (2 in) wide and 2½ cm (1 in) thick
2 medium potatoes, cut into cubes 5 cm (2 in) wide and 2½ cm (1 in) thick
2 medium courgettes, cut into cubes 5 cm (2 in) wide and 2½ cm (1 in) thick
½ butternut squash, peeled and cut into cubes 5 cm (2 in) wide and 2½ cm
(1 in) thick
500 ml (17 fl oz) vegetable stock
400 ml (14 fl oz) tin coconut milk
handful curry leaves
2 cinnamon sticks
¼–½ tbsp concentrated apple juice or honey
120 g (4 oz) green beans, topped and tailed
250 g (9 oz) cooked butterbeans or 400 g (14 oz) tin butterbeans, drained
120 g (4 oz) cashew nuts, toasted
handful fresh coriander

Heat the oil in a large pan and gently fry the onion for about 3 minutes, until soft. Add the garlic, chillies, ginger, turmeric and ground cinnamon and cook for a further 3 minutes. Add all the vegetables except the green beans and stir well. Sauté for 2 minutes. Add the vegetable stock, coconut milk, curry leaves, cinnamon sticks and concentrated apple juice, cover and simmer for 20 minutes, until the vegetables are cooked.

Meanwhile, blanch the green beans by placing them in a bowl of boiling water for 5 minutes. Drain and run under the cold tap until completely cold.

Add the green beans, butterbeans and nuts to the pan and heat through. Remove the cinnamon sticks, season and add the fresh coriander. Serve with long-grain brown rice.

Vegan. Dairy, gluten, sugar, wheat and yeast free.
Freezing: Suitable for freezing.
Cook's Tips: You can use light coconut milk if you're concerned about fat content.
Nutritional Content: Antioxidants, copper, dietary fibre, fat, folate, manganese, molybdenum, protein, tryptophan and vitamins A, C and K.
Note to the Senses: Just yummy – creamy beans, creamy sauce and subtle spices – perfect!

Quick and Easy Thai Green Vegetable Curry

serves 4
ready in 50 minutes

Thai cuisine is unique on the Asian continent. Thai cuisine is essentially a marriage of centuries-old Eastern and Western influences harmoniously combined into something uniquely Thai. Of course, each region is distinctive. In the south, coconut plays a prominent role in many dishes, its milk tempering the heat of chilli-laced soups and curries. The sauces are flavoured by many spices, such as basil, chilli, coriander, garlic, ginger, lemongrass and tamarind, as well as peanuts. The most popular or best-known dish is the Thai curry. Below I give you a simple recipe for a delicious Thai green curry.

for the sauce:

1½ tsp sunflower oil

1 tsp sesame oil

2 sticks lemongrass, thinly sliced (outer skin removed)

1¼ cm (½ in) piece of fresh ginger, finely grated

4 garlic cloves, finely chopped

4 medium onions, thinly sliced

3 red or green chillies, finely chopped

2 tbsp Thai green curry paste

4–5 tbsp water

400 ml (14 fl oz) tin coconut milk (light if you prefer)

½ bunch Thai basil, chopped

½ bunch fresh coriander, chopped

1 tbsp Basil Pesto (see p. 3)

for the curry:

1½ tsp sesame oil

4 green peppers, thinly sliced

1 red pepper, thinly sliced

3 courgettes, cut into slices 2 cm (1 in) thick

100 g (4 oz) green beans or mangetout

1 medium head of broccoli, broken into small florets

400 g (14 oz) tin cooked chickpeas

handful fresh coriander, finely chopped

To make the sauce, heat both oils together over a gentle heat. Sauté the lemongrass, ginger and garlic together. Add the onions and sauté until the onions are soft and translucent, about 15 minutes. Add the chillies and sauté for another 5 minutes. Add the curry paste and water and mix well. Add the coconut milk, Thai basil and coriander, and cook for 10 minutes. Blend and add the Basil Pesto. Taste and season if needed.

To make the curry, heat the remaining sesame oil in a pot and lightly sauté the peppers for 5 minutes, until softened. Add the courgettes and cook for another few minutes.

Blanch the green beans and broccoli by placing them in a bowl of boiling water for 5 minutes. Drain and run under the cold tap until completely cold.

Add the sauce to the peppers and courgettes in the pot. Add the green beans and broccoli and combine well. Add the chickpeas and heat through.

Add the fresh coriander and mix well into the sauce. Serve with freshly cooked basmati rice.

Vegan. Dairy, gluten, sugar, wheat and yeast free.
Freezing: Suitable for freezing.
Cook's Tips: This sauce is best made the day before and then reheated. If you do this, the sauce thickens overnight and the flavours develop beautifully. It's a really good idea to make double the quantity of sauce and freeze half for the following week. If you can't get Thai basil, use regular fresh basil.
Nutritional Content: Antioxidants, dietary fibre, fat, folate, manganese, molybdenum, protein, tryptophan and vitamins A and C.
Note to the Senses: This curry is the most popular curry in Café Fresh. The wonderful green colour and ingredients just scream nutrients. The red peppers balance the green and are a perfect colour combination, and so immediately appeal.

Indian Potato, Pea and Carrot Curry with Tomato Relish and Basmati and Wild Rice

serves 4–6
ready in 40 minutes

for the sauce:
1 tbsp sunflower oil
2 medium onions, thinly sliced
1 tsp cumin seeds
3 garlic cloves, finely chopped
1½ cm (½ in) piece of fresh ginger, finely chopped
2 red chillies, finely chopped
1 tsp turmeric

1 tsp curry powder

½ tsp ground coriander

½ tsp ground cumin

½ tsp garam masala

½ tsp ground cardamom

2 × 400 g (14 oz) tins chopped tomatoes

for the curry:

1 tbsp sunflower oil

2 large potatoes or 3–4 small potatoes, peeled and cut into small cubes, or if using new baby potatoes, approx. 8 unpeeled and cut into cubes

6 carrots, peeled and thinly sliced into 5 cm (2 in) lengths

100 g (4 oz) fresh or frozen peas

handful of freshly chopped coriander

for the tomato relish:

6 ripe tomatoes, quartered, deseeded and diced

1 small red onion, finely chopped

200 g (7 oz) tub of Greek-style yoghurt (optional)

bunch of fresh coriander, roughly chopped

squeeze of lemon or lime juice

for the rice:

175 g (6 oz) basmati rice

50 g (2 oz) wild rice

To make the sauce, heat the oil and sauté the onions and cumin seeds together for 5–7 minutes, until the onion is cooked but not brown. Add the garlic and ginger and cook for a further 2 minutes. Add the chillies and all other spices, combining well with the onion mix, and cook over a low heat for 2 more minutes. Add the tinned tomatoes, mix well, cover and bring to the boil. Reduce the heat and allow to simmer for 20 minutes. Remove from the heat, allow to cool slightly, then blend to a smooth consistency. Taste and season if required.

To make the curry, heat the sunflower oil in a medium pot. Add the potatoes and carrots and sauté for 5 minutes. Add a tablespoon of the curry sauce, cover the pot and simmer for 10 minutes, stirring occasionally. Add the remaining sauce, mix well, cover and cook for a further 10–15 minutes, until the vegetables are cooked. Add the fresh peas. (If using frozen peas, immerse the peas in hot water, strain and add to the curry sauce. Heat the peas thoroughly.)

To make the tomato relish, mix together the tomatoes, onion, yoghurt, coriander and lemon or lime juice and season to taste.

To make the rice, in large pot of lightly salted boiling water, add the basmati rice and wild rice. Bring to the boil, reduce the heat, simmer for 15 minutes and strain. To remove any starch, rinse the rice with fresh boiling water, return to the pot and cover until ready to serve.

When ready to serve, add the fresh coriander to the curry and serve with the rice and the tomato relish on the side.

Vegan. Dairy, gluten, sugar, wheat and yeast free.
Freezing: Suitable for freezing.
Cook's Tips: As with all curry sauces, there's a huge benefit from making the sauce a day in advance. In saying that, this is a great quick curry recipe and has a good flavour when made anyway. Leave overnight if using for a party to really impress.
Nutritional Content: Antioxidants, carbohydrate, fibre, folate, lycopene, niacin, potassium and vitamins A, B_6 and K.
Note to the Senses: It's amazing what you can do with tomatoes when you add various spices and flavourings. This is hugely different from the chilli recipes and equally as satisfying.

Cauliflower and Spinach Dhansak

serves 4–6
ready in 30–40 minutes

Dhansak has its origins in a Parsee (Middle Eastern, Persia) dish and was probably a special dish presented at a feast. The dish served in Indian restaurants today is based on the addition of a lentil purée to the cooking process. Below we have a very simple version for you to enjoy.

1 tbsp sunflower oil
1 Spanish onion, roughly chopped
3 large garlic cloves, finely chopped
5 cm (2 in) piece of fresh ginger, finely chopped
2 red chillies, finely chopped
1 tsp ground coriander
1 tsp cumin seeds
1 tsp turmeric
1 tsp ground cinnamon
1 tbsp tomato purée
110 g (4 oz) Puy lentils
400 g (14 oz) tin chopped tomatoes
570 ml (1 pint) water
1 medium or 2 small heads of cauliflower, broken into small florets
500 g (18 oz) fresh spinach, finely chopped
1 tsp fresh chopped coriander
basmati rice, to serve
pistachio nuts, finely chopped, to serve

Heat the oil in a large, heavy-based pan and sauté the onions, garlic and ginger for 5 minutes. Add all the spices and sauté for a further 2 minutes. Add the tomato purée and sauté with the onions and spices for a further 5 minutes, until the paste becomes a dark red colour.

Add the lentils, tinned tomatoes and water. Season, cover and bring to the boil, reduce the heat and simmer for 15 minutes. Stir occasionally to ensure the lentils don't stick to the bottom of the pot.

Stir in the cauliflower and simmer for a further 15 minutes, until the lentils and cauliflower are tender. Remove from the heat and stir in the spinach and allow to wilt. Sprinkle the fresh coriander on top. Serve immediately with basmati rice tossed with finely chopped pistachio nuts.

Vegan. Dairy, gluten, sugar, wheat and yeast free.

Freezing: Suitable for freezing up to 2 months.

Cook's Tips: Puy lentils are the best lentil for this curry, as they hold their shape. If you can't get them, you can use brown or green lentils.

Nutritional Content: Antioxidants, dietary fibre, folate, iron, manganese, molybdenum, protein, tryptophan and vitamins A, B$_6$, C and K.

Note to the Senses: Dhansak should have a good spice in it and have a fairly thick consistency. It's most suitable as a winter dish because it's filling, satisfying and nutritious.

Caribbean Plantain, Cashew Nut and Spinach Curry with Creole Rice and Mango Relish

serves 4–6
ready in 30 minutes

Caribbean cuisine is full of exotic ingredients such as coconut, mangos, papaya and plantain. This curry isn't an everyday curry. You'll have to source the ingredients in an ethnic shop or market. This is one for a special occasion and is well worth the effort for the terrific end result.

for the curry:
1 tbsp vegetable oil
1 onion, finely chopped
2 garlic cloves, chopped
2 tsp medium curry powder
1 tsp ground cardamom
1 tsp ground cumin
4 cm (1½ in) piece of fresh ginger, peeled and finely chopped
2 sweet potatoes, peeled and cut into medium chunks
4 green cooking plantains, peeled and cut into medium chunks
1 glass white wine
500 ml (17 fl oz) light vegetable stock

400 g (14 oz) spinach, washed and roughly chopped

50 g (2 oz) desiccated coconut

handful roasted cashew nuts, finely chopped

1½ tsp raisins

1½ tsp concentrated apple juice or honey, to sweeten

for the Creole rice:

225 g (8 oz) long-grain white rice

570 ml (1 pint) water

½ small carrot, peeled

½ onion, peeled

¼ tsp salt

1 sprig fresh parsley

1 sprig fresh thyme

for the mango relish:

1 tbsp vegetable oil

½ mango, peeled, stoned and diced

dash of white wine

3 cardamom pods, crushed

1½ tsp balsamic vinegar

splash of white wine vinegar

½ garlic clove, finely chopped

To make the curry, heat the oil in a pan and fry the onion, garlic, curry powder, cardamom and cumin over a gentle heat for 3–4 minutes. Add the ginger, sweet
potato and plantain and fry for another 5 minutes.

Add the wine, stock and a tablespoon of water and simmer until the vegetables are tender, 15–20 minutes.

Stir in the chopped spinach, allowing it to wilt and heat through. Add the desiccated coconut, cashew nuts, raisins and apple juice and season to taste. The
consistency should be fairly thick. Stir well, allowing the coconut to break down
and add thickness to the sauce.

To make the rice, soak the rice in cold water for 15 minutes, then drain. In a large saucepan, bring the water to the boil. Add the carrot, onion, salt, parsley and thyme. Add the rice and simmer over a medium heat for 20 minutes.

Remove the carrot, onion, parsley and thyme. Drain the rice in a colander. Rinse under cold running water. Drain again and turn into the saucepan. Simmer over a low heat for 5 minutes, until the rice grains are completely dry.

To make the mango relish, heat the oil in a small pan. Add the mango, wine, cardamom and vinegars and cook for 5–6 minutes. Add the garlic and continue to cook gently, until soft. Allow to cool slightly.

Serve the curry with the rice and relish on the side.

Vegan. Dairy, gluten, wheat and yeast free.
Freezing: Suitable for freezing.
Cook's Tips: Desiccated coconut is different to coconut milk in texture. It's the dehydrated form of white coconut meat and has a gritty texture. When added and blended into the curry, the texture isn't smooth, like when adding coconut milk. This complements the plantain perfectly and adds a slightly gritty texture.
Nutritional Content: Antioxidant, carbohydrate, fibre, manganese, potassium and vitamins A and C.
Note to the Senses: A very different-flavoured curry to the other curry recipes. It's an aromatic, slightly sweet curry.

DK's Vegetable and Buckwheat Noodle Korma

serves 4–6
ready in 40 minutes

For most Westerners, 'korma' means a very mild dish with a heavy cream sauce. The word 'korma' actually means 'braising', and the dish can be either very mild or very fiery, depending on the region. Korma is Mogul in origin, and in the north of India, where Moguls became established, a wide array of kormas are served. This recipe is a mild korma sauce using almonds to enrich the sauce and omitting the cream to reduce the calories. My friend DK tried this recipe with noodles as an experiment and it worked wonderfully, so here's how we do it.

350 g (12 oz) buckwheat noodles

1 head of broccoli, broken into small florets

200 g (7 oz) mangetout or green beans, topped and tailed

1½ tsp sunflower oil

1 carrot, peeled and chopped into thin strips

1 green pepper, deseeded and sliced into thin strips

1 red pepper, deseeded and sliced into thin strips

for the sauce:

1½ tsp sunflower oil

1 Spanish onion, sliced

3 garlic cloves, finely chopped

1¼ cm (½ in) piece of fresh ginger, peeled and finely chopped

2 chillies, finely chopped

1 tsp mild curry powder

1 tsp ground cumin

½ tsp garam masala

½ tsp ground coriander

½ tsp turmeric

400 g (14 oz) tin chopped tomatoes

200 g (7 oz) blanched almonds

1 tbsp water

To make the sauce, heat the oil and gently sauté the onions until soft, 5–7 minutes. Add the garlic, ginger and chillies and sauté for 5 minutes more. Add all the spices and sauté for 1 minute. Add the tomatoes, season with 1 tsp sea salt, cover and cook for 15 minutes.

Meanwhile, blend the almonds with the water until a smooth paste forms. You can use a food processor or hand blender for this.

Once the tomato is heated through, blend to a smooth sauce. Add the blended nuts and combine well. Taste and season as required. Leave to stand for 10 minutes.

Meanwhile, cook the buckwheat noodles according to packet instructions. Drain and run under a cold tap until cold. Leave to drain.

Blanch the broccoli and mangetout by placing in a bowl of boiling water for 7 minutes. Drain and run under a cold tap until cold. Leave aside to drain.

Heat the remaining oil in a pot and add the carrot and peppers. Sauté until soft, about 7 minutes. Add the sauce to the pot and gently reheat. Add the broccoli and mangetout and mix through. Add the buckwheat noodles and combine well to heat thoroughly. Check the seasoning and adjust if necessary. Serve immediately.

Vegan. Dairy, gluten, sugar, wheat and yeast free.

Freezing: Sauce is suitable for freezing.

Cook's Tips: 100 per cent buckwheat noodles cook in just 5 minutes when added to boiling water. If you overcook them, they get soggy and sticky. If you use the noodles with some wheat, they cook more easily. It just takes a little practice and keeping a close eye on the noodles. Make sure you cool them properly so they won't cook any more.

Nutritional Content: Antioxidants, dietary fibre, magnesium, manganese, tryptophan and vitamins B_6, C and K.

Note to the Senses: This combination of noodles and curry is delicious. Buckwheat noodles have a nice texture when cooked properly and combine with the curry sauce for an interesting and addictive curry.

breads and everyday cakes

Introduction

Baking is the more technical of the cooking categories. You must weigh and measure accurately to get a good end result. Personally, I'm a savoury person and love the freedom that cooking savoury dishes allows me. When it comes to baking, I've devised some recipes that allow me the freedom to alter and adjust at will and avoid weighing. This only applies to brown bread, scones, muffins, crumbles and easy cakes like the ones in this chapter. All other cakes need careful attention to measurements and baking techniques to create successful cakes and desserts.

When baking with brown flour, I always choose Doves Farm organic wholemeal flour. The 1984 UK Bread and Flour Regulations provide a definition of wholemeal flour, saying that 'wholemeal consists of the whole of the product obtained from the milling of cleaned wheat.' The terms 'whole wheat' and '100 per cent' aren't actually mentioned, although you could assume they refer to wholemeal.

When using white flour, I always use strong white flour. This type of flour should be made from hard wheat varieties and produces elastic dough because it has a high gluten and protein content. Again, I use Doves Farm, as they don't add any other improvers, enzymes or bleaches to their strong flours.

Don't forget that cakes and breads are a carbohydrate. Wholemeal flour is a complex carbohydrate.

Rita's Brown Bread

makes 1 loaf
ready in 1 hour

This bread is quick and easy and oh so wholesome, perfect with lentil soup.

450 g (1 lb) stone-ground wholemeal flour
60 g (2 oz) strong white flour
2 tsp baking powder
½ tsp sea salt
90 g (3 oz) organic oat bran
90 g (3 oz) organic wheat germ
60 g (2 oz) organic sesame seeds
60 g (2 oz) organic sunflower seeds
60 g (2 oz) organic pumpkin seeds
500 ml (18 fl oz) organic soy milk

Preheat the oven to 200°C/400°F/gas 6. Oil and lightly flour a 2-lb loaf tin.

Sieve the flours, baking powder and salt together into a large bowl. Add the oat bran, wheat germ and seeds. Combine well.

Make a well in the centre of the flour mix and add in half the soy milk. With a wooden spoon, combine the milk with the flours. If needed, add more milk, enough to get a loose, sticky consistency.

Transfer to the prepared loaf tin. Bake on the centre shelf in the oven for 20 minutes. The bread should have risen and the crust should be getting brown. Reduce the heat to 180°C/350°F/gas 4 and continue baking for 25–30 minutes. The bread is done when the base sounds hollow when tapped.

Remove from the tin and allow to cool on a wire rack. For a soft crust, wrap bread in a clean tea towel.

Vegan. Dairy, sugar and yeast free.
Freezing: Will freeze well for up to 1 month.
Cook's Tips: All ingredients should be at room temperature. Wholemeal flour is

available in fine or coarse varieties. I've found that a lot of the coarse wholemeal flour available in supermarkets is very coarse and doesn't produce a nice bread. The stone-ground organic wholemeal flours available in health food stores are infinitely superior and I would advise using this flour if you want a good bread. Strong white flour is added to lighten the bread. If you want less milk, you can use half water and half soy milk. Crucially, for good brown bread, the oven must be at the right temperature and the oven door must not be opened for the first 15 minutes of baking time so that the bread rises properly.

Nutritional Content: Calcium, carbohydrate, dietary fibre, folate, phosphorous, thiamin and vitamins B_1, B_2, B_3, B_6 and E and the minerals copper, magnesium, manganese and zinc.

Note to the Senses: Making bread reminds me of my mother, who has made bread every day since I can remember. There's nothing so homely as the smell of freshly baked bread. When making bread, don't be afraid to get your hands dirty and feel the texture of the grains and seeds. When combining the flours and the seeds, use your hands to mix the dry ingredients together. It's a good way to ensure the ingredients are well combined and the heat from your hands helps to keep the ingredients at room temperature.

Cheddar and Chive Scones

makes 10–12 scones
ready in 35 minutes

450 g (1 lb) stone-ground wholemeal flour
3 tsp baking powder
1 tsp sea salt
180 g (6 oz) cheddar, grated
handful of chopped chives
3 free-range eggs, lightly beaten
about 185 ml (7 fl oz) milk/soy milk, to bind

Preheat the oven to 200°C/400°F/gas 6. Grease and lightly flour a baking tray.

Mix the flour, baking powder, salt, cheese and chives together in a bowl. Stir in the beaten eggs and enough milk to form a smooth, firm dough (not sticky).

Turn onto a lightly floured surface and knead. Roll out to 2½ cm (1 in) thickness. Using a medium-sized chef's ring or cutter (5 cm/2½ in), cut out rounds and place on the prepared baking tray. Brush the top of the scones with a little milk.

Bake for 15–20 minutes, or until risen and golden brown. Leave to rest for 5 minutes, then transfer to a wire rack to cool.

Sugar free.
Freezing: Freezes well for up to 1 month.
Cook's Tips: Don't add all the milk at once, as you may not need it all. It will depend on the flour you're using. You don't want a sticky dough; it should come together well and roll out easily.
Nutritional Content: Calcium, carbohydrate, fat, folate, protein, thiamin and vitamin B_6, and the minerals magnesium, manganese and zinc.
Note to the Senses: These scones are quite obviously savoury. They have a hard crust and are more bread-like in texture than other scones. They are delicious served warm with a hearty soup.

Sugar-Free Date and Orange Muffins

makes 8–10 muffins
ready in 35 minutes

Muffins are a pretty recent addition to the Irish diet, and much of this influence has come from the US. A muffin is a small cake-like bread that can be made with a variety of flours and many combinations of fruits and nuts. This muffin is baked in a muffin tin, which is deeper than the traditional queen cake baking tray. You can buy the tray with six or twelve cup-shaped depressions that hold the muffin batter. Each standard muffin cup is about 6 cm (2½ in) in diameter. They are widely available in homeware/kitchen stores.

This is the most popular muffin in Café Fresh. It's a very satisfying muffin, with plenty of sweetness from the dates. It's a great mid-morning or mid-afternoon snack.

600 g (1 lb 5 oz) stone-ground wholemeal flour

2 tsp baking powder

¼ tsp salt

rind and juice of 1 orange

170 g (6 oz) chopped dates

200 g (7 oz) butter or margarine, melted and cooled

2 large free-range eggs, lightly beaten

about 170 ml (6 fl oz) milk/soy milk

Preheat the oven to 190°C/375°F/gas 5. Lightly grease 12 deep muffin tins and sprinkle with a little flour. Alternatively, you can use paper cases in the tin, in which case you don't need to grease the tins.

Mix the flour, baking powder, salt, orange rind and chopped dates together.

Make a well in the centre of the flour and add the melted butter and lightly beaten eggs and orange juice. Mix lightly with a wooden spoon – do not beat.

Finally, add in half the milk and gently combine with a wooden spoon. Add more milk as needed to form a moist consistency, but not too soft.

Transfer to the prepared muffin tray and bake for 20–25 minutes, until golden brown and firm to the touch. Transfer to a wire rack to cool.

Sugar free.

Freezing: Not suitable for freezing.

Cook's Tips: You can, of course, change the fruit as you like. Other alternatives are:

Banana and Cinnamon Muffins: Replace the dates with 6 very ripe mashed bananas; add ½ tsp cinnamon to the flour; and add 3 tbsp honey/concentrated apple juice after you add the eggs. You may need to add less milk here, as the banana changes the consistency. Add the milk in stages until you get a moist consistency, but not too soft or runny.

Raspberry or Strawberry and Pine Nut Muffins: 1 medium punnet raspberries or strawberries, sliced; add 1 tbsp roughly chopped pine nuts to the flour; and add 3 tbsp honey/concentrated apple juice after you add the eggs.

Plum or Pear Muffins with Almond: Add 170 g (6 oz) finely chopped plums or pears; add ½ tsp almond extract to eggs; and add 3 tbsp honey/concentrated apple juice after you add the eggs.

Apple and Cinnamon: Add 170 g (6 oz) finely chopped apples with ½ tsp cinnamon; and add 3 tbsp honey/concentrated apple juice after you add the eggs.

Nutritional Content: By using wholemeal flour, you get the goodness of the whole grain, including calcium, copper, fibre, folic acid, iron, phosphorus, zinc and vitamins B_1, B_2, B_3 and E.

Note to the Senses: There's no sugar in these muffins, but you'd never know it. The wonderful sweetness from the dates and the subtleness of the orange are a great combination of flavours. These muffins are very filling and don't keep very well, so eat them quickly.

Apricot and Almond Buns

makes 12 buns
ready in 50 minutes

I found this recipe in an American food magazine in 2003 and I absolutely love it. It takes a little more effort than regular scone recipes, but it's really worth it. Perfect for Sunday morning family breakfast or brunch.

for the apricot swirl:
225 g (8 oz) apricots
6 tbsp water
2 tbsp muscovado brown sugar
2 tbsp whole almonds, roughly chopped

for the buns:
680 g (1½ lb) white flour
100 g (4 oz) butter or margarine, cut into small cubes
60 g (2 oz) caster sugar
3 tsp baking powder
½ tsp sea salt

50 g (2 oz) sliced almonds (or use whole almonds, roughly chopped)

2 large eggs

170 ml (6 fl oz) buttermilk

½ tsp almond extract

To make the apricot swirl, simmer the apricots and water over a low heat until all the water is absorbed. Transfer to a food processor, add the sugar and pulse to a coarse purée. Add the almonds and pulse once or twice more. Store in a labelled tub in the fridge.

To make the buns, preheat the oven to 190°C/375°F/gas 5. Lightly grease 12 deep muffin tins and sprinkle with a little flour. Alternatively, you can use paper cases in the tin, in which case you don't need to grease the tins.

Place the flour, butter, sugar, baking powder and salt in a food processor and pulse until the mixture resembles coarse breadcrumbs. Transfer to a bowl and add the almonds.

Whisk the eggs, buttermilk and almond extract together. Make a well in the centre of the flour mix and add the liquid ingredients to the dry ingredients. Mix well to form a scone texture. Add the apricot purée and gently incorporate to mix well.

Spoon into the prepared muffin tin and bake for 20–25 minutes, until golden brown and a wooden pick or skewer inserted in the centre of a bun comes out clean.

Freezing: Will freeze well for up to 1 month.

Cook's Tips: You can use brown flour for this recipe, but it just isn't the same! Don't make the bun mixture too wet, or it will overflow in the oven – not good! Just add the milk in stages until you get a moist but stiff-ish consistency. You don't want a runny, dropping consistency.

Nutritional Content: A big carbohydrate rush.

Note to the Senses: This recipe is a cross between a scone and a muffin. All you need to add here is some butter, fruity jam and maybe a little whipped cream or cashew nut cream.

Carrot Cake

makes 2 × 2-lb loaves or one 28 cm (11 in) round cake
ready in 1 hour 30 minutes

Carrot cake recipes are wide and varied. Many would say it's a bit out of date now. If this is the case, then my customers aren't impressed by the removal of carrot cake from the cake selection during the summer months. It's the most popular cake in the restaurant. I think this has something to do with its similarity to the old Irish fruit cakes. It's very moist and rich in fruit and spices.

This is a substantial recipe. I've set it out like this because this recipe is absolutely perfect for freezing. You can make 2 × 2- lb loaf tins with this recipe and freeze it, or you can make one large 28 cm (11 in) round cake, which is an impressive cake for a family get-together.

3 medium free-range eggs
285 g (10 oz) dark muscovado brown sugar (or you can substitute 200 ml/
7 fl oz concentrated apple juice for a sugar-free recipe)
215 ml (7 fl oz) sunflower oil
285 g (10 oz) stone-ground wholemeal flour
2½ tsp baking powder
1 tsp ground cinnamon
½ tsp freshly grated nutmeg
425 g (15 oz) grated carrots, plus extra for decorating
85 g (3 oz) desiccated coconut
145 g (5 oz) raisins
2 tbsp Greek-style yoghurt, to decorate
a handful of toasted flaked almonds, to decorate

Preheat the oven to 190°C/375°F/gas 5. Grease a 28 cm (11 in) round spring-form tin (base lined) or 2 × 2-lb cake tins (base lined).

Whisk the eggs and sugar together in a blender until thick and creamy. Alternatively, use a hand whisk and whisk in a large bowl. Slowly add in the oil, whisking all the time.

Sieve the flour, baking powder, cinnamon and nutmeg together in a large bowl. Add the grated carrots, desiccated coconut and raisins. Combine well.

Add the creamy sugar and egg mix to the dry ingredients and combine very well. The mixture should be quite thick.

Transfer to the greased and lined tin and bake for 40–50 minutes, until golden brown and a skewer inserted in the centre of the cake comes out clean.

Allow to cool in the tin for 5 minutes, then turn onto a wire rack to finish cooling.

Decorate by spreading the Greek yoghurt over the top, and sprinkle the grated carrot and toasted flaked almonds over the yoghurt.

Freezing: Perfect for freezing.
Cook's Tips: You can use a little of the lemon icing from the Apricot and Almond Cake on p. 207 for a lemony, tangy alternative.
Nutritional Content: This cake has vitamins A and K from the carrots. By using wholemeal flour, you get the goodness of the whole grain, including calcium, copper, fibre, folic acid, iron, phosphorus, zinc and vitamins B_1, B_2, B_3 and E.
Note to the Senses: This is a wonderfully moist cake which gets better over a few days. The carrots keep this cake moist. In *The Oxford Companion to Food*, Alan Davidson tells us that carrots were used in sweet cakes in Europe in the Middle Ages, when other sweeteners were hard to find or just too expensive. In fact, carrots, along with beets, contain more sugar than other vegetables, which may explain their use in desserts.

Rosie's Orange, Almond and Coconut Cake

serves 12
ready in 55–60 minutes

This is a wonderful, simple recipe which was given to us by Rosie from Seattle, who baked delicious cakes for Café Fresh in 2004. Like the carrot cake recipe, you can make 2 × 2-lb loaves from this recipe and freeze one.

450 g (1 lb) strong white flour or wholemeal flour

1 tsp baking powder

½ tsp salt

½ tsp ground cinnamon

170 g (6 oz) brown sugar

170 g (6 oz) desiccated coconut

170 g (6 oz) ground almonds

3 ripe bananas, mashed

juice and zest of 2 oranges

1 tsp vanilla extract

Preheat the oven to 180°C/350°F/gas 4. Grease and base line a 23 cm (1 inch) round springform tin or 2 × 2-lb loaf tins.

Sift the flour, baking powder, salt, cinnamon and brown sugar together. Add the coconut and almonds.

Mash the banana in a bowl until smooth. Add the orange juice, rind and vanilla. Add the wet ingredients to the dry ingredients and combine well.

Bake for 35–40 minutes, until golden brown and a skewer inserted in the centre of the cake comes out clean.

Vegan. Dairy free.

Freezing: Perfect for freezing.

Cook's Tips: This cake is delicious warm, if a bit crumbly. It slices better when left to cool and will last well for up to 3 days wrapped in greaseproof paper and kept in an airtight container. This cake is not too sweet, so it's better as an everyday cake than as a rich dessert cake.

Nutritional Content: Carbohydrate, potassium. If using wholemeal flour, you'll get the additional nutritional benefits.

Note to the Senses: If you like orange flavours, you'll love this cake. It's a great dairy-free cake recipe.

Green Leaf and Seed Salad

Berries

Chocolate Truffles

Chocolate Brownies

Apricot and Almond Cake

serves 8
ready in 1 hour

250 g (9 oz) butter or margarine
200 g (7 oz) sugar
4 eggs, lightly beaten
75 g (3 oz) ground almonds
100 g (4 oz) maize flour
zest and juice of 1 lemon
100 g (4 oz) dried apricots, finely chopped

Preheat the oven to 180°C/350°F/gas 4. Lightly grease the sides of a shallow 23 cm (9 in) round springform cake tin and line the base with baking parchment or greaseproof paper.

Beat the butter and sugar together in a food processor or with an electric hand whisk until white and fluffy. Add one-third of the beaten eggs to the butter mix, gently folding in – do not beat. If using a food processor, use the pulse button so that the mixture isn't beaten. Repeat twice more until all the eggs are incorporated.

Combine the ground almonds and maize flour, then gently fold in one-third of the flour mixture. As before, repeat twice until all the flour is incorporated.

Fold in the lemon zest and juice. Lastly, gently fold in the chopped apricots.

Bake for 35 minutes. Gently remove from the tin by first loosening the edges, then turn onto a sheet of greaseproof paper to cool. Serve with a blop of crème fraîche and a cup of tea.

Gluten and wheat free.
Freezing: Freezes well for up to 1 month.
Cook's Tips: Whiz the apricots in a food processor until finely chopped, then soak in a little water for half an hour before use to soften. The folding process is very important to ensure a light cake.

This is a thin cake. If you want to make this for a special occasion for someone with gluten and wheat intolerance, you can make two cakes and sandwich them together with a simple lemon icing:

675 g (1½ lb) icing sugar, sieved
350 g (12 oz) butter or margarine, softened
juice of 12 lemons

Cream the icing sugar and butter together to a smooth consistency. Add the lemon juice and whisk to combine well.

This is very rich, so you can compromise by using the icing just for sandwiching the two cakes together and then dusting the top with icing sugar.

Nutritional Content: A carbohydrate sugar cake, just indulgence.
Note to the Senses: This is a perfect sweet cake for tea time. This cake doesn't rise very much, so it's a good idea to top it with crème fraîche or Greek-style yoghurt, which also serves to cut through the sweetness of the cake. The sweetness is also well balanced with the lemon flavour, which comes through beautifully. The only problem with this cake is that you feel you can have a few pieces because the cake looks flat, but remember, it's very rich – one piece is all you need! This cakes keeps very well wrapped in foil in an airtight container. The almonds ensure the cake remains moist.

Tea Time Loaves

The following three recipes are really good, sweet loaves that are ideal for tea time or when you need a sweet fix. They are simple to make and freeze very well. I always think it's worthwhile making two loaves and freezing one of them. If you're baking for one or two and you don't feel you will get through a whole loaf in 4 days, you can make the loaf, allow it to cool, cut it in half or in slices, wrap each slice very well in greaseproof paper, then in foil and freeze the slices. Then you can take them out as you need them.

These cakes can be made with wholemeal brown flour or white flour, as you prefer.

Cherry Almond Loaf

makes 1 loaf
ready in 1 hour 30 minutes

200 g (7 oz) glacé cherries
200 g (7 oz) butter, softened
135 g (5 oz) caster sugar
3 eggs, beaten
¼ tsp almond essence
250 g (9 oz) wholemeal or strong white flour
1 tsp baking powder
135 g (5 oz) ground almonds
50 ml (2 fl oz) milk

Preheat the oven to 180°C/350°F/gas 4. Grease and line a 2-lb loaf tin.

Halve the cherries, rinse with cold water, pat dry and dust with some flour, shaking well to get rid of the excess flour.

Cream the butter and sugar together until light and fluffy. Gradually add in the beaten eggs and almond essence.

Combine the flour and baking powder together. Gently fold in the flour and ground almonds. Fold in the cherries and then the milk. Spoon the thick mixture into the prepared loaf tin.

Bake for 50–60 minutes, until a skewer inserted in the centre of the loaf comes out clean. Leave to cool for 10 minutes before removing from tin.

Freezing: Freezes well for up to 1 month.
Cook's Tips: If using white flour, the cherries really stand out and look very nice, ideal for a tea party.
Nutritional Content: Carbohydrate based. By using wholemeal flour you get the goodness of the whole grain, including traces of calcium, copper, fibre, folic acid, iron, phosphorus, vitamins B_1, B_2, B_3 and E, and zinc. Ground almonds add some vitamin E and B_{12}.

Note to the Senses: A simple, light cake that is perfect for sharing with family with a cup of tea.

Granny Leonard's Ginger Bread

makes 1 loaf
ready in 2 hours

350 g (12 oz) wholemeal or strong white flour
1 tsp baking powder
1 tsp bicarbonate of soda
¼ tsp ground ginger
8 globes of preserved stem ginger in syrup, strained and chopped
125 g (4½ oz) unsalted butter or margarine, softened, plus extra for greasing
100 g (3½ oz) light muscovado sugar
225 g (8 oz) golden or maple syrup
1 free-range egg, beaten
75 ml (3 fl oz) milk

Preheat oven to 160°C/320°F/gas 3. Grease and line a 2-lb loaf tin.

Sift the flour, baking powder, bicarbonate of soda and ground ginger together. Add half the chopped ginger to the flour mixture. Finely slice the rest of ginger and leave aside.

Melt the butter, sugar and golden syrup in a pan. Set aside and allow to cool for about 15 minutes. Beat the egg and milk together.

Stir the cooled butter mixture into the dry ingredients, followed by the milk mixture, and beat well. Spoon into the tin and arrange the remaining ginger overlapping on top.

Bake for 1½ hours, until firm to the touch or until a skewer inserted in the centre of the loaf comes out clean. Cool on a wire rack.

Freezing: Freezes well for up to 1 month.
Cook's Tips: Preserved stem ginger can be found in good delicatessens and in

some Asian food shops.

Nutritional Content: By using wholemeal flour you get the goodness of the whole grain, including traces of calcium, copper, fibre, folic acid, iron, phosphorus, vitamins B_1, B_2, B_3 and E, and zinc.

Note to the Senses: A wonderful ginger flavour which is more delicate than a normal ginger cake.

Granny Farrell's Tea Brack

makes 1 loaf
ready in 2 hours

180 ml (6 fl oz) strong tea
450 g (1 lb) mixed fruit (sultanas, raisins, currants)
170 g (6 oz) brown sugar
1 free-range egg, lightly beaten
25 g (1 oz) butter or margarine, melted
255 g (9 oz) wholemeal flour, sieved
1½ tsp bread soda
1 tsp mixed spice

Preheat the oven to 180°C/350°F/gas 4. Grease and line a 2-lb loaf tin.

Mix the tea, fruit and sugar together, cover and leave to soak overnight.

Add the egg and melted butter to the fruit mix. Fold in the sieved flour, bread soda and mixed spice.

Transfer to the tin and bake for 1–1½ hours, until a skewer inserted in the centre of the cake comes out clean. Leave to cool for 10 minutes before removing from tin.

Freezing: Freezes well for up to 1 month.

Cook's Tips: My grandmother was fond of adding alcohol to her cakes, so if you like, add 2 tbsp of whiskey to the fruit and tea before soaking.

Nutritional Content: By using the wholemeal flour you get the goodness of the whole grain, including traces of calcium, copper, fibre, folic acid, iron, phosphorus, vitamins B_1, B_2, B_3 and E, and zinc. Raisins have been the subject of phytonutrient research primarily for their unique phenol content. They are also one of the top sources of the trace mineral boron in the US diet.

Note to the Senses: This cake couldn't be simpler, and is an ideal accompaniment to tea in the winter months. Reminds me of my childhood.

Date and Oat Slice

serves 6–8
ready in 40 minutes

This slice has proven to be very popular in Café Fresh. It seems to have some addictive qualities, as customers keep coming back for more. It's very filling, with plenty of sweetness from the dates.

475 g (1 lb 1 oz) chopped dates
juice and rind of 1 orange
3 tbsp water
285 g (10 oz) rolled oats
60 g (2 oz) sesame seeds
60 g (2 oz) sunflower seeds
60 g (2 oz) pumpkin seeds
225 g (8 oz) vegan margarine

Preheat the oven to 180°C/375°F/gas 4.

Place the dates, orange juice and water in a saucepan and heat until the dates have softened, about 7 minutes.

Mix all the dry ingredients together and rub in the margarine until the mix sticks together. You may need to add a little more margarine to get the correct consistency. Alternatively, you can place all the ingredients in a food processor and pulse until the margarine has been incorporated. Don't overdo this, or the topping will be too fine.

Put half the oat mixture in a greaseproof dish. Pour the softened dates on top of the oats and finish with the last of the oat mix on top. Bake for 20 minutes, until golden brown. Allow to cool before slicing. You'll find that some of this crumbles and falls apart – simply add more to the serving.

This slice will keep very well for up to 4 days in an airtight container. It's a good afternoon snack.

Vegan. Dairy and wheat free. No added sugar.
Freezing: Not suitable for freezing.
Cook's Tips: You can use different fruit, such as figs or apricots, as an alternative if you like.
Nutritional Content: Carbohydrate based, with some calcium, copper, magnesium, manganese, phosphorus, potassium, selenium, tryptophan and vitamins B_1 and E.
Note to the Senses: This slice has a wonderful richness with a delicate hint of orange. An ideal snack and quite addictive!

Raspberry and Pine Nut Bars

serves 6
ready in 40 minutes

This is a delicious fruity summer snack. You can substitute strawberries for the raspberries if you like.

285 g (10 oz) plain flour
285 g (10 oz) porridge oats
225 g (8 oz) butter or margarine
85 g (3 oz) light muscovado sugar
finely grated zest of 1 lemon
100 g (4 oz) pine nuts
225 g (8 oz) raspberries

Preheat the oven to 180°C/350°F/gas 4. Grease a 23 cm (9 in) baking tin.

Sieve the flour, then add the oats. Rub in the butter and work to a coarse breadcrumb texture. Mix in the sugar and lemon zest. Add three-quarters of the pine nuts and press the mixture together until it forms large, lumpy clumps.

Place two-thirds of the oat mixture in the tin, pressing down lightly. Scatter the raspberries on top and sprinkle the rest of the oat mixture over them.

Bake for 25 minutes, until pale golden in colour. Sprinkle the remaining pine nuts on top and return to the oven for a further 5 minutes to toast the pine nuts. Cut into bars. These keep for 2 to 3 days in an airtight container in the fridge.

Freezing: Not suitable for freezing.

Cook's Tips: The fruit can be changed according to the seasons. Chopped rhubarb is a very good alternative here. I would advise sprinkling 85 g (3 oz) of muscovado sugar over the rhubarb before putting the topping on the fruit. You will need this extra sweetness to counteract the bitterness of the rhubarb. Remember, there's fresh fruit in the centre, so the bars must be kept in the fridge or they'll go mouldy.

Nutritional Content: Carbohydrate based, with traces of copper, magnesium, manganese, phosphorus, selenium, trypophan and vitamin C.

Note to the Senses: Summer is here when raspberries appear! This bar is a perfect combination of sweetness from the oat mix and tartness from the raspberries.

sweet cakes and desserts

Introduction

I'm not a big dessert person. I'm naturally drawn to the savouries. This isn't typical of women, I have to admit. Most, if not all, of my female friends are automatically drawn to the desserts on the menu before they look at anything else. If given a choice of two courses – a starter and main or main and dessert – I will always choose the former. That said, I love making sweet cakes and desserts and get great pleasure discovering new quick and easy dessert recipes.

I haven't included the nutritional content of the desserts in this chapter. Let's be honest – they're desserts, and we aren't really concerned about how good or bad they are for us. They are treats, so let's enjoy them without the guilt!

chocolate

So much has been written about chocolate. It's bad for you, it's good for you, it's an aphrodisiac. Some even claim chocolate is the most endorphin-inducing food on earth, which is why it's so satisfying. One thing is for sure – my female friends, not to mention some male friends, will always enjoy a good chocolate dessert.

When using chocolate in cooking, don't compromise – buy the best available (at least 70 per cent cocoa solids).

Vegan Chocolate Cake

This is a super-easy vegan cake, very moist and rich in flavour. Interestingly, vinegar is used in this cake, and it works!

150 g (5 oz) bar vegan chocolate, such as Green & Black's
350 g (12 oz) wholemeal flour
225 g (8 oz) raw cane sugar
½ tsp baking powder
pinch sea salt
175 ml (6 fl oz) sunflower oil
1 tsp vanilla extract
1 tsp cider vinegar
400 ml (14 fl oz) cold water

for the icing:
50 g (2 oz) vegan sunflower margarine
100 g (4 oz) vegan chocolate

Preheat the oven to 180°C/350°F/gas 4. Grease and line a 23 cm (9 in) spring-form baking tin.

Place the chocolate in a small bowl and melt over a pot of simmering water over a low heat. Allow to cool.

Thoroughly mix the flour, sugar, baking powder and salt in a bowl. Pour in the melted chocolate. Slowly add the oil, stirring to incorporate well. Add the vanilla extract and vinegar.

Pour in the cold water and stir well with a wooden spoon until completely incorporated. Do not beat. The consistency will be quite runny, which is exactly how it should be.

Pour into the greased tin and bake for 30 minutes, until a skewer inserted in the centre of the cake comes out clean. Allow to cool for 5 minutes before removing from the tin. Gently turn onto a wire rack to cool completely.

To ice the cake, simply melt the margarine with the chocolate and drizzle over the cooled cake, letting it run down the side. Leave to set for 30 minutes. Serve with cashew nut cream.

Vegan. Dairy free.
Freezing: Freezes well for 1 month.
Cook's Tips: This cake is best eaten fresh. It tends to lose its flavour as the days go by. If you have a little left over, warm up the cake in the oven to bring it back to life.
Note to the Senses: This cake doesn't rise very well, so it can look a little flat. Never fear – if you ice it and cut a good big slice of it, you will taste the wonderful richness of chocolate.

Really Rich Chocolate Cake

serves 8–10
ready in 1 hour 15 minutes

750 g (1 lb 10 oz) dark muscovado sugar
450 g (1 lb) sunflower margarine
4 large eggs, lightly beaten
1 tsp vanilla extract
200 g (7 oz) dark chocolate, melted
400 g (14 oz) wholemeal flour
2 tsp baking powder
500 ml (17 fl oz) boiling water

Preheat the oven to 180°C/350°F/gas 4. Grease and line a 23 cm (9 in) spring-form baking tin.

Cream the sugar and margarine together until soft and fluffy. Add the eggs and vanilla, beating well. Fold in the melted chocolate. Blend well but do not overbeat.

Gently add the flour and baking powder, alternating spoon by spoon with the boiling water until you have a smooth and fairly liquid batter.

Pour the batter into the lined baking tin and bake for 30 minutes on the top shelf in the oven. Switch to the lower shelf and bake for a further 15 minutes.

Note: A skewer will not come out clean, as the cake will be sticky inside.

Freezing: Freezes well for up to 1 month.
Cook's Tips: This is a very rich cake that lasts well. I like to serve this with crème fraîche or Greek-style yoghurt and some fresh berries to cut through the sweetness.
Note to the Senses: As the name suggests, this is a really rich chocolate cake. The chocolate quality is vital for the flavour of the cake. You can smell the chocolate as the cake bakes in the oven, preparing your taste buds for the delicious experience.

Chocolate Brownies

makes 8
ready in 40 minutes

375 g (13 oz) butter or sunflower margarine
100 g (4 oz) dark chocolate (70 per cent cocoa solids), such as Green & Black's or Valrhona
6 large eggs
250 g (9 oz) caster sugar
1 tsp vanilla extract
225 g (8 oz) wholemeal flour
½ tsp salt
275 g (10 oz) drinking chocolate
200 g (7 oz) chopped walnuts

Preheat the oven to 180°C/350°F/gas 4.

Line a medium brownie tray (33 cm × 25 cm × 10 cm) with parchment paper.

Place the butter or margarine and chocolate in a bowl and melt over a pot of simmering water over a low heat. Allow to cool. Beat the eggs with the sugar and vanilla extract. Sieve the flour and salt together. Add in the drinking chocolate.

With a wooden spoon, mix the melted and slightly cooled chocolate mix into the egg and sugar mix, along with the nuts. Fold in the flour mix.

Place in the baking tray and bake for 25 minutes, or until the top is crusty.

Freezing: Freezes well for up to 1 month.

Cook's Tips: Replace the walnuts with pecans or hazelnuts if preferred. If you have a nut allergy, just leave them out.

Note to the Senses: Brownies should have a gooey centre and you should be instantly pleased with the first mouthful. Best served warm.

Chocolate Puddings

makes 4
ready in 50 minutes

100 g (4 oz) plain flour
75 g (3 oz) caster sugar
1 tbsp cocoa powder
1½ tsp baking powder
1 egg
1 tbsp golden syrup or maple syrup
100 ml (3½ fl oz) milk
80 ml (3 fl oz) light olive oil or sunflower oil
2 tbsp roasted chopped hazelnuts, to decorate

for the fudge sauce:
100 g (4 oz) good-quality chocolate, chopped
25 g (1 oz) unsalted butter or margarine
25 g (1 oz) icing sugar
284 ml (10 oz) carton double cream
1 tbsp brandy

Preheat the oven to 150°C/300°F/gas 2 and grease 4 individual pudding moulds.

Sift the dry ingredients together.

Mix the egg, golden syrup, milk and oil together in a separate bowl. Add to the dry ingredients and stir until soft.

Pour the batter into moulds, put the moulds on a baking tray and bake for 30 minutes.

To make the fudge sauce, place all the ingredients in a pan over a low heat and cook, stirring until thick. Run a knife around each pudding and turn out onto a plate. Pour over the sauce and decorate with nuts.

Freezing: Not suitable for freezing.

Cook's Tips: Take care removing the puddings from the moulds. A warm knife inserted around the edge of the mould helps loosen the pudding.

Note to the Senses: Pure indulgence – the fudge sauce really finishes this off!

Easy Chocolate Truffles

makes approx. 25
ready in 45 minutes

225 g (8 oz) vegan drinking chocolate, such as Green & Black's
225 g (8 oz) vegan sunflower margarine, softened
225 g (8 oz) icing sugar
175 g (6 oz) desiccated coconut
100 g (4 oz) hazelnuts
100 g (4 oz) raisins
1 tbsp water
1 tsp vanilla extract

Place all the ingredients in a food processor and blend to a smooth consistency. Place in a bowl and refrigerate for 30 minutes. Remove from fridge and roll into small truffle shapes.

The truffles will keep in the fridge for up to a week.

Vegan. Dairy, gluten and wheat free.

Freezing: Can be frozen for up to 1 month, but much better made fresh, as they can be kept in the fridge for up to 1 week.

Cook's Tips: When rolling the truffles, you can coat them with a little desiccated coconut or some vegan cocoa/chocolate powder, or both.

Note to the Senses: Chocolate truffles are always pleasing to the eye. Once you bite one you will enjoy the rich flavour, which is enhanced by the hazelnuts and raisins.

pastry

Pastry is always considered tricky or difficult. It takes practice and a knowledge of the important basic rules. When making pastry, all your utensils must be cold. Cold ingredients are necessary for a crisp pastry. When the recipe requires water or eggs, always take them straight from the fridge. Use a metal spoon or knife when mixing ingredients. You shouldn't handle the pastry too much, as the heat from your hands will warm the pastry too much. Once pastry is made, it should be refrigerated for 30 minutes before rolling. When rolling pastry, use the least amount of flour possible to flour your work surface. The pastry will shrink slightly in the oven. To avoid having a greatly reduced pastry edge, when lining the pastry case, push the pastry up around the edges after trimming.

Blind Baking

Blind baking is the best way to bake pastry before adding a filling. First, preheat the oven to 200°C/400°F/gas 6.

Line the pastry with foil or greaseproof paper. Fill with baking beans or any dried beans, such as kidney beans or chickpeas. Bake for 15 minutes, remove the beans and paper/foil and return to the oven for a further 5 minutes, until the pastry is dry to touch. It's now ready for the filling.

Apple Pie with Cashew Nut Topping

makes 8
ready in 1 hour 15 minutes

for the shortcrust pastry:
225 g (8 oz) plain white flour
¼ tsp salt
110 g (4 oz) sunflower margarine, cut into small cubes
3–4 tbsp cold water

for the filling:
900 g (2 lb) red eating apples
1 tbsp water
1 tbsp concentrated apple juice or 1½ tsp maple syrup (optional)
1½ punnets blueberries

for the topping:
110 g (4 oz) cashew nuts
1 tbsp water

To make the pastry, grease a 23 cm (9 in) fluted pastry case. Sieve the flour and salt together. Rub in the margarine until a breadcrumb consistency is formed. Add water and combine until the flour forms a ball. Wrap in cling film and refrigerate for 30 minutes. Blind bake as per the instructions on p. 221.

To prepare the filling, peel and core the apples, then thinly slice and place in a saucepan with the water. Add sweetener if required. Place the pot over a medium heat and cover until the water begins to boil. Reduce the temperature to its lowest point and simmer for about 10 minutes. Remove from the heat and allow to cool.

To make the cashew nut topping, place the nuts in a blender and add water until a paste-like mixture has formed. You can add a little sweetener at this point if you wish, but it's not necessary.

To assemble the pie, place the cooked apples into the pre-baked pastry case.

Sprinkle the blueberries indiscriminately on top of the apples. Pour the cashew nut topping over the fruit.

Bake at 180°C/350°F/gas mark 4 for 15–20 minutes, until brown on top. Serve warm or cold.

Vegan. Dairy and sugar free.

Freezing: Not suitable for freezing.

Cook's Tips: Sprinkle the tart with toasted flaked almonds for added flavour.

Note to the Senses: This apple pie is quite different to a traditional apple pie. It has a lovely cashew nut crust, looks very appealing and is not very sweet. If you don't like overly sweet dishes, then this is the dessert for you!

Plum and Almond Tart

serves 8–10
ready in 1 hour 30 minutes

for the shortcrust pastry:
225 g (8 oz) plain white flour
¼ tsp salt
110 g (4 oz) sunflower margarine, cut into small cubes
3–4 tbsp cold water

for the filling:
6 ripe plums
175 g (6 oz) butter, very soft
175 g (6 oz) golden caster sugar
3 large eggs at room temperature, lightly beaten
175 g (6 oz) ground almonds
½ tsp vanilla extract
1 tbsp apricot jam

To make the pastry, grease a 23 cm (9 in) fluted pastry case. Sieve the flour and salt together. Rub in the margarine until a breadcrumb consistency is formed. Add water and combine until the flour forms a ball. Wrap in cling film and refrigerate for 30 minutes. Blind bake as per the instructions on p. 221.

Cut the plums in half and remove the stones. Set aside.

Cream the butter and sugar together until light and fluffy. Gently fold in one third of the eggs and one third of the almonds. Repeat until all egg and almonds are incorporated. Do not beat or whisk. Add the vanilla extract.

Spread the halved plums over the pre-baked pastry case and pour the almond mixture over the top of the plums.

Bake for 40–45 minutes, until the frangipane is set. It should be golden brown and firm. When cooled, warm the apricot jam and brush over the top of the tart.

Freezing: Best made fresh.

Cook's Tips: Pears are a perfect substitute here. Just remember you will need to peel them.

Note to the Senses: I love this tart. The richness of the almond filling combined with the sharpness of the plum is perfect. Add a spoon of cream or crème fraîche to a warm slice of tart for a wonderful treat.

Zingy Lemon Tart

serves 8
ready in 1 hour

for the rich shortcrust pastry:
225 g (8 oz) strong white flour
110 g (4 oz) cold butter, broken into pieces
1 egg, beaten

for the filling:
juice and rind of 3 large lemons
175 g (6 oz) caster sugar
3 eggs

5 egg yolks
150 g (5 oz) sunflower margarine

Preheat the oven to 200°C/400°F/gas 6 and grease a 28 cm (9 in) fluted loose-bottom tart case.

To make the pastry, sieve the flour and rub in the butter until a breadcrumb texture is formed. (You can use a food processor to do this.) Add the beaten egg and combine with a knife. The pastry should come together in a ball. Cover and refrigerate for 30 minutes, then roll out the pastry and line the prepared tart case. Trim the edges. Blind bake the pastry as per the instructions on p. 221.

Reduce the oven to 160°C/325°F/gas 2.

Meanwhile, place the lemon juice and rind, sugar and eggs in a pot over the lowest possible heat. Start whisking immediately until the sugar has dissolved. Add in half the margarine and continue whisking until the margarine has dissolved.

Add the remaining margarine and continue whisking until you get a custard-like consistency, which takes about 8 minutes. *Do not boil* – keep the temperature low at all times.

Pour the mixture through a sieve to remove the lemon rind and to ensure the filling is smooth.

Pour the lemon filling into the prepared pastry case and bake for 20 minutes. It should be only slightly darker than the colour the filling originally was. It may not be fully set, but it will set as it cools. Leave to cool completely.

Freezing: Not suitable for freezing.
Cook's Tips: If you're feeling adventurous and are comfortable making pastry, try replacing half the flour with an equal quantity of crushed pine nuts for an interesting alternative. The pastry will be a little more crumbly, but it's really delicious.
Note to the Senses: Lemon tart is a classic. This tart will appeal to all those who like to be reminded of French pastries.

Pecan Pie

serves 8
ready in 1 hour

for the rich shortcrust pastry:
225 g (8 oz) strong white flour
110 g (4 oz) cold butter, broken into pieces
1 egg, beaten
4 small, deep tartlet cases or 1 × 9 in fluted tart case

for the filling:
50 g (2 oz) muscovado sugar
110 g (4 oz) butter
110 ml (4 fl oz) honey
65 g (2½ oz) pecans, finely chopped
1 egg, beaten
pinch of ground cinnamon
pecan halves, to decorate
maple syrup, to decorate

To make the pastry, sieve the flour and rub in the butter until a breadcrumb texture is formed. (You can use a food processor to do this.) Add the beaten egg and combine with a knife. The pastry should come together in a ball. Cover and refrigerate for 30 minutes, then roll out the pastry and line the prepared tart cases. Trim the edges. Blind bake the pastry as per the instructions on p. 221.

Preheat the oven to 170°C/325°F/gas 3.

In a saucepan, melt together the sugar and butter. Remove from the heat and stir in the honey, chopped pecans, beaten egg and cinnamon. Mix together thoroughly.

Pour the pecan mixture into the tartlet cases and top with the whole pecans. Bake for 20 minutes. Decorate the serving plates with pecans and a drizzle of maple syrup.

Freezing: Freezes well for up to 1 month.

Cook's Tips: It is worth sourcing good quality maple syrup for this pie, as it has an excellent, rich flavour.

Note to the Senses: A delicious, nutty pie, which is not too sweet.

Hazelnut Torte

serves 8

ready in 1 hour

250 g (9 oz) hazelnuts

225 g (8 oz) butter, softened

250 g (9 oz) sugar

8 large eggs, separated

zest of 2 oranges

50 g (2 oz) ground almonds

250 g (9 oz) ricotta cheese

2 tbsp poppy seeds

pinch of salt

3 heaped tbsp jam, preferably apricot

4 tbsp water

50 g (2 oz) best-quality cooking chocolate (70 per cent cocoa solids), finely grated

Preheat the oven to 190°C/375°F/gas 5. Grease a 28 cm (11 in) springform tin, line with greaseproof paper and place in the fridge.

Put the hazelnuts on a baking tray and toast for 5 minutes, or until golden brown. Allow to cool, then whiz in a food processor until you have a fine powder, similar to ground almonds. Don't overdo this, or you'll end up with a paste.

Beat the butter and sugar together until pale and thick. Add the egg yolks one by one, then add the orange zest. Add the ground almonds, crumble in the ricotta and stir in the powdered hazelnuts, poppy seeds and salt.

In a separate bowl, beat the egg whites until they're very stiff. Fold them slowly into the hazelnut mixture.

Pour the mixture into the chilled tin and bake for 25–30 minutes, until there's a little colour on the top of the torte. Remove from the oven and allow to cool.

While the tart is cooling, place the jam and water in a pan and bring slowly to the boil. Brush the jam over the top of the cooled torte, then sprinkle the grated chocolate over it. Serve with some crème fraîche or fromage frais.

Gluten and wheat free.

Freezing: Will freeze well for 1 month – do not glaze until serving.

Cook's Tips: This cake has cheese in it, so it should be kept in the fridge if it's not being eaten immediately, or if you have some leftover slices.

Note to the Senses: This cake looks quite light, but remember the ingredients are rich, so you don't need a big slice. It is delicious with a spoon of Greek yoghurt.

Baked Strawberry Cheesecake

serves 12
ready in 1 hour

250 g (9 oz) digestive biscuits or similar
1½ tsp sunflower oil
600 g (1 lb 5 oz) cream cheese
200 g (7 oz) crème fraîche
1 tbsp maple syrup
4 eggs, separated
225 g (8 oz) strawberries, sliced

Preheat the oven to 180°C/350°F/gas 4. Grease and line a 28 cm (11 in) spring-form tin.

Place the biscuits in a food processor and pulse until they are completely broken up. Alternatively, place the biscuits in a bag and crush with a rolling pin. Add the oil to the biscuits and pulse to combine. Place in the bottom of the greased and lined baking tin.

Blend the cream cheese, crème fraîche, maple syrup and egg yolks together until smooth.

In a separate bowl, whisk the egg whites until light and fluffy. Fold into the cheese mixture.

Place the sliced strawberries over the biscuit base, then pour the cheese mixture over the fruit.

Bake for 45–50 minutes, until golden brown and stiff when the tin is shaken. Allow to cool completely before removing from tin. Decorate with fresh strawberries and a dusting of icing sugar, if desired.

Freezing: Not suitable for freezing.

Cook's Tips: This is a perfect dinner party dessert for any time of year. Substitute any seasonal fruit, such as plums, mixed berries, blackberries, etc.

Note to the Senses: Everyone loves cheesecake. This cheesecake has less sweetness than traditional cheesecake so it has a sharpness that reminds me of German Quark cake.

Berry and Apple Crumble

serves 6
ready in 35 minutes

8 medium eating apples, peeled, cored and thinly sliced
1 tbsp water
2 tbsp organic maple syrup, concentrated apple juice or honey (optional)
450 g (1 lb) mixed berries

for the topping:
100 g (4 oz) rolled oats, oat flakes or rice flakes
50 g (2 oz) flaked almonds
50 g (2 oz) ground almonds
50 g (2 oz) sesame seeds
50 g (2 oz) sunflower seeds
2 tbsp sunflower oil

Preheat the oven to 180°C/350°F/gas 4.

Place the apples in a saucepan with the water and your choice of sweetener (if necessary), cover and allow to cook for 5 minutes. Add half the berries and continue cooking for a further 5 minutes. Make sure the fruit is soft but hasn't lost its shape completely.

For the topping, mix all the dry ingredients together. Add the sunflower oil and combine well. If you wish, you can add a little sweetener, such as 1½ tsp concentrated apple juice.

Place the cooked fruit in a medium-sized oven dish and sprinkle over with the remaining uncooked berries. Cover with the crumble topping and bake for 15–20 minutes, until the topping is golden brown and the fruit is bubbling at the sides of the dish. Serve with whipped cream, natural yoghurt or vegan cream.

Dairy, sugar and yeast free. Gluten and wheat free if using rice flakes.
Freezing: Not ideal for freezing.
Cook's Tips: Substitute fruit as the season changes.
Note to the Senses: A crunchy topping and a juicy, fruity base gives a very satisfactory and comforting dessert.

Baked Stuffed Apples

serves 4–6
ready in 40 minutes

6 large Bramley cooking apples, decored and scored
110 g (4 oz) soft brown sugar
50 g (2 oz) flaked almonds
50 g (2 oz) chopped pecans
50 g (2 oz) unsalted butter or vegan sunflower margarine
2 tbsp raisins
1 tsp cinnamon
1 tbsp rum (optional)
3 cinnamon sticks, halved

Preheat the oven to 190°C/375°F/gas 5.

Mix the brown sugar, almonds, pecans, butter, raisins, cinnamon and rum together and spoon it into the cavities of the apples. Place the excess filling in the bottom of a buttered baking dish. Place half a cinnamon stick in the filling of each apple.

Place the apples in the dish. Dot the tops with butter, cover and bake for 20 minutes. Remove the cover, spoon the juices from the bottom of the dish over the apples and continue baking for a further 10 minutes, or until the apples are soft. Serve piping hot with cashew nut cream or double cream.

Vegan. Dairy, gluten, wheat and yeast free.
Freezing: Not suitable for freezing.
Cook's Tips: This is an ideal dessert for children during the winter months.
Note to the Senses: Cinnamon and apples marry perfectly together. The visual effect of the baked apples with the wonderful aromas of the cinnamon and nuts really awaken the senses to a delicious, simple dessert.

Fruit Fool

serves 2
ready in 10 minutes

1 apple, cut into bite-sized pieces
1 pear, cut into bite-sized pieces
1 plum, cut into bite-sized pieces
50 g (2 oz) Greek-style yoghurt
25 g (1 oz) chopped nuts (almonds, walnuts, pine nuts)
1 tsp maple syrup, honey or concentrated apple juice

Divide the fruit in half and place in the bottom of 2 wine glasses. Add a soup spoon of yoghurt and top with the rest of the fruit. Add the remaining yoghurt and top with the nuts. Drizzle sweetener on top and allow to run down the inside of the glass.

Gluten and wheat free. Sugar free if using concentrated apple juice.

Freezing: Not suitable for freezing.

Cook's Tips: Alternate fruit according to the changing seasons, e.g. stewed rhubarb, strawberry and apple is a good combination for May.

Note to the Senses: Beautifully presented in glasses, fruit fool immediately stimulates the taste buds. The combined tartness of the Greek yoghurt and fruit is well balanced by the rich sweetness of the maple syrup.

glossary

Cheese

Cheese is a popular protein for many vegetarians, though not all cheeses are suitable for vegetarians. Rennet is a protein that's added to milk in cheese manufacture. It curdles the milk, separating the milk into solids (curds) and liquids (whey). The curds are then packed in cheese cloths and after further mould colonisation and maturing, they eventually produce blocks of cheese. The rennet has traditionally been animal sourced, though there's now a microbial alternative (suitable for vegetarians) that's more commonly used in cheese making. There is a wide variety of cheeses suitable for vegetarians. If you go to the farmers' markets, you can talk to the producers themselves and they will inform you. I never have any problem getting excellent vegetarian cheeses for the restaurant and for home. One cheese that does pose a problem for recipes is Parmesan. If you're looking for an alternative to Parmesan, I suggest Gabriel cheese, which is made in Schull, Co. Cork and is available in good cheesemongers or at farmers' markets. You can also use a non-dairy substitute, Florentino Parmazano, found in good health food shops.

Dried and Canned Beans

Dried beans are available pre-packaged or in bulk. Some of the more popular dried beans are black beans, cannellini beans, chickpeas, haricot beans, kidney beans and pinto beans. Store dried beans in an airtight container. The flatulence caused by dried beans is created by oligosaccharides, complex sugars that are indigestible by normal stomach enzymes. They therefore proceed into the lower intestine, where they're eaten (and fermented) by friendly bacteria, the result of which is gas. This is seen by many people as the greatest disadvantage of eating beans. It is best to cook the beans very well to the point that they are soft so as to minimise flatulence and make them more digestible.

Cooking Dried Beans

Wash dried beans thoroughly before use. Dried beans must be soaked in double the amount of water overnight. Rinse, place in a medium pot with double the amount of water, bring to the boil, reduce the heat and simmer for 1–1½ hours.

Canned beans are a quick and easy alternative to soaking and boiling dried beans, which may be too troublesome for a busy lifestyle. I suggest you buy the organic varieties in health food stores. They are slightly more expensive, but the quality is superior. Many of the standard canned varieties have salt or sugar added and the quality of the beans is generally poor.

When introducing beans into your diet, you'll initially find that your digestive system will take a week or so to get used to the high-fibre nature of the beans.

Dried beans are rich in calcium, iron, phosphorus and protein. Their high protein content, along with the fact that they're easily grown and stored, make them a staple throughout many parts of the world where animal protein is scarce or expensive. For vegetarians, they're a highly nutritious and inexpensive food source and a cheap alternative to many other protein foods. For people who need to reduce their intake of animal protein, bean dishes are a very healthy alternative. Bean dishes can be included a few times a week in the diet in various ways. In this book, interesting and tasty dishes are detailed to help you on your way.

Lentils

Lentils have been used as a meat substitute for a long time. They are popular in many parts of Europe and are a staple throughout much of the Middle East and India. Historically, however, in this part of the globe they have been associated with a bland vegetarian diet. This notion harks back to the 1970s, when vegetarian fare wasn't the most inspiring. If you go to France or many other European countries, lentils are included in many dishes on menus and are always tasty, interesting and nutritious. In India and Middle Eastern countries, they are used with spices and vegetables, creating dishes that excite and delight.

There are three main common varieties of lentils – the reddish orange/red lentil, yellow lentil and brown lentil. Then there's the French Puy lentil, also known as the king of lentils. It has a dark green speckled coat and a rich flavour. None of these varieties are used fresh, but are dried as soon as they're ripe. Though available in some supermarkets, lentils are best sourced in health food shops or ethnic food shops. Lentils should be stored in an airtight containter at room temperature for up to six months. Lentils are used in soups, salads, main dishes and stews. In this book there are many recipes using lentils that allow you to enjoy the humble lentil as it should be – bursting with flavour and filled with goodness. In Cafe Fresh we use the red lentil and Puy lentil.

Cooking Red Lentils

In contrast to dried beans, lentils don't need to be soaked and they take much less time to cook. Wash dried lentils thoroughly before use. Place lentils in double the amount of water, bring to the boil, reduce the heat and simmer for 15–20 minutes.

Cooking Puy Lentils

These take longer to cook – 30 minutes – but retain their shape and are great for making pies and soups.

Lentils contain dietary fibre, folate, molybdenum, protein and vitamin B_1 and are a good source of copper, iron, phosphorus and potassium.

Miso

Miso is a Japanese culinary mainstay and is a basic flavouring in Japanese cooking. It has the consistency of peanut butter and comes in a wide variety of flavours and colours. Miso is a fermented soy bean paste which can be divided into three basic categories – barley miso, rice miso and soy bean miso, all of which are developed by injecting cooked soy beans with a mould cultivated in either a barley, rice or soy bean base.

Additionally, the miso's colour, flavour and texture are affected by the amounts of soy beans and salt used. It's further influenced by the length of time it's aged, which can range from six months to three years. Shinshu miso is a golden yellow, all-purpose variety with a mellow flavour and rather high salt content. There are regional favourites such as sendai miso, a fragrant, reddish-brown variety found in northern Japan, and the dark brown hatcho miso, popular in central Japan. Miso is used in sauces, soups, marinades, dips, main dishes, salad dressings and as a table condiment. Miso can be found in Japanese markets and health food stores. It should be refrigerated in an airtight container. It's easily digested and extremely nutritious, having rich amounts of B vitamins, calcium, oestrogens and protein. Miso is used in recipes for flavour and nutrition.

Rice

Rice has been cultivated since at least 5000 BC, and archaeological explorations in China have uncovered sealed pots of rice that are almost 8,000 years old. Today, rice is a staple for almost half the world's population, particularly in parts of China, India, Indonesia, Japan and Southeast Asia. The 7,000-plus varieties of rice are grown in one of two ways. Paddy-grown rice is cultivated in flooded fields. The lower-yielding, lower-quality 'hill-grown' rice can be grown on almost any tropical or subtropical terrain.

Rice is commercially classified by its size into three categories: long-, medium- or short-grain.

Long-grain rice is four to five times that of its width. When cooked, it produces light, dry grains that separate easily. Basmati rice is the most exotic of the long grains.

Medium-grain rice has a size and character between the other two. It's shorter and moister than long-grain rice and generally not as starchy as short-grain rice. Though fairly fluffy right after being cooked, medium-grain rice begins to clump once it starts to cool.

Short-grain rice has fat, almost round grains that have a higher starch content than the long- or medium-grain varieties. When cooked, it tends to be quite moist and viscous, causing the grains to stick together. Italian arborio rice is an example.

Rice varieties are available in white or brown form. **White rice** has had the husk, bran and germ removed, making it less nutritious than its brown counterpart. **Brown rice** is the entire grain with only the inedible outer husk removed. Brown rice is a perfect example of a whole food. The nutritious, high-fibre bran coating gives it a light tan colour, nutlike flavour and chewy texture. The presence of the bran means that brown rice is subject to rancidity, which limits its shelf life to about six months. It also takes slightly longer to cook, generally 50–60 minutes.

Rice, which is cholesterol and gluten free, is low in sodium, contains only a trace of fat and is an excellent source of complex carbohydrates. Organic brown rice contains calcium, iron and many B-complex vitamins and is a great source of roughage.

Buying Rice

I always buy organic brown rice in my local health food store. The quality is superb and you can choose from organic short grain, long grain or brown basmati. Organic brown rice is one of my favourite foods. Generally I have it every day. On the days that I don't have it, I never manage to feel completely full after any meal.

Cooking Brown Rice

1 part brown rice, thoroughly washed
2 parts cold water

Place the rice and water in a large pot and bring to the boil. Reduce the heat and simmer for 50–60 minutes. I personally never add salt when cooking rice.

Cooking Basmati Rice

1 part basmati rice
2 parts boiling water

Place the water and a pinch salt in a large pot and bring to the boil. Add the rice and return to the boil. Reduce the heat and simmer for 15 minutes.

Cooking Basmati and Wild Rice

In a large pot of lightly salted boiling water, add 1 cup basmati rice and ⅛ cup wild rice. Bring to the boil, reduce the heat and simmer for 15 minutes. Strain. To remove any starch, rinse the rice with fresh boiling water, return to the pot and cover until ready to serve.

Kitchen Equipment

Today you can shop in any of the main department stores and kit your kitchen out with the most elaborate equipment and accessories. It's important to remember that you don't need to spend vast amounts of money on lots of gadgets to get yourself started in the kitchen. For me, there are a few absolute essentials. I have found that I always use six items in the kitchen, and after that, others are used very intermittently. Of course, like everyone else I indulge myself with the non-essentials from time to time, and why not?

The Six Essentials

1. Knives: A chopping knife is an absolute necessity in any kitchen. Choose a good-qualify knife with a handle that suits your hand. It's important that the knife feels comfortable in your hand. I have found that the best knives are the Wusthof-Gourmet model, a German brand. You don't need to buy the most expensive knife – spend around €40 to €50 and you'll get a good knife that will last you many years; all you need to do is sharpen it every so often. The department stores or a catering supply shop will stock good-quality knives.

A small **paring/peeling knife** is very handy for tackling fruits and vegetables, e.g. for peeling ginger.

A small **serrated-edge knife** is perfect for chopping tomatoes, peppers, fruit or basically anything with a skin that tends to be hard to slice through with a straight-edged knife.

2. Chopping board: I only use wooden chopping boards at home. I have one for vegetables and one for fruit. A wooden board is the best surface for your knife. A glass chopping board will result in a blunt knife. Plastic boards are okay, but a good wooden board is far superior. To clean them, wash/scrub with hot soapy water, rinse and dry immediately. A good wooden board shouldn't be put into a dishwasher. I find that rubbing a little vegetable oil into the board every so often keeps it in tip top shape.

3. Spatula: This is one of the best inventions for a cook. You can be sure there's no waste if you use the spatula to get the last bit of sauce, cake mix, etc. out of the pot or bowl. If you have children, they won't appreciate cleaning the cake bowl with the spatula, as they generally think this is their job!

4. Hand soup blender: A compact, cheap hand blender that can be used for blending anything from soup to hummus and pestos.

5. Mixing bowl: A medium-sized mixing bowl is handy for everything from mixing salads to making cakes.

6. Saucepans: I find that three different-sized pots is a good general rule in the kitchen. There is a huge selection to choose from.

Enjoy the Fruits of Your Labour

I have often heard the main cook in the house complain that she never enjoys the meal she's prepared. I think this is down to picking too much and getting too stressed when cooking. It's easy for me to say this, you may comment. Indeed it is, but you should enjoy the act of cooking and look forward to your meal. If you're learning to cook or are feeling a little unsure of what you're doing, it's a good idea not to have too many distractions in the kitchen. Keep the pokey noses out. I love people in the kitchen when I'm cooking, but if I'm trying a new recipe, I like to be left alone so I can concentrate. And don't have a glass of wine until the dish is cooked.

Always sit down at the table and enjoy your meal. A meal that you've cooked yourself should be something you sit down and enjoy with a partner, friends, family or on your own. It's important to take your time when eating to savour the flavours of the food and relish in a job well done. Sitting down and taking the time to enjoy your meal also has beneficial effects on your digestive system.

Creating the Atmosphere

When inviting people to your home for a meal, whether it's a lunch, dinner or barbeque, I think it's important that you take the time to present the food well. You've spent some time in the kitchen preparing the dishes, but this can be let down if you don't go to the trouble of presenting the dishes and the table layout well. Whether casual or formal, I really think it's important to take the time to create the right atmosphere and impress. This doesn't mean that you have to spend a lot of time constructing masterpieces. For a buffet lunch, a nice presentation consists of bowls of salad with fresh herbs, a fresh basket of bread and a well-browned dish of lasagne. Your food will impress, so why not present it beautifully? I always appreciate this when I'm invited to dinner. It's all about creating the atmosphere and mood for the wonderful food and eating. Lots of conversation and a pleasant time will be had by all.

Wine

Don't forget the wine, red, white or sparking. There's a wine for every occasion, and meatless fare is no exception.

Index

garlic
    aioli, 8–9
    garlic mayonnaise, 59–60
ginger, miso, tofu and bean stew, 171–2
ginger bread, 210–11
goulash, butterbean, 176–8
green beans, butterbean and basil pesto salad,
    51–3
guacamole, 14–15

hazelnuts
    easy chocolate truffles, 220–1
    hazelnut torte, 227–8
    roast butternut/pumpkin, spinach and hazel-
    nut lasagne, 156
hotpot, winter vegetable, 165–6
hummus, 11
Hungarian-style butterbean goulash, 176–8

Indian potato, pea and carrot curry, 188–90

jambalaya, kidney bean and vegetable, 138–9

kale, beetroot and fennel stack, 148–9
kidney beans
    kidney bean and vegetable jambalaya,
        138–9
    Mexican bean stack, 146–8
    vegetable and kidney bean chilli, 182–3
korma, vegetable and buckwheat noodle,
    194–6

lasagne, 150
    roast butternut/pumpkin, spinach and hazel-
        nut, 156
    roast Mediterranean vegetable, 151–2
    roast root vegetable, 152–3
    spinach, fennel and goat's cheese, 155–6
    spinach, leek and feta cheese, 153–4
Lebanese courgette filo pie, 143–4
leeks
    leek, pine nut and feta tart, 120–1
    mushroom, leek, tofu and cashew stack,
        144–6
    saffron and leek risotto, 129
    spinach, leek and feta cheese lasagne,
        153–4

lemons
    tahini and lemon dip/dressing, 7
    zingy lemon tart, 224–5
lentils, 49–50, 159, 234–5
    cauliflower and spinach dhansak, 190–2
    lentil soup, 79–81
    Puy lentil and vegetable moussaka, 162–4
    Puy lentil shepherd's pie with celeriac mash,
        160–1
    tomato, Puy lentil and red onion soup, 81–2
    warm winter salad of rosemary roast root
        vegetable and Puy lentils, 50–1
lettuce: green leaf and seed salad, 47–8

mango relish, 192–4
mayonnaise, 27–9
    egg-based mayonnaise, 28
    garlic mayonnaise, 59–60
    tofu dressing, 7–8
    tofu mayonnaise, 29
Mediterranean couscous, 69–70
Mediterranean vegetable, basil pesto and brie
    tart, 122–3
Mediterranean vegetable lasagne, 151–2
Mexican bean stack, 146–8
Middle Eastern filo rice torte, 140–2
minestrone, 93–4
miso, 75, 235
    miso soup, 76
    miso, tofu, ginger and bean stew, 171–2
Moroccan chickpea tagine with herb couscous,
    178–80
Moroccan spiced vegetable quinoa pilaf,
    134–5
moussaka, Puy lentil and vegetable, 162–4
muffins, 200
    apple and cinnamon, 202
    banana and cinnamon, 201
    plum/pear with almond, 201–2
    raspberry/strawberry and pine nut, 201
    sugar-free date and orange, 200–1
mushrooms, 101, 103
    broccoli, mushroom and tofu cashew nut
        bake, 164–5
    courgette and mushroom risotto, 128–9
    marjoram-infused mushroom and shallot
        couscous salad, 71–2